Thank You
Colle

MW00576741

"Bill Ehrhart is *the* poet perhaps of the Vietnam War."
—**Studs Terkel** (WBEZ-FM, 2001)

"Amazing; just amazing. Profound, powerful, startling. I'd be glad to be able to write these poems. I'm glad you can. And do. They're *really* good. And good to read. Thank you for what you write, for what you remember."—**Daniel Ellsberg** (*Secrets*, 2002, and *The Doomsday Machine*, 2017)

"When I organized a course at West Point on the best artists of the Vietnam War, in addition to Oliver Stone for film, Phil Caputo for nonfiction, and Tim O'Brien for fiction, I invited Bill for poetry. He is the finest combat veteran poet to come out of the war. Bill is brutally honest in the revelation of his own and society's flaws. He is a master of sharing complex truths in seemingly simple language and is a poet who will represent the important truths of our time for generations"—**Joseph T. Cox** (Colonel, U.S. Army, retired; *The Written Wars*, 1996)

"A hunger for honesty and a charged lyricism have always made Bill Ehrhart's poetry remarkably his own. Though he's best known for his Vietnam War poems with their sharp moral outcry and humane insight, this collection includes many lovely poems not about Vietnam."—**John Balaban** (Poet-in-Residence, North Carolina State University; *Remembering Heaven's Face*, 1991)

"W. D. Ehrhart is one of the most important and enduring writers to have emerged from the war. Since his first collection, *A Generation of Peace*, in 1975, his prodigious production has earned him a reputation as one of the preeminent poets of a war that provoked an exceptional outpouring of poetry. The significance of his contribution to this body of work cannot be overstated. His pieces offer interesting reflections on many aspects of American life, and those poems are no less penetrating in their vision, skilled in their description, profound in their thinking, or powerful in their emotion than the war works."—**Adam Gilbert** (University of Sussex; *A Shadow on Our Hearts*, 2018)

"The poetry of W. D. Ehrhart is sublime, earthy, gritty and delicate, precise and original, uniquely appealing to both the heart and the intellect."—**M.L. Liebler** (*Wide Awake in Someone Else's Dream*, 2008)

"Ehrhart takes the elemental experiences of our daily lives and transforms them into moments of compelling insight. His poems resonate with grace and decency."—**Dale Ritterbusch** (*Far from the Temple of Heaven*, 2005)

"Welded in the fires of Vietnam, Bill Ehrhart's strong, sure, memorable poems encompass love, family, and supple lyrics like 'The Way Light Bends.'"—(**Daniel Hoffman**, Poetry Consultant to the Library of Congress, a post now known as Poet Laureate of the United States)

"Bill Ehrhart is a wonderful poet, a force of nature, a conscience that won't let us off the hook. His writing is not the fashionable embroidery that these days too often passes for poetry. There are neither ready-made emotions nor ready-made answers here, only authentic experience, transmitted indelibly by Ehrhart's craft and art."—**Philip Appleman** (professor emeritus, Indiana University)

Thank You for Your Service: Collected Poems

W. D. Ehrhart

McFarland & Company, Inc., Publishers

Jefferson, North Carolina

Over the years, the poems in this collection have been published in the following journals and magazines in addition to multiple anthologies and online publications: *Acoma* (Italy); *American Poetry Review; Another Chicago Magazine; ASHA; Asphodel; Big Hammer; Big Sky Journal; Bucks County Writer; Caprice; Cedar Hill Review; Chiron Review; Christian Science Monitor; Cimarron Review; College English; Colorado Review; Connecticut Poetry Review; Connections; Cultural Critique; Cycnos* (France); *Deadly Writers' Patrol; The Drunken Boat; Earth Ethics; Eleven; Epoch Poetry Quarterly* (Taiwan); *Fellowship; 5 AM; Friends Journal; Front 'n' Center; Great River Review; Greater Philadelphia Group Newspapers; Greenfield Review; Hollow Spring Review; Interchange* (UK); *Journal of American Culture; The Kindred Spirit; Kurungabaa* (Australia); *Long Island Review; Long Shot; Lummox Journal; Mad Poets Review; Many Smokes; Michigan Quarterly Review; Modern Times; Negative Capability; New Hampshire Gazette; New Letters; North American Review; Northeast; O-Dark-Thirty; One Trick Pony; Owen Wister Review; Painted Bride Quarterly; Paterson Literary Review; Piedmont Literary Review; Pocket Pal; Poet Lore; Poetry Australia* (Australia); *Poetry East; Poetry International; Poetry Wales* (UK); *The Pub; Puerto del Sol; Rattle; River Poets Journal; Samisdat; San Pedro River Review; Santa Fe Literary Review; Schuylkill Valley Journal; Shantih; The Signal; The Smudge; The Socialist Tribune; South Boston Literary Gazette; Spafaswap, Stone Country; Studies in Education; Swarthmore College Bulletin; Syncline; Tulane Literary Magazine; Underground Rag Mag; U.S. 1 Worksheets; VAFW Newsletter; VFP Newsletter; VVAW Veteran; Virginia Quarterly Review; Visions; Voices Israel* (Israel); *Voices West; Vooys* (The Netherlands); *War, Literature & the Arts; Washington Post Magazine; WIN; Wind; Yarrow; Z Miscellaneous;* and *Zeitschrift fur Australien Studien* (Austria).

FIRST EDITION, *first printing*

LIBRARY OF CONGRESS CATALOGUING-IN-PUBLICATION DATA

Names: Ehrhart, W. D. (William Daniel), 1948– author.
Title: Thank you for your service : collected poems / W. D. Ehrhart.
Description: Jefferson, North Carolina : McFarland & Company, Inc., 2019 |
    Includes bibliographical references and index.
Identifiers: LCCN 2018059309 | ISBN 9781476678535
    (softcover : acid free paper) ∞
Subjects: LCSH: American poetry—21st century.
Classification: LCC PS3555.H67 A6 2019 | DDC 811/.54—dc23
LC record available at https://lccn.loc.gov/2018059309

BRITISH LIBRARY CATALOGUING DATA ARE AVAILABLE

ISBN (print) 978-1-4766-7853-5. ISBN (ebook) 978-1-4766-3662-7

The front cover image is of W. D. Ehrhart during the Vietnam War

Printed in the United States of America

McFarland & Company, Inc., Publishers
  Box 611, Jefferson, North Carolina 28640
  www.mcfarlandpub.com

For Anne,
and for Leela

Table of Contents

Preface and Acknowledgments   xv
Introduction by Lorrie Goldensohn   xix

Juvenilia, 1963–1967

So Much Time   1

Excerpts from the Mind of
    the Writer   1

Friendship   2

Viet Nam—February 1967   2

1969–1971

Listening Post   3

One Night on Guard Duty   4

The Sniper's Mark   4

The Generals' War   4

Hunting   5

Christ   5

Gettysburg   5

Dancing   6

Starships   6

To Swarthmore   7

1971–1973

Perimeter Guard   12

Souvenirs   13

Sergeant Jones   13

The Rat   14

Mail Call   14

The One That Died   14

Night Patrol   15

The Next Step   15

Guerrilla War   16

Time on Target   16

The Hawk and Two Suns   17

The Ambush   17

Another Life   18

The Bob Hope Christmas
    Special   19

Coming Home   19

A Relative Thing   20

Old Myths   21

A Generation of Peace   22

Imagine   22

Rehoboth   23

The Living   24

September   25

Yours   26

Charleston   26

1974

Rhythm   29

The Flying Gypsy   29

Myers, Messick & Me   30

1975

The Last Day   31

The Obsession   31

The Traveler   32

Granddad   33

To the Asian Victors   33

The Fool   34

Geese   35

Bicentennial   36

Money in the Bank   37

Shadows   38

Making the Children Behave   39

The Silent   39

1976

Vietnam Veterans, After All   40

To Those Who Have Gone
Home Tired   41

Going Home with the
Monkeys   42

Ghosts   43

Going Down Off Columbia
Bar   43

To Maynard on the Long
Road Home   44

The Death of Kings   45

Colorado   46

Rootless   46

Letters   47

Cascais   47

Jimmy   48

1977

The Trial   49

Leaving the Guns Behind   50

Helpless   51

Coma   51

Letter   51

Portrait of Friends   52

After the Fire   53

Desire   54

Cast Out   54

Twodot, Montana   55

Growing Older Alone   56

The Last Prayer of
Michelangelo   57

Sanctuary   57

Welcome   58

Empire   59

1978

Vietnamese-Cambodian
Border War   61

The Spiders' White Dream
of Peace   61

An Exorcism   62

A Confirmation   63

Driving Through
Wisconsin   66

Great Horned Owl   67

Eighteen Months in Chicago   67

Waking Alone in Darkness   68

Peary & Henson Reach
the North Pole   68

The Teacher   69

Turning Thirty   70

Again, Rehoboth   71

Companions   73

Last of the Hard-hearted
Ladies   74

1979

Fog	75
Another Way of Seeing	76
The Grim Art of Teaching	77
The Dancers	77
Lost at Sea	78
Afraid of the Dark	79
The Dream	79
Driving into the Future	81
Sunset	82

1980

The Farmer	83
Near-sighted	84
Channel Fever	85
The World As It Is	86
The Vision	87
The Eruption of Mount St. Helens	88
Matters of the Heart	89
Briana	90

1981

Gifts	91
Sound Advice	92
Continuity	93
New Jersey Pine Barrens	94
Pagan	95
Deer	96
A Warning to My Students	96

1982

Surviving the Bomb One More Day	98
The Blizzard of Sixty-six	98
Letter to the Survivors	99

Everett Dirksen, His Wife, You & Me	100
High Country	101
Cowgirls, Teachers & Dreams	102
Canoeing the Potomac	103
"...the light that cannot fade..."	104
The Outer Banks	105
The Suicide	110

1983

Climbing to Heaven	110
Moments When the World Consents	111
Letter from an Old Lover	112
Appearances	113
Responsibility	113
The Reason Why	114
The Invasion of Grenada	115

1984

On the Right to Vote	115

1985

Winter Bells	116
Parade	117
POW/MIA	118

1986

Apples	119
For Mrs. Na	120
The Ducks on Wissahickon Creek	121
Twice Betrayed	121
Water	122
Adoquinas	123
Heather	124

1987

The Beech Tree	124
Some Other World	125
Nicaragua Libre	126
Why I Don't Mind Rocking Leela to Sleep	127
The Trouble with Poets	128
What Keeps Me Going	129
Small Song for Daddy	130
The Storm	130
Starting Over	131
Second Thoughts	132

1988

Lost Years	133
Chasing Locomotives	134
Secrets	134
Lenin	135
Keeping My Distance	136
Just for Laughs	137
The Next World War	138
Not Your Problem	138
For Anne, Approaching Thirty-five	139

1989

For a Coming Extinction	139
What You Gave Me	140
The Origins of Passion	141
America Enters the 1990s	142
The Way Light Bends	142
The Poet as Athlete	143
In the Valley of the Shadow	144
How I Live	145
The Facts of Life	146

The Heart of the Poem	147
What We're Buying	147

1990

A Scientific Treatise for My Wife	148
Song for Leela, Bobby & Me	149
The Old Soldiers	150
Love in an Evil Time	150
A Small Romance	151
The Children of Hanoi	152
Who Did What to Whom	152
The Lotus Cutters of Hồ Tây	153
Guns	153
Singing Hymns in Church	154

1991

The Cradle of Civilization	155
Finding My Old Battalion Command Post	156
The Simple Lives of Cats	157
After the Latest Victory	157
A Vietnamese Bidding Farewell to the Remains of an American	158
Star Light, Star Bright	159
More Than You Ever Imagined	160
America in the Late 20th Century	160
The Exercise of Power	161
The Open Door	162
Governor Rhodes Keeps His Word	162

1992

The Distance We Travel	163

What War Does 165

Sleeping with General Chi 166

Making Love in the Garden 168

What I Know About Myself 168

On Any Given Day 169

Guatemala 170

Long Shot O'Leary Ain't
Dead Yet 170

Midnight at the Vietnam
Veterans Memorial 171

The Last Time I Dreamed
About the War 172

1993

Small Talk 173

How It All Comes Back 173

Purple Heart 174

Red-tailed Hawks 175

Mostly Nothing Happens 176

1994

Beautiful Wreckage 180

Strangers 180

Not for You 181

Prayer for My Enemies 182

Suffer the Little Children 182

Sarajevo 183

Dropping Leela Off
at School 184

After the Winter of 1994 185

1995

Drought 186

Variations on Squam Lake 186

The Perversion of Faith 187

Reading Out Loud 188

1996

Christmas Miracles 188

The First French Kiss 189

Visiting My Parents'
Graves 189

Cycling the Rosental 191

The Rocker 192

Ginger 193

Rehoboth, One Last Time 194

Night Sailing 194

Is It Always This Hard? 195

What Goes Around Comes
Around 197

Because It's Important 198

I Just Want You to Know 198

The Sergeant 199

Jogging with the
Philosopher 200

A Meditation on Family
Geography and a Prayer
for My Daughter 201

1997

Cliches Become Cliches
Because They're True 202

Detroit River Blues 203

Artsy Fartsy Whiskey &
Girls 204

Pabst Blue Ribbon Beer 205

The Orphan 206

1998

Music Lessons 206

1999

For My Daughter, Alone
in the World 207

Gravestones at Oxwich Bay   208
Sins of the Fathers   208

2000
What Better Way to Begin   209
Letting Go   210
Sleeping with the Dead   211
On the Eve of Destruction   212
The Wreckage Along the
    Road   212

2001
The Damage We Do   213
September 11th   215
The Bombing of
    Afghanistan   216

2002
Seminar on the Nature
    of Reality   218

2003
Home Before Morning   219
Breakfast with You and
    Emily Dickinson   220

2004
Kosovo   222
Manning the Walls   223
Meditations on Pedagogy   225
All About Death   226
All About Love   227
Golfing with My Father   228

2005
Coaching Winter Track
    in Time of War   229
Reflections on the Papacy   230
Oh, Canada   231

Primitive Art, or: The Art
    of the Primitive   232
Home on the Range   233

2006
What the Fuss Is All About   234
Temple Poem   235
Down and Out in Darfur   235

2007
The Work of Love   236
The Bodies Beneath the
    Table   237
Turning Sixty   237

2008
What Makes a Man   239
Extra! Extra!   240
Epiphany   240
The Secret Lives of Boys   240

2009
Burning Leaves   242
Life in the Neighborhood   242

2010
Redipuglia   243
Children of Adam & Eve   245

2011
How History Gets Written   246

2012
Patrick   247
Judas Joyful   247
Cheating the Reaper   248

2013
What It Signifies   249
First Day of School   250

2014

The Baby in the Box 251
Long Time Gone 252

2015

Praying at the Altar 252
Spontaneous Combustion 253
It's About You 254
The Amish Boys on Sunday 254

2016

Here's to Us 255
I Dream of Alternate
Histories 256

Old Men Bodysurfing 257
The Poetry of Science 258
Lunch at the A&N Diner 258
Making America Great
Again 259

2017

Dancing in the Streets 260
Silver Linings 261

2018

The Right to Bear Arms 262
Playing It Safe 262
Thank You for Your Service 263

Also by W. D. Ehrhart 265
Military History of W. D. Ehrhart 267
About the Poet 269
Index of Titles 271
Index of First Lines 275

Preface and Acknowledgments

The poems in this collection span fifty-five years of my life, beginning with "So Much Time," which I wrote in the ninth grade in response to an assignment from my English teacher, Miss Hersperger, and which was "published" in a mimeographed class collection called *Agony and Ecstasy*. I have included just two other poems from my high school years, both of which appeared in the 1966 Pennridge High School literary magazine *Ramblings*. Other poems in that same magazine are so obviously knock-offs of Stephen Crane and Kahlil Gibran that I cannot bring myself to include them here even as juvenilia, even to indicate where and how I began writing. The two poems I've included should suffice.

I've also included "Viet Nam—February 1967" in the juvenilia section because I did indeed write it in February 1967, only days after I arrived in Vietnam at the age of 18 and only eight months after I graduated from high school. Many years later, Philip Beidler, in his landmark study *American Literature and the Experience of Vietnam*, singled out the poem as paradigmatic of the worst poetry to come out of the Vietnam War (which was probably an accurate assessment, though he might have had the courtesy to tell his readers that I had since written some better poetry in the intervening fifteen years).

But there you go: You put stuff into print, and then you have to live with it. In addition to that poem, which was published in the 1972 anthology *Winning Hearts and Minds*, I published two other poems in that anthology that have also come back to haunt me time and again. I have not included them in this collection because they add nothing to understanding the trajectory of my growth as a poet and they are embarrassingly terrible poems. If anyone is actually interested in seeing more of the stuff I wrote in my teens and early twenties, but never published, you can find a bunch of it housed in the W. D. Ehrhart Collections at LaSalle University, part of the Imaginative Representations of the Vietnam War archive created and curated by John Baky, himself a veteran of the American War in Vietnam, and another person I need to thank for supporting and encouraging me in both tangible and intangible ways over the years.

As one can already surmise then, not all of the poems I've published over the course of my life have ended up in this "collected" volume. Most of the poems I omitted were published in my twenties and early thirties in little magazines, but never made it into even my earliest *Samisdat* chapbooks because they aren't very good poems. I have also omitted some of the poems that did make it into one or another of my previous collections, though at Tom Stambaugh's urging, I included most of what is found in those earlier books and chapbooks.

As for sequencing the poems, most of my early work is difficult to date accurately. I know I wrote "So Much Time" in 1963, the two poems from my high school lit mag sometime prior to the late spring of 1966, and that first Vietnam War poem in February 1967. I know that the second through sixth poems in the 1969–1971 section had to have been written prior to the late winter of 1971 because that's when I sent them to the editors of *WHAM*. "Listening Post" was not published until 1973 in an anthology called *Listen. The War*, but it just feels like something I wrote very early on in my post–Marine Corps life, so I have placed it where you find it. (I stopped writing within a few months of my arrival in Vietnam, when the war became so disturbing that I did not want to think about it; it was hard enough just to survive from day to day without thinking about what you were doing or why, and how none of it matched what I had been told the war was about by everyone I'd ever trusted. And if you don't think, you can't write, so I wrote nothing until the spring of 1969, just before I got off active duty from the Marines.) I do know that I wrote the long rambling "To Swarthmore" in the spring of 1971 at the request of the editor of the *Swarthmore College Bulletin* as part of a collection of essays by students reflecting on their college experiences.

The only poems in the 1971–1973 section that I can date with any accuracy are "A Relative Thing," which I wrote after Henry Kissinger announced in late October 1972 that peace was at hand (as usual, he was lying), "A Generation of Peace," which I wrote shortly after the signing of the Paris Peace Accords that allowed Richard Nixon to claim "peace with honor" while the war itself went on, and "Yours" and "Charleston," both of which I wrote in the fall of 1972.

Beginning in December 1974, however, when I first began systematically to submit poems to journals for publication, and ever since, I have kept logbooks of every poem I've written, where I sent it, when I sent it, and when it came back rejected. (In the much rarer times when one would be accepted, I'd write "A Cigar" on that page, a tradition I have maintained to this day.) Indeed, from 1974 on, all of the poems included here are in the exact chronological order in which they were written. It should therefore be apparent that while the American War in Vietnam and its continuing echoes and repercussions have always been a subject of mine, it has hardly been my only subject.

Though it was tempting to do so, I have not made any revisions to these poems, even the earliest of them. I have only standardized some of the punctuation—in my twenties, I was much enamored of the semi-colon, and regularly overused and misused it—and I have eliminated my original capitalization of the first letter of each line in poems written before 1974, when Merritt C ifton persuaded me to abandon that archaic habit.

One can also glean from scanning the table of contents that while my annual output has varied widely from year to year, there has been a distinct decline over the past twenty years. I'm not sure to what that can be attributed, but I take solace in the fact that a higher percentage of the poems I do write are "keepers" than was true when I was younger, and I take pleasure in the number of poems I've written over the years that I still like. Moreover, four decades ago, when I used to think that three weeks without a new poem constituted a "dry spell," Merritt Clifton gave me some sage advice that I've relied on ever since. "You can't rape the Muse," he wrote to me, "If you do, you'll have sex, but it won't be love." So I write when the spirit moves me, or the Muse inspires me, or however one explains it, but when I'm not writing, I try not to worry about it. That approach has held me in good stead all these years. I might yet have a few more poems in me before I finally shuffle off this mortal coil, which would be just fine with me. But if I never write another poem, well, I've had a good run.

I want to thank—and I mean THANK in huge neon letters—McFarland & Company, Inc., for affording me this privilege. Thirty-six years ago, Robbie Franklin took a chance on me, and it has resulted in nine books and a relationship that has lasted more than half my life.

I owe thanks also to a number of people who have shaped and fostered and supported my life as a writer and poet: Robert Hollenbach and John Diehl, my high school English teachers who taught me to value literature and who made it safe for a boy to love poetry; Margaret Geosits, my high school journalism teacher, who encouraged me to write poetry; Daniel Hoffman, poetry consultant to the Library of Congress (a position since renamed poet laureate of the United States), the first poet who made me believe that I too might actually be a poet; Jan Barry, poet, journalist, and one of the founders of Vietnam Veterans Against the War, who showed me how to channel my postwar anger and pain in constructive ways; Merritt Clifton of *Samisdat*, who published me for nearly a decade when few others were interested; Gary Metras of Adastra Press, who took up where Merritt left off, and with whom I have had a productive and warm relationship even longer than the one I've had with McFarland; and finally Tom Stambaugh, my colleague and friend at the Haverford School, who bravely waded through the entire body of my published poetry and helped to shape this volume.

Introduction
by Lorrie Goldensohn

W. D. Ehrhart's "Curious Grace"

While he has been a prolific and hard-charging essayist, editor, and memoirist, the backbone of William D. Ehrhart's career as a writer has nonetheless always been poetry. Even before the lure of a romantic patriotism drew him as a 17-year-old to enlist in the U.S. Marine Corps during the Vietnam War, he was also, paradoxically, a minister's son who with other boys stuffed firecrackers down a frog's throat, a runaway to California the summer before his senior year, and a high school rebel who went to church every Sunday but challenged his teachers at every turn. Graduating as a straight-A student, he put four college acceptances aside because of a burning desire to try his mettle as a Marine. Beyond all these warring elements of personal history, each examined later in his writing, Ehrhart was also fascinated from his earliest years by the powers of lyric poetry. This volume collects more than five decades of Ehrhart's poems, drawn from nearly a hundred journals. While adding a small number of juvenilia and poems from on-line sources, the collection is mostly gathered from U.S. print publications, although it compiles work from eight different countries, including the United Kingdom, as well as translations and adaptations from Vietnamese and Japanese sources. In *Thank You for Your Service*, we have between the covers of one book the full arc of a poet's work—work that is as compelling as it is unique in American literary history.

Ehrhart's poems, gradually but steadily appearing in print from 1972 and beyond, helped to shape our enduring ideas of the psycho-social, political and historical impact of the Vietnam War on American consciousness. Poems like "Guerrilla War" and "The Next Step," both widely reprinted, came to define what it was like to be a clueless and jumpy 18-year-old who had every reason to be afraid of the landscape he was moving through, and every reason to fear the unfathomable alignments of friend and foe to which every moment of his life in Vietnam was being subjected. The handful of very early poems published here, like "Viet Nam—February 1967," "Listening Post," and "One Night on Guard Duty," lean a bit too exclusively on the natural detail that still underpins Ehrhart's mature poems. But poems like "Guerrilla War" and "Time on Target" were also written early, some of them from as early as 1971, only three years after Ehrhart arrived home from Vietnam. These and other poems in this collection mark a steeply rising developmental curve. Later pieces stress the sensory envelope of Ehrhart's experience but perform the further work of reflective commentary, identifying the painful ironies of the larger personal and historical perspective that became his signature stance.

In "Souvenirs," written early in the 1970s, there is a barebones account of an incident that has haunted Ehrhart's poetry and prose over decades, in which a mindless bunch of adolescent Marines, among whom the narrator includes himself, finds in a war zone an intact Buddhist temple:

> It must have taken more than half an hour,
> but at last we battered in
> the concrete walls so badly
> that the roof collapsed.

Ehrhart completes the poem by describing how the narrator takes "two painted vases" and says: "One I kept, / and one I offered proudly to the captain." As readers, we can stand behind the distancing shelter of a literary term like "narrator," but a strength of Ehrhart's poetry is the rarity with which he allows himself to take comfort from that distance, and the techniques he adopts and refines to widen the scope of first-person sensibility. Contravening that ever-present *I*, and the generalized ownership of its more comfortable *We*, Ehrhart splits his voice into a Then and Now: *we* did all this determined battering together—the temple collapsed—and after that, offered a souvenir to my captain "proudly." That adverb cuts a space, an interval, between the kid who battered and the kid who forced himself to think about it all, and to question later exactly what proud thing he had done. In its telescoped time, deftly managed pronouns, and spare but pointed modifiers, "Souvenirs" bears witness, and does so within the disquieting moral urgency of individual accountability. Ehrhart's directness and urgency only amplify, growing fuller, wiser, and more passionate over decades of practice.

W. D. Ehrhart's first full collection of poems, *A Generation of Peace*, appeared in 1975, becoming noticeable in the wake of a growing awareness of the poets of the Vietnam War as a distinctive class. *A Generation of* Peace was published a few years after the 1972 groundbreaking anthology (in which several of Ehrhart's poems were included) *Winning Hearts & Minds*, edited by Jan Barry, Larry Rottmann and Basil Paquet. Staking out the ground for the Vietnam war poets, the three editors declared: "Previous war poets have traditionally placed the blame directly on others. What distinguishes the voices in this volume is their progression toward an active identification of themselves as agents of pain and war—as 'agent-victims' of their own atrocities. This recognition came quickly to some and haltingly to others, but it always came with pain and the conviction that there is no return to innocence." In short, these poems held to the anti-war ethos of World War I poets like Wilfred Owen, Siegfried Sassoon, Isaac Rosenberg and many others, but broke decisively with the one-sided view that adopted the soldier as a passive innocent enduring the impact of political and military forces beyond his control. In two ways, the Vietnam War poets also resembled many World War II poets like Randall Jarrell, Howard Nemerov and John Ciardi: they recognized the changing industrialized battlefields of modern war, which removed agency from the old warriors of sword, bow, and spear, and displaced power onto the greater kill ratios of machine guns, tanks, and airplanes. They also acknowledged the blurring of conflict boundaries that with increasing fatality punished both civilian and soldier alike.

But the uniqueness of the Vietnam War poets like Ehrhart was their insistence nonetheless on re-drawing the moral responsibility for death and injury back onto the soldier himself, as well as up and down the chain of command, on all sides of the conflict. "You" become, writes Ehrhart in "What War Does," "the straightleg grunts and boonie rats. The trigger men"—those who are "held hostage by time, forced to look and look and look till what you are seeing is burned into your retinas, until it is tattooed on your soul. And what you are seeing is the bottom line, the cold butchery upon which civilization is built." Both those in the field and those at headquarters home and abroad became answerable, however uneasily so, for death and destruction. In "A Relative Thing," a 1972 poem, W. D. Ehrhart writes:

> We are the ones you sent to fight a war
> you didn't know a thing about.
>
> It didn't take us long to realize
> the only land that we controlled
> was covered by the bottom of our boots.
> ....
> We have been Democracy on Zippo raids,
> burning houses to the ground,
> driving eager amtracs through new-sown fields.
>
> We are the ones who have to live
> with the memory that we were the instruments
> of your pigeon-breasted fantasies.
> We are inextricable accomplices
> in this travesty of dreams:
> but we are not alone.

In 1980, in his preface to *In the Shadow of Vietnam: Essays, 1979–1997*, Ehrhart wrote: "I never intended to be a 'Vietnam writer,' and I have never thought of myself as a 'Vietnam writer.' That label has largely been imposed on me by others. But it is also true, in looking at the body of my work, that nearly all of it, in one way or another, directly or indirectly … has been informed by my irrevocable decision as a teenager to become a Marine and fight in Vietnam" (ix).

The first collection of Ehrhart's poems appeared in the 1989 anthology he edited, *Carrying the Darkness: The Poetry of the Vietnam War*. As Adam Gilbert writes in *A Shadow on Our Hearts: Soldier Poetry, Morality, and the American War in Vietnam*, we hear in these poems combat survivors like Ehrhart, for whom "morality becomes a process of thinking rather than a pre-digested set of answer" (17). In writing a poetry like no other in its unflinching willingness to probe the wounds of all the people who were trapped inside the war, these men produced a poetry, in Ehrhart's words, that also came to represent "the terrible beauty that Vietnam engendered in sensitive hearts, the curious grace with which the human spirit can endow even the ugliest of realities" (*Unaccustomed Mercy*, 4).

After long study of the war poetry within which his work has often been too narrowly confined, Ehrhart continues to clarify how Vietnam War poetry both merged with and differed from other war poetry. In 2001, in *The Madness of It All: Essays on War, Literature and American Life*, he writes, "What one does not find in the poetry of World War Two is any challenge to the need to fight this particular war. It may have been ugly, it may have been brutal, it may have been butchery and stupidity and madness, it may have exacted a hideous price from everyone engaged in it, but one need only consider the alternative to not fighting—Adolf Hitler and the Japanese Imperial General Staff—and the debate is over…, [World War Two] was necessary. It was unavoidable" (229). About his war: "What sets Vietnam War poetry apart is the unavoidable realization that all suffering and death and destruction was for nothing. Just nothing" (231). The "nothing" theme, in Vietnam so often colloquially rendered by American soldiers as "It don't mean nuthin'," was sounded by a plurality of Vietnam War poets. For Ehrhart and his cohort, "Nothing" meant the betrayal of American values, which led consequentially to the scorching sense of self-betrayal and the confession of psychic self-wounding that infuse the singular war poetry he and his peers wrote.

The developing shape of Ehrhart's poems, their point of view, the keenness of the extreme experience they transcribed, emerged within the same crucible that eventually produced his memoirs, including *Vietnam–Perkasie: A Combat Marine Memoir* (1983) and *Passing Time* (1986), the latter quoting two poems written in the 1970s, "Hunting" and "A Relative Thing." Yet another crucial overlap with these two initial memoirs and the early Vietnam War anthologies was a further collection of war poetry, *Demilitarized Zones: Veterans After Vietnam*, that Ehrhart edited in 1976 with Jan Barry. The work he was plunged into writing and editing in the ferment of contemporary American political protest inevitably contributed to his thinking about war. His memoirs detail the progression of his involvement in anti-war protest: simultaneously, he increased his own political activity in organizations like Vietnam Veterans Against the War, finding that his writing deepened his awareness of the potential dimensions of war poetry as a morally expressive genre.

While putting his own war experience into poetry, Ehrhart, acutely aware of his own historical positioning, reached out to veterans of other American wars, especially to those of the Korean War. He was one of the first to connect the deep debt that the poets of that earlier Asian war owed, in shaping their own approach, to the veterans of Vietnam; in an odd chronological twist, the insights of the Korean War poets were entangled with the war that postdated theirs. Ehrhart notes that "none of the soldier poets began writing poetry about the Korean War until the 1960s" (*The Madness of It All*, 236), adding elsewhere that "if the Korean War poets are closer in age to their World War Two counterparts, they respond to their experiences in the Korean War with a sense of disillusionment and betrayal that much more closely resembles the poets of the Vietnam War" (*Dead on a High Hill*, 161).

Ehrhart's own prodigious efforts in discovering and editing war poets were especially evident in the savvy application of literary principles that resulted in the 1989 anthology *Carrying the Darkness*. Additionally, writing his powerful and unsettling nonfiction narratives contributed to the streams of language and experience forming W. D. Ehrhart's own style, and its emphatic siting within a given political and historical perspective.

H. Bruce Franklin, in his foreword to the 1995 edition of Ehrhart's *Busted: A Vietnam Veteran in Nixon's America*, describes the impact of this memoir when assigned to his students: they had been so taken by the life story they had read that, notwithstanding an institutional cutback on funding for speakers that year, they pooled their finances to bring him live into their classroom. The quality of their undivided attention is something Ehrhart, a sharp-eyed and skillful narrator in all literary forms, has always elicited.

Franklin remarks, "Even as a high school student, Ehrhart was committed to the belief in a crucial relationship between American history and the role of each individual American." In Ehrhart's persistent and enduring need to tell the whole truth, whether in speaking truth to power in his unvarnished prose and poetical responses to *The Pentagon Papers* or in acknowledging the personal shame of his acts as a grunt in Vietnam, his convictions are morally grounded. But they issue from a belief in the power of individual voice, and in an unwavering sense of the relation between private and public act; we are always ourselves, and the dimensions of self are inevitably traceable in how we behave toward others in events both small and large. Our lives are witness and beholden to something beyond ourselves that belongs to family and community. Throughout Ehrhart's professional career, there has been an unwearying and generous effort to write the times, and without stint, to write the whole life, the whole man.

The largeness of the force that drives this ambition emerges in Ehrhart's prose, poetry, and public life. It surfaces in several poems, as when he describes inadvertently shooting an old peasant woman while on patrol or writes in poem and memoir about the agony of blowing up a 10-year-old boy who threw a grenade at him, or when he admits on public television to being part of a gang-bang in a mortar pit, with other Marines. After having written many passionate and loving poems for his wife, in mid-career Ehrhart wrote "The Simple Lives of Cats," a painful poem that winds up: "the only danger here is me. / Once again I've lost it, temper flaring, / patience at a too-quick end, my daughter / crying, and my wife's heart sinking / in the sadness of another day gone bad." There's no withholding of emotion.

Here is the additional dimension, as Bruce Franklin notes in the foreword to *Busted*, finding "from within the distinctive flat voice speaking in a deceptively plain style, the painful honesty and insights, the visceral power, *the rare fusion of personal and historical vision*" (xv–xvi; italics mine). There's no palliative explanation of a smoldering personal anger, an explosive and ungovernable rage, appearing in episodes in both Ehrhart's poetry and prose as part of the Vietnam War veteran's burden of post-traumatic stress disorder. Rather, Ehrhart's broad labor is to place the sources of that anger within a more nuanced family and generational perspective—and not simply to advance his war experience as the lever of release. As a result, the story of rage disperses into several finely nuanced poems about himself, his father, and his brother that show the ramifying origins of family angers. In "The Damage We Do," he writes,

> I don't remember a time when the house
> I grew up in wasn't crackling with rage.
> ....
> you learn to be angry all the time.
> ....
> By then you've got a child of your own
> who's angry all the time....

Many of Ehrhart's best poems are tributes to women. Whether he writes of charged relations with mother, grandmother, wife, daughter, friend, colleague, or enemy civilian, a vortex of feelings—lusty, tender, comic, grieving, penitent, admiring, regretful—comes into play. In a poetry so often dark and disturbing, the playfulness and humor that also streak through it are refreshing.

In "The Origins of Passion," a speech offered as Senior Dinner Remarks at the Haverford School in 2010, Ehrhart guesses that he has been invited to speak on that occasion "because you figure that there's a good chance I'll say something entertainingly outrageous" (*Dead on a High Hill*, 133). And he obliges, reading out loud from his poem "The Origins of Passion," which opens with Ehrhart at age eight, alone in his mother's bedroom, greedily pressing his nose into the folds of her white lace slip: He says he lifts "my trembling arms and drop it / over me, aching with desire." This bit of cross-dressing is followed by the ex–Marine sergeant's homage to the future women of his life who will bless him "with hands adept at rituals I want / to share but don't know how or why: / lipsticks, brushes, combs and stockings." He notes that he's not allowed to read this poem when his wife is present, because it embarrasses her, and says that an old friend has warned him against reading the piece—because of the questions it potentially raises for an audience about the poet's "sexual orientation." Ehrhart repeats his response to that reaction to the waiting Haverford seniors: "This made me laugh because by that point in my life I had long since ceased to give a big rat's backside if people think I'm a gay transvestite fan dancer or a left-handed Belizian parrot lover" (*Dead on a High Hill*, 134).

He explains what the poem is about: "It's a poem about what our culture forces boys to deny in and about themselves as they mature into what our culture passes off as manhood" (134). He goes on to meditate about what his Marine Corps training, intent on building men, mostly ignored or saw fit to dismiss. His own evolving definition of manhood included being a college water ballet swimmer, and later a stay-at-home Dad, who turned the major breadwinning over to his wife for twenty years. Poems and prose vividly describe the gender inflections of his life through friendships and working relations with women like Vietnam War nurse Lynda van Devanter and journalist Gloria Emerson.

But the same drive that prompted Ehrhart to seek out the details of his anger in his personal life, to narrow and deepen the sources of his understanding of both love and war, rather than to explain personal burdens solely by his war history, finally leads him, by virtue of the same ambitious honesty, to broaden his understanding of that war by looking at other wars, and other war veterans. In a large poetry copiously devoted to the work of memory, many piercing poems deal with recalling the war dead of Vietnam, whether singly or in group poems. But a 1992 poem like "Midnight at the Vietnam Veteran's Memorial," with its "silent wall of kids, this / smell of rotting dreams," shows him nearly ten years later still unable to drop or modify the bitterness of "The Invasion of Grenada" (1983), which ended, "What I wanted / was an end to monuments." Yet perhaps the final comment on all formal efforts at commemoration occurs in the immensely moving late poem

"Redipuglia," where Ehrhart, without referring to Hemingway's famous World War I statement reifying only names, places and dates for the lost, merely reiterates the names and military assignment of the Italian dead of World War I. Finally, after each refrain, "*Presente* Present. We are here." Ehrhart writes, "mocking the Duce's own design,"

> The steps are so arranged
> That all you see is the single word PRESENTE
> rising out of the stone
> over again, and over and over again....
> PRESENTE Present. We are here.

Whatever any leader designs, the names summoning the persons remain the reality in view.

We might guess that in an attempt to deal with the inadequacy of cere-monies of mourning to compensate for the cruelties of war loss, Ehrhart's poems are the more highly inventive in style and situation—from the blunt-ness of "How It All Comes Back" to the defeated irony of "Beautiful Wreck-age," to the notation of the physical horror of death in "The Bodies Beneath the Table." What persists is the need to span it all, and to compass a restless man's craving for elegy, who says in "Eighteen Months in Chicago": "I don't know why I always go, / for everywhere I am / it's always where I've been / that I remember."

If you look at this work with an eye open to its variety and plenitude of incident, including its many elegies for civilians, what becomes striking is the lack of emphasis on traditional battlefield encounter. Mostly, in these war poems, there is nothing like the gas attack in Wilfred Owen's "Dulce et Deco-rum Est," or the kind of battlefield experience Isaac Rosenberg gives in suc-cinct summary within these lines from "Dead Man's Dump":

> The air is loud with death,
> The dark air spurts with fire
> The explosions ceaseless are.

Ehrhart saves such experience for prose. For the most part, his poems reflect the equally deadly, equally wearing frustrations of the guerrilla warfare he described bitterly in a 1990 poem dedicated to a dead fellow Marine, "Song for Leela, Bobby and Me":

> chickenshit guerrilla fight:
> farmers, women, booby traps and snipers,
> dead Marines, and not a Viet Cong in sight.

It is not as if battle engagement were lacking from Ehrhart's service as a Marine. Twice, his own combat experience was extended and horrific during his Vietnam service. First, near the DMZ in Con Thien, where for 33 days Ehrhart was pinned down in concentrated exposure to enemy fire, and second, while he fought from street to house and back again in Hue City during the Tet Offensive before being wounded by a North Vietnamese B-40 RPG. Deafened by his injury, but mostly on his feet, Ehrhart stayed in the fight with his unit until the day that a jeep flew up the road; while scouts laid down a covering fire, he ran for the jeep, which took him to a waiting helicopter. Before leaving for home, he's handed a U.S. Marine Corps Certificate of Commendation and a promotion to sergeant. All the pulse-quickening, heart-thumping events are detailed in three memoirs, *Vietnam–Perkasie: A Combat Marine Memoir* (1983), *Passing Time: Memoir of a Vietnam Veteran Against the War* (1986), and *Going Back: An Ex-Marine Returns to Vietnam* (1987). A fourth postwar account, *Busted: A Vietnam Veteran in Nixon's America* (1995), updates his postwar experience. Like a mason choosing stones, or a contractor selecting different timbers, Ehrhart will weigh, measure, and cut different materials to build an original story. But the style of these four battle memoirs owes more to the elaborations of fiction and non-fiction narrative technique than to the lyric compression of poetry. It is striking that Ehrhart so divides his writing about war.

Decade by decade, an increasingly split perspective invests an anonymous and mostly invisible enemy with maximum fright and terror in prose narrative but then surges forward in poems and essays to re-see the heretofore enemy as a man like himself. In one of his brilliantly clarifying essays, "They Want Enough Rice: Reflections on the Late American War in Vietnam," he writes:

> [W]e killed a man in an ambush who was dressed in thin cotton shirt and pants with sandals made from discarded tires (we called them Ho Chi Minh sandals). He had in one pocket a few balls of rice wrapped in a banana leaf. His weapon was a 1936 French bolt action MAS-36 with a bent hide-away bayonet, a stock held together with wire and a bamboo strip to replace the leather sling that had rotted away a decade or more earlier. He had five bullets, and the barrel of his rifle was so pitted that I dared not fire it for fear it would explode in my face. And that is how that man had gone out to do battle with the most powerful army on earth. You can kill people like that, but you cannot defeat them [*Dead on a High Hill*, 121].

That respect for an enemy would mutate into an elegiac desire to return to Vietnam to engage with both an earlier self as well as with his ultimately victorious enemy. Most of Ehrhart's poetry, properly speaking, is *not* war poetry, but postwar reflection on the need for reparation, with a lot of flashback and flashforward into postwar Vietnam. As early as 1978, in "Letter," he wrote to the unknown gunner who shot him, asking him to "build houses; build villages, / dikes and schools, songs / and children in that green land / I blackened with my shadow / and the shadow of my flag."

Even in his combat narratives, however, Ehrhart's need to complete the observation, to drive his language into the exact sensation, the precise event, is present in masses of detail that ultimately eat away at the heroic. He isn't embarrassed to report that he's pissed his pants after an ambush in Con Thien:

> A set up! The whole hedgerow was sewn with exploding booby-traps. A man ran into the hedgerow just in front of me, and came flying out in pieces. I hit the deck. "Jesus Christ! Jesus Christ!" I thought. Mortar rounds were falling among us now. Guys were running for cover, and guys were lying all over the field, and rounds kept exploding, and men shouted meaningless orders, and men hollered for corpsmen. No more than sixty seconds had elapsed since the first mortar rounds had left their tubes. I lay there trying to hide and trying to look around at the same time…. You could hear some of the wounded moaning, and one guy who'd had his thigh ripped open was still screaming, but the vitality of his cries indicated that he was not fatally wounded in spite of the bone-sh'ivering screams. It was always the quiet ones who were close to the edge. I lit a cigarette, took a few puffs, and calmed down enough to notice that I'd wet my pants [*Vietnam–Perkasie*, 223–224].

The note-taking, at once both wide-angle in scope and narrow in focus, is undoubtedly essential for survival. But the impact of fear itself is also carefully charted, and all the soldiers come to know that after sundown NVA fire ceases, because the source of their fire can be traced in the darkness. Ehrhart writes that "after sundown, my teeth didn't grind so much and my jaws stopped aching from the constant effort of clenching my teeth to keep them from grinding in the daytime" (214).

All the memoirs follow the same pattern of unrelenting, almost self-crucifying honesty as the poems and essays: one man speaks his life with a frequently harsh and unnerving consistency. From the details offered in *Vietnam–Perkasie* and also in the battle narrative offered in portions of the other three books, as well, a paradoxical pattern of value emerges: William Daniel Ehrhart's war record is that of an exemplary U.S. Marine, who carried out orders intelligently and meticulously, and insofar as that was possible, stood by his fellow Marines with courage in critical moments of risk, and received the commendations, promotions, citations and medals that any ardently committed Marine would covet. Each of Ehrhart's prose books appends his military history, and nothing is conveyed that is not honorable, nor contains anything which could not be the accompanying biographical detail for a professional warrior.

It becomes clear that shame and dishonor lodge, and may not be dislodged, from the writer's view of the profession of arms itself. If a retroactively shaming cruelty and indifference to human beings exists in these narratives, and if a dissolving and disorienting fear exists that crumbles military resolve, it originates in the inhuman practices of modern industrial warfare. Yet

Ehrh rt can be found sourly observing time and again that this inhumanity is inherent in the age-old onslaughts of human against human that constitutes all war—of that intractable "butchery" on which "civilization is built." In this belief, Ehrhart deviates from the narrower conviction of the editors of *Winning Hearts & Minds*; the shame and guilt by which Rottmann, Paquet and Barry define the Vietnam War veteran is something Ehrhart broadens to a black conception of human nature against which he persistently, and with frequent success, struggles.

At the outset, from the very first poem Ehrhart wrote in-country, "Viet Nam—February 1967," he made a concentrated effort to see the people around him—Marines, South Vietnamese soldiers, and ordinary peasants—and to allow himself to hear, smell, feel the tropical heat, and register totally what excited the senses of an 18-year-old in the first foreign country of his life. It became a scene that might have been recorded by a journalist as well as a combatant. Other poems follow suit, sidelining battle: they cover random death on patrol, the look of a dead body killed in an unspecified mode, and the traumatic experience of being around when a fellow Marine gets notification that his wife is suing for divorce and promptly shoots himself in the head. The sort of poem that Wilfred Owen and others wrote about trench warfare and battlefields is not a Vietnam lyric specialty, perhaps because prose began to seem a better, suitably more expansive vehicle for later generations.

But a poem that zeroes in on the random brutality of Vietnam warfare, on the voracious quest for any victim, was there from the beginning in Ehrhart's work. In "Time on Target":

> One day, while on patrol,
> we passed the ruins of a house;
> beside it sat a woman
> with her left breast torn away;
> beside her lay a child, dead.
>
> When I got back to base,
> I told the fellows in the COC;
> it gave us all a lift to know
> all those shells we fired every night
> were hitting something.

Yet while Ehrhart's poetic career initiated in war, we need to notice how steadily the war poems morph into aftermath, reconciliation with the enemy, and meditation on the causes and consequences of his and any war. Since he began writing seriously only after returning from Vietnam, the poems he subsequently published trace the ineradicable injury of memory—the bad dreams, the jarring reintegration with the poet's American homeland—

as well as his proliferating engagements with communal and political life. Coming into prominence were Ehrhart's several trips back to an ever more thriving and peaceful Vietnam.

Immersion in politics and history has always characterized Ehrhart's poetry. It is unexpectedly true, for someone who has made his mark as a war poet, that the bulk of his poems over a long career have favored subjects not directly related to war. But often the many poems written about friendship, domestic relations and the interplay of generations within the mid–Atlantic state of Pennsylvania, about sky, sea, fishing, animals, and traveling in places as distant from Perkasie, Pennsylvania, as Twodot, Montana, or Vietnam or El Salvador or Nicaragua—as well as the frequent meditations on the nature of teaching, masculinity, personal wanderlust, parenting, and citizenship— have become the poems that fully contextualize his work. All have the added benefit of bearing directly on his status as a combat survivor of an unforgettably particular war.

Many of Ehrhart's poems deal with education. It is not surprising that some of his most vivid essays and poems originate in encounters with students of all ages and gender; behind the urgency of his concern is his own bitterly earned knowledge that it is young people who fight wars. As early as 1978, he wrote in "The Teacher," "I swore an oath to teach you / all I know— / And I know things / worth knowing." In 1989, in "A Letter to McGeorge Bundy," he writes, "I was lucky." But others? "I have friends whose names were carved into that ugly black slab in Washington, D.C. I have friends who were dumped into wheelchairs at nineteen and won't be taken out again until they are laid in their coffins. I have friends who still can't see an Asian face without trembling. I have friends who live in shacks deep in the forests of the Olympic Peninsula. I have friends whose wives are afraid to touch them when are sleeping." Written in 2005, the poem "Coaching Winter Track in Time of War," brings that knowledge of young men, war, and teaching all together. The poem begins:

> You could fall in love with boys
> like these: so earnest, so eager, so
> ready to do whatever you ask, so
> full of themselves and the world.

He goes on to ask them to question everything, even the coach, and tells them,

> Ask the young dead soldiers coming home
> each night in aluminum boxes
> none of us is allowed to see,
> an army of shades.

The poem concludes after the boys have been dismissed, while the coach stands alone "in fading light while / memory's phantoms circle the track / like weary athletes running a race without a finish line."

It is a resonant place for Ehrhart to stand.

Lorrie Goldensohn's most recent work on poetry of the American-Vietnamese War, "Lifting the Darkness," has been published in the on-line *Asia Pacific Journal* (spring 2018). In October 2018, she gave a talk connecting American poets of the Vietnam War to the poetry of Wilfred Owen at Oxford University's commemorative conference "Wilfred Owen and Beyond." Goldensohn is a poet who has published books and articles on modern and contemporary poetry, including *Dismantling Glory: 20th Century English and American Soldier Poetry* (2004).

Juvenilia, 1963–1967

So Much Time

So much time, so little to do,
Comes the chant on a hot afternoon;
A boy sits alone, time seems to drag,
A day like this could not end too soon.

So much time, so little to do,
The little boy sighs, and time stands still;
The hours drag by; lonely and sad,
The little boy sits on top of a hill.

Oh little boy, why sit so still?
There are many things waiting for you;
When you grow old, you'll look back and say:
So little time, so much to do.

Excerpts from the Mind of the Writer

100 minus three is 97 is 94 is 91 is 88 is 85 is 82,
82 ends in two
And one and one is two is you and me
And you are going and I am one
And everything is going and I am one and all alone.
Here I sit and it is dark,
I see the colors—red and blue and green and yellow
Terribly loud, too loud for music,
They sound like music, I can't hear it,
They must be drums pounding in my skull.
I hear laughter and people having fun,
I wonder where they are hiding,
The laughter is getting louder,

1

It rises from a hideous moan that comes from my quivering mouth,
My head splits in two—
Two—we are two, I am two,
You and I are two and you are going and I am one
And nothing is me and I am nothing,
I can't say my name, there it is written on the wall
Beside the gravestone over in the corner,
Written in blood.
I can't read it, the tears in my eyes,
It's raining—bricks and bullets and blood.
The moon explodes, it must be sick,
The room is spinning very fast,
So is my head, there you go and here I stay,
I want to call, I cannot shout, I cannot reach you,
And so you go and two minus one is one
And I am one and one is zero and zero is nothing
And I am nothing and nothing is me.

Friendship

We walk together in a free land,
We can be friends and smile,
Through the streets we stride,
Without mocking jeers;
Our hands clasp in friendship,
One black and one white—
Perhaps, someday, perhaps.

Viet Nam—February 1967

Air heavy with rain and humidity,
sky full of ominous clouds,
dank smell of refuse,
mosquitoes and flies like carpets on the wind.

Patchwork quilt of rice paddies,
winding rivers and swollen streams,
water buffalo lumbering through the field,
high mountains on the horizon.

Thundering roar of aircraft on the prowl,
roads clogged with troops and trucks,

distant growl of artillery,
crackling whine of small arms.

Ramshackle busses crammed with people,
bamboo huts with straw-thatched roofs,
women bearing baskets to market;
a ragged child stares at passing soldiers.

1969–1971

Listening Post

The grass is wet,
but the rain has stopped.
The air is fresh and still.
The moon is a pale circle
behind a thin film of clouds.
I sit, half thinking, half dreaming.
Sleep is sweet, but life is sweeter;

I dare not close my eyes.
Cool leaves dangle before me.
The damp ground chills my body.
Nighttime sounds in my ears.
It is almost as if—

Looking for adventure,
we troop into a neighbor's wood
and pitch our camp.
We are too young for guns,
but we have knives and axes and fire.
We huddle close around the fire
and dare the fiercest enemy to come near.

Strange, though only for a moment,
as though the time between boy and man
were but a rising and setting of the sun.

A shadow moves;
my heart begins to pound:

cold eyes and colder steel peer into the darkness.
It is different now—
the fire has gone out.

One Night on Guard Duty

The first salvo is gone before I can turn,
but there is still time to see the guns
hurl a second wave of steel against the dark.

The shells arc up,
tearing through the air like some invisible hand
crinkling giant sheets of cellophane among the stars.

The night waits, breathless,
till the far horizon erupts in brilliant
pulsing silence.

The Sniper's Mark

He seemed in a curious hurry
to burn up what was left
of the energy inside—

a brainless, savage flurry
of arms and legs and eyes.

The Generals' War

Paper orders passed down and executed;

straggling back in plum-colored rags,
one-legged, in slings, on stretchers,
in green plastic bags,
with stubbled faces
and gaunt eyes hung in sockets;

returned to paper
for some general to read about
and pin a medal to.

Hunting

Sighting down the long black barrel,
I wait till front and rear sights
form a perfect line on his body,
then slowly squeeze the trigger.

The thought occurs
that I have never hunted anything in my whole life
except other men.

But I have learned by now
where such thoughts lead,
and soon pass on
to chow, and sleep,
and how much long till I change my socks.

Christ

I saw the Crucified Christ three days ago.
He did not hang on the cross,
but lay instead on the shambled terrace
of what had been a house.
There were no nails in His limbs,
no crown of thorns, no open wounds.
The soldiers had left nothing
but a small black hole upon His cheek.
And He did not cry, "Forgive them, Lord,"
but only lay there, gazing at a monsoon sky.

Today, angelic hosts
of flies caress His brow,
and from His swollen body comes
the sick-sweet stench of rotting flesh.

Gettysburg

Yankee day
picnicking by an old stone wall
where cannons ranged once in fury.
Waving colored flags
and blue felt hats,

we interrupt our meal
to watch
the President's long black motorcade
pass by.
He doesn't notice,
but his wife does,
and smiles at us
from behind the closed window.

Dancing

Having been where contrasts meet,
I perceive reality to be
whatever looms largest in the mind.

Thus, truths are never absolute;
nebulous, they never lose the shifting
beat of music changing time.

Books I read, and faces seen
in sunlight tell me where I am;
at night, this truth melts away;

an older truth looms within
and I submit, take my rifle,
rejoin comrades on patrol

until the sun returns the books,
and faces, and the other truth
I dance with to a kinder beat.

Starships

The stars are faces;
they are far away.
But at night, sometimes,
while traveling in our starships,
we pass by more closely,
and, gazing through the portholes,
catch a wisp of hair
or the turned-up corner of a smile
before they slip away and are gone.

In the daytime,
we cannot see the stars,
but we know they are there.

Today is cold and crackling.
The wind tugs at the cuffs of our coats
and tells us there is nowhere to hide.

But the wind doesn't know about our starships.
We laugh at the frozen sun
and think of faces in the sky
that touch us briefly as we sail by
on the long passage of our dreams.

And the wind doesn't know of our desire
to collide one night
with the stars that are faces in the sky
and will consume us in their heat

if only we sail far enough.

To Swarthmore

The night I got here,
The mosquitos formed a solid black carpet
On the ceiling of the Meeting House,
And I was so busy warding off
Massed squadron attacks upon my body
I don't even remember who spoke.
That was almost two years ago.

Orientation Week is for orienting—
Not bad, this place;
Eat, talk, lie on the grass,
Sing songs on the tower steps,
Go to parties: "Hi! What's your name?"
                        "Where you from?"
                        "Uh, well ..." (shuffle feet, shove
hands in pockets, scratch behind the ear, stare at the
fascinating light fixture)
Which way is the punchbowl?
Get up, take showers, stroll around;
Easy living—not bad, this place.

Then came an Introduction to Sociology-Anthropology;
The professor opened his mouth
And left it open for nearly an hour—
He wasn't even talking English:
"Africanus Australopithecus utilized
bipedal locomotion andonandonandon ..."
"What did that man say?"
"Cavemen walked on two feet."
"Oh, really—why can't he just *say* that?"
"Not scientific, you know."
I left that class with my hair standing on end,
Wondering what happened to Orientation Week.
I didn't wonder long—there wasn't time;
We "learned" the Russian alphabet in 23 minutes flat;
Covered 400 years of the Roman Empire in an hour;
I was terrified.

But the pace comes;
Not easily, not consciously,
(You can't turn your back on a book
or it will bite you in the neck),
It just seems to come
Somewhere along in those first confused months.
Ed stops in and asks me about the Marines;
We talk.
Worm comes in and Chris and Steve;
Four hours—2:00 A.M.
And you feel guilty about the work
You didn't do that *has* to be done,
But you're getting to know the people in Pitt
And they're not just people now,
They're faces with names that you know—
They're friends.

Friends.
Friends, Green's, Sharples, roses, Delta Upsilon,
Wharton, girls, swimming, English, autumn,
Chaplin, cider, study, Coltraine, mid-terms,
Walk, laugh, worry, beards, eyes, Parrish, dates,
Snow.

The week before Christmas, it snowed.
Papers to write—snow.
Books to read—snow.

Notes to study—snow.
Snow—the Crum—snow—midnight—snow;
Snow, snow, turn off your mind
And walk and walk for hours
Through the snow in the dark glowing half-white
And talk to your friend who's walking with you.
(And somehow the work gets done anyway
before the end of the term, though it takes
three weeks of madness
that cost you four or five years
off the good end of your life,
you're sure of that—
But you smile)

And you start all over again and again too and the
Courses run head-on into one another—Medieval European
History Comparative Politics Poetry Workshop Russian
Thought and Literature in the Quest for Truth Elements
Of Politics Political Anthropology Ethnic Groups in
American History International Politics Contemporary
Poetry Problems and Principles of Modern Technology
Non-Philosophy Europe of the Dictators Scream
Choke Suffocate Go Crazy
Watch the daffodils come bursting into the sunlight
With a sunlight of their own
Along Magill Walk and stop
To play stretch on the lawn and
Feel Springtime reaching back
Into the stuffy corners of your mind
And you feel alive
And good
And not so hassled as you always think you are.

You are, in fact, Commodore of a yacht
Maneuvering for a starting position in
The First Annual Head of the Crum Regatta
For non-motorized vessels,
Which means surfboards and canoes and innertubes
And plastic boats and rafts and baggies
And planks and frisbee paddles and
Flippers and some people even managed to finish.
Everyone got wet.
We had fun.

Fun. "American and South Vietnamese forces
Have crossed the border into Cambodia in order to ..."
And then the fun stopped for a lot of people for awhile at least
And a lot of people did some sober thinking
On what was happening and at least tried:
Strike, mass meetings, pamphleteering, committees,
workshops, Rotary Clubs, Black Panthers, speeches,
discussions, non-violence, energy, passion.
But the year ended and the momentum stalled,
And I wondered what we had really accomplished;
But I have an idea now that it was not time wasted.
Most of us grew a little,
Became more aware,
Changed in quiet, irreversible ways.
I still remember the feeling of being in a room
With 700 people trying very hard to work together.

There was, too, Water Ballet and Rap Sessions and Yeats
And the riotous storming of Fortress McCabe
When, reportedly, one night a skeleton was found
Who had suffered amid the stacks and books and cobwebs
And shadows of corners where he had gone unnoticed
And had forgotten it was lunchtime
until he finally starved to death
Over a copy of Shakespeare to the glory of Honors
And they laid him to rest in the Treasure Room;
And pain and problems unsolvable solved or forgotten,
Skipping class to throw stones that sail
Across the water and rattle
In the bushes on the other side And

the President's Tea was Far Out
David and I thought.
"Would you like a cookie?"
"No thanks, would *you* like a cookie?"
Coats and ties and tie-dyed T-shirts
And a whole new batch of faces
To find names for;
And Charlie is from Wilmington.
Good old Wilmington.
Good old Charlie.
"'That's Catch-22!' he cried," which could be
22 people celebrating my 22nd birthday,

All stuffed into one small room and all talking
At once.
Or it could be 22 eggs;
But it wasn't.
It was D.K., C.J. and me in political science
At 8:30 in the morning with 37 eggs between us
And pencil lines running off the page:
(Hey, look. Look! It's *them* again!
—and it was).

And just when your brain is fried beyond redemption
And you have nothing to look forward to
But another Saga in culinary delight,
You find the tables pushed back
And a rock band
Playing music
And you dance off five hours in the library
And things are o.k. again;
At least until you have to write a paper
In four days (and nights)
And your kidneys are drowning in coffee,
And you float away to the three-ring circus in your dorm
At two o'clock on a Wednesday night/morning
That won't keep you awake—
if you're a clown,
or a Tiger,
or one of an assorted crew of maniacs
who have no eardrums and never sleep,
or like circuses.
My hearing is bad;
The people aren't.

> The people are all kinds.
> The people are fine.
> The people are friends.
> The friends are together.
> Together is a nice way to be.

Also happy, laughing, harried, hassled, searching,
Wanting, sharing, helping, listening, working;
The Three Stooges in a homemade steam shower;
Tarbs, Tarot cards, Lee Michaels, Willets,
King Kong, Sandy Bull, Starships, Alone;

Soap operas on Friday afternoon;
Water balloons from "C" Section;
"We have the most advanced International
Politics Simulation in the country,"
(except the computer program won't run);
Road rallyes, brownies, pressure;
Ten Years After at the Spectrum;
Nairobi, Swarthmore, Trucking, Trotter,
unsungs, Kerouac, Tin Pan Bands,
Fine Red California Wine;
The harvest Moon and half a toilet seat;
Hello in the morning with clean white teeth
On the way to the mail box
And late again for class,
And Rainbow Riders on the way to the sun.

The sun sets easy beyond Clothier Tower
As I sit alone in the pink-orange glow
That spreads across the campus
like some soft sea of safety and reflection and
Mood that goes deep and is inside me
And always has been, it seems, or at least
Always will be:

This place is all right.

1971–1973

Perimeter Guard

Crouched in a corner,
shivering, damp,
Gerry asleep beside me,
I stand the last
two-hour watch
of a long, tired night.
To the east,
the stars are fading:
gray appears,
then pink, red, and blue.

Souvenirs

"Bring me back a souvenir," the captain called.
"Sure thing," I shouted back above the amtrac's roar.

Later that day,
the column halted,
we found a Buddhist temple by the trail.
Combing through a nearby wood,
we found a heavy log as well.

It must have taken more than half an hour,
but at last we battered in
the concrete walls so badly
that the roof collapsed.

Before it did,
I took two painted vases
Buddhists use for burning incense.

One vase I kept,
and one I offered proudly to the captain.

Sergeant Jones

And then there's Sergeant Jones.
He's hard, but knows the ways
to handle other men
when they're afraid.

Always has a good word, too.

Not just for us either—
speaks Vietnamese fluently,
makes the girls at the district office
giggle with delight
every time we go there.

The kind of guy the young enlisted men
admire:
he can hit a gook at 50 yards
with a fuckin' .45.

The Rat

Flashing jagged teeth,
he squealed and shrieked and tried
to break the circle of our flailing rifle butts.

But he couldn't, and at last,
trapped in a corner of the bunker,
he only glared at us through wild
uncomprehending eyes.

His final glimpse of life
was the bottom of a cinderblock.

Mail Call

It's strange, the obstacles
that fail to break the will:
boredom, body rot, pervasive fear of death.
Stranger still, the unanticipated breath
that tips the scales:

    Private Thomas married
only weeks before he left. Now, ten months past,
he was our point man—unscathed, unharried,
though constantly exposed. Ten months unmarked—

and over in an instant with a single shot
that punched a hole in the hot day; with Thomas,
lifeless, sprawled across his cot;
with the lawyer's note,
blood-spattered, crumpled in his fist;
with his last "I love you" trapped inside his throat
by the barrel of a pistol.

The One That Died

You bet we'll soon forget the one that died;
he isn't welcome anymore.
He could too easily take our place
for us to think about him
any longer than it takes
to sort his personal effects:

a pack of letters,
cigarettes,
photos and a wallet.
We'll keep the cigarettes,
divide them up among us.
His parents have no use for them,
and cigarettes are hard to get.

Night Patrol

Another night coats the nose and ears:
smells of fish and paddy water,
smoke from cooking fires and stale urine
drift uneasily, cloaked in silence;
the marketplace deserted, shuttered
houses, empty paths, all cloaked in silence.
Shadows bristle.

Our gravel-crunching boots tear great
holes in the darkness, make us wince
with every step. A mangy dog
pits the stomach; rifles level;
nervous fingers hit the safety catch.

The Next Step

The next step you take
may lead you into an ambush.

The next step you take
may trigger a tripwire.

The next step you take
may detonate a mine.

The next step you take
may tear your leg off at the hip.

The next step you take
may split your belly open.

The next step you take
may send a sniper's bullet through your brain.

The next step you take.
The next step you take.

The next step.
The next step.

The next step.

Guerrilla War

It's practically impossible
to tell civilians
from the Viet Cong.

Nobody wears uniforms.
They all talk
the same language
(and you couldn't understand them
even if they didn't).

They tape grenades
inside their clothes,
and carry satchel charges
in their market baskets.

Even their women fight.
And young boys.
And girls.

It's practically impossible
to tell civilians
from the Viet Cong.

After awhile,
you quit trying.

Time on Target

We used to get intelligence reports
from the Vietnamese district offices.
Every night, I'd make a list
of targets for artillery to hit.

It used to give me quite a kick
to know that I, a corporal,

could command an entire battery
to fire anywhere I said.

One day, while on patrol,
we passed the ruins of a house;
beside it sat a woman
with her left breast torn away;
beside her lay a child, dead.

When I got back to base,
I told the fellows in the COC;
it gave us all a lift to know
all those shells we fired every night
were hitting something.

The Hawk and Two Suns

The silver hawk swoops 300 miles per hour
almost standing still,
locks his grid-coordinate prey
between his cross-haired eyes,
holds, extends twin silver talons—
cannisters that tumble through the air—
almost horizontal, they strike the ground together.

Coming from the sun, the hawk creates another sun
that spreads a brilliant orange sun-storm
that billows out and rolls along the earth;
billows, then recedes;
leaves behind burnt-black bodies and lungs
burst outward in frantic search of oxygen.

The hawk shrieks his predatory victory cry,
and wheels away to join the greater sun
he drains with every raid.

The Ambush

Illusion:
waiting come to an end.

The target:
black shape
against the bluer black of night.

Response:
extremities converge inside the chest,
burst outward through the arms,
explode
from the muzzle of an automatic rifle
toward the lurching, speechless figure
caught mid-sentence
by the fury of an inability to hate.

 (The target is a pretext;
 it has a hundred names.
 none belong to it;
 all are out of reach.)

Respite:
through the long night after,
sleep—the deep and total sleep
that swallows one whose mind is without thought,
empty, drained, at peace.

Illusion shattered:
daylight;
things remain as they were.

Another Life

The long day's march is over.
Ten thousand meters through the bush
with flak jacket, rifle, helmet,
three hundred rounds of ammunition,
three days' rations, two canteens,
hand grenades, a cartridge belt,
pack straps grinding at the shoulders,
feet stuffed in boots that stumble forward
mile after hill after hour,
the sun a crushing hundred-and-two,
sweat in the eyes and salt on the lips,
and always aware that Charlie only waits.

The march is over for today.
Now, heaped against a paddy dike
and fighting back the sweetness of exhaustion,
I close my eyes
and struggle to recall
another life.

The Bob Hope Christmas Special

They went to Cam Ranh Bay,
to Saigon, and Danang—
to anywhere that was secure,
and had good roads, and showers.

They made the headlines
with their bombshell girls
and dedication to the boys.

They never got to where the fighting was,
to where the face of yesterday
looked exactly like today.

They never gave a show for those
who found relief in cigarettes,
dry socks, and no patrol today.

In thirteen months,
I never saw the USO.
But once in August, near Hoi An,
Floyd Patterson shook my hand.

Coming Home

San Francisco airport—

no more corpsmen stuffing ruptured chests
with cotton balls and not enough heat tabs
to eat a decent meal.

I asked some girl to sit
and have a Coke with me.
She thought I was crazy;
I thought she was going to call a cop.

I bought a ticket for Philadelphia.
At the loading gate, they told me:
"Thank you for flying TWA;
we hope you will enjoy your flight."

No brass bands,
no flags,
no girls,
no cameramen.

Only a small boy who asked me
what the ribbons on my jacket meant.

A Relative Thing

We are the ones you sent to fight a war
you didn't know a thing about.

It didn't take us long to realize
the only land that we controlled
was covered by the bottoms of our boots.

When the newsmen said that naval ships
had shelled a VC staging point,
we saw a breastless woman
and her still born child.

We laughed at old men stumbling
in the dust in frenzied terror
to avoid our three-ton trucks.

We fought outnumbered in Hue City
while the ARVN soldiers looted bodies
in the safety of the rear.
The cookies from the wives of Local 104
did not soften our awareness.

We have seen the pacified supporters
of the Saigon government
sitting in their jampacked cardboard towns,
their wasted hands placed limply in their laps,
their empty bellies waiting for the rice
some district chief has sold
for profit to the Viet Cong.

We have been Democracy on Zippo raids,
burning houses to the ground,
driving eager amtracs through new-sown fields.

We are the ones who have to live
with the memory that we were the instruments

of your pigeon-breasted fantasies.
We are inextricable accomplices
in this travesty of dreams:
but we are not alone.

We are the ones you sent to fight a war
you did not know a thing about—
those of us that lived
have tried to tell you what went wrong.
Now you think you do not have to listen.

Just because we will not fit
into the uniforms of photographs
of you at twenty-one
does not mean you can disown us.

We are your sons, America,
and you cannot change that.
When you awake,
we will still be here.

Old Myths

Citations, medals, warrants of promotion:

all the things I ever earned I framed
and tacked up in the attic room
I used to use for studying.

That was many years ago—
before events began to show
how deeply they were etched.

Now the room is cluttered with old clothes
and broken toys and boxes.
I don't go up there anymore:
I've lived the myth, and know
what lies are made of.

Yet even now, sometimes I find
traces of an older pride:

I guess old myths die hard.

A Generation of Peace

The longest war is over, so they say;
now there is peace. And it was hard going:
these last four years especially, when we
could not understand, sometimes, exactly
how invasions and blockades and bombing
could bring a quicker end. But others knew,
and they were right, weren't they?
Now there is peace.

Now there is peace for a generation
of Americans molded by the war;
peace for a nation split to the bones;
peace for the dead and peace for the crippled;
peace for the homeless, for those who went mad;
peace for the men whose dreams have stolen sleep;
peace for the gassed and peace for the clubbed;
peace for expatriots who cannot come home;
peace for the guardsmen and peace for the cops;
peace for a battered people who were fighting
long before we got there, who will
go on fighting long after we are gone;
peace that justifies the search for the light
at the end of an endless tunnel.

Yes, the longest war is finally over.
And it was hard going for awhile,
but it was worth it after all, wasn't it?
For now there is peace.

Imagine

The conversation turned to Vietnam.
He'd been there, and they asked him
what it had been like:
had he been in battle?
Had he ever been afraid?

Patiently, he tried to answer
questions he had tried to answer
many times before.

They listened, and they strained
to visualize the words:
newsreels and photographs, books
and Wilfred Owen tumbled
through their minds.
Pulses quickened.

They didn't notice, as he talked,
his eyes, as he talked,
his eyes begin to focus
through the wall, at nothing,
or at something inside.

When he finished speaking,
someone asked him:
had he ever killed?

Rehoboth

The bay is calm tonight.
Three miles south, the Bethany lights
float midway to the sky.
Green and white, shimmering and shy,
they dance their silent dance.
The dark bay sparkles with a crystal chance
to sail a highway moon, and only
where that broad path ends, we know
the sky begins. Farther east,
the wide Atlantic moans beneath
the stars. Two concrete towers stand
abandoned on the salt-swept beach;
their sightless eyes still strain to reach
beyond the breakers. The sand
outside the window is a luminescent band
behind the seawall.
      My friends and I
sit inside the house, silent
as those towers, silent as those colored lights,
absorbed in the passage of the night.
All day our laughter has been shadowed
by tomorrow and today and the gulf between,
and now the rising sadness can be seen

on dim-lit faces. We have not even
laughter for a shield tonight, for the boundless
beauty that encloses us and holds us
gently in its arms is but a stark reminder
that our years together
will be over all too soon,
that with the coming of the morning sun
each of us must go his separate way.
We know we cannot stay
here any longer, for the shifting world
that long since passed those towers by
is more than frail desires can deny.
We cannot change what has come.
    So we sit amid a speechless gale
and search our minds for some
bond to take away with us, labor to inhale
each other's presence, that we may not forget.
    Yet we are more than quiet nights;
more even than moving water and the fairy lights.
That we can be together now and share
this moment without words is care
and bond enough. We have each other's love.
Friendship, though apart, shall still be common
to us all. We have, because we live,
the irrepressible will to go on.
And while we may not be this way again,
still we have the undiminishable
gift of our interwoven lives to help us fill
those days and nights we are alone.
    Tonight is not an end:
though we depart, we begin again.

The Living

for Amy Vedder

I heard tonight a boy you knew
is dead. I tried to think of words
I could say or write to help you—
nothing came but painted birds.
The dark admitted only silence
and at last—reversion to the truth:

the dead are dead and that is changeless.
Your friend has passed beyond poor breath;
beyond love and hope and fear,
pain, sorrow, or your tears.
You have this obligation to be kept:
to realize the way things are, accept,
and never without laughter pass
blind daffodils or thoughtless grass.

September

The long night hangs above these woods
like fog that waits the passing of the sun.
Scarcely visible, it chills the body
with the subtle breath of mist at evening.

The sun, in full-blown afternoon,
still makes a pleasant bed of grass,
and lovers need no blankets yet.
Blooming flowers wander on the breeze.

But now the breeze reveals
faint traces of a sharper edge
the sun is powerless to hide,
and the leaves, though green, are pale and
fading with the onset of a cancerous end.

Another sign: though you can hear a rustling
in the murmur of the falls, the squirrels
no longer play. They have begun their search.
Tonight, the first chevroned geese appeared
and disappeared above the trees.

The long dead night approaches,
and though I know it will not last,
I still am haunted by a mute, compelling fear:

as though, within a dream, I were sole witness
to the expiration of a tired world,
all memory, the light.

Yours

So now it has come to this:
through dark tunnels, arm-in-arm,
the damp walls cracked
and echoing our footsteps;
on past highways paved
with the harbor of night,
where the sound of tires,
though close, is now intangible,
like unseen ships along the Delaware
whose foghorns conjure
worlds of ice, exotic markets,
lions on a beach,
or rails that hum
with melancholy travelers
miles to the east;
through the shadows of trees,
and branches startling in the dark,
and cold wet grass;
past buildings swallowed by the hour,
empty of all but dreams;
on, and still on
to an old stone bench
carved at the edge of a wood
where we sit and shiver together,
reluctant, but unable to return.

Yes, it has come to an old stone bench,
and to an end of an old life
in an older, simpler world,
and to a harsh
yet undeniably desired
awakening.

Charleston

As it is now
the twenty-fourth year since
the resurrection,

I have decided to
celebrate.

First, I shall
dress up
like an evergreen

with pine cones
in my ears and

needles in my arms.
Then, I'll call all

the winemakers
of the world together

and treat them to
ice cream
on the French Riviera.

As it will then be
nearing noon,

I will leave
for Kansas,
arriving

just in time
for tea.

Beyond
this, I have
envisioned

painting moustaches on
the faces of Mount Rushmore,

the demolition of
the Brooklyn Bridge,
and a campaign to

initiate
Take-a-Policeman-to-Breakfast Week,

all of which should be
completed
before six o'clock.

After supper at
Bookbinder's

(escorted by
the Mayor of East
St. Louis and

half a dozen
alcoholic concert

pianists),
I shall go motoring
along the Industrial Highway

for thirty-five minutes.
Then it's off

to Colorado to
watch the long-awaited collapse
of the Rocky Mountains,

purchase land, and
visit with my brother.

A short hop
by covered wagon
will find

me
in San Francisco,

this time dressed
as a penguin
and hawking

pornographically illustrated
single-volume

copies of
*The Complete Works of
William Shakespeare.*

Sometime around
midnight,

I intend to
turn into
a three-pound jar of

Skippy peanut butter,
and live

incognito
with Italian friends
in Sausalito

until the next
millennium arrives.

1974

Rhythm

The rhythm
comes through his hands.
That's what the old man told me.

Sits all day by the waterfront
catching fish.
Big fish.
Twelve inches long.

Pulls living creatures
from this stagnant
oil-encrusted
cesspool of a harbor
where the last fish
must have died
thirty years ago.

I asked him how he does it.

"It's the rhythm that gets 'em,"
he said, "and the rhythm
comes through my hands."

The Flying Gypsy

I. Windward

She sits each night near Market Street.
And every night she wears the same
old dress and faded flowered hat
that must have fired young men's dreams
fifty years ago.
A battered Gimbels shopping bag
holds everything she owns.

II. Leeward

Once, many years ago, I came
by chance upon a clipper ship
tied up beside an unused dock.
The Flying Gypsy was her name,
and in her time, white canvas bent
before the wind, she must have been
the swiftest lady on the sea,
for even then her rotting shrouds
and broken spars stretched anxious
fingers to the gentlest breeze.

III. Windward

I pass that way each night at ten.
No matter that I know by now,
before I see her, she'll be there;
in the quiet, empty street
her solitary presence always startles:
saying nothing, she demands her place
with eyes that stare through pounding waves
and lips still tasting salt.

Myers, Messick & Me

Three men deliberately posed:
two sit on steps;
one stands beside a keg
resting by the door
of an old stone lodge;
all hold beer mugs.

Like the last sad gunfighters
of another day,
made obsolete
by time and circumstance,
and bending visibly
beneath the weight
of recognition,
their eyes burn softly

with a blue proud flame
of tired dignity.

Though the posse closes in,
Butch Cassidy
and the Sundance Twins
still drink their beer
in measured drafts
and dream of Panama,
Bolivia, and Peru.

1975

The Last Day

Night drifts coldly into dawn.
Stark slate turns
first grey, then red.
The sea lies flat;
the hills breathless.

Terror and alarm, confusion,
fire, death, apocalyptic change—
all these we imagined.
In the darkest alleys of our minds
we covered every possibility.

No one thought of this.

The sun climbs in the east;
still the streets and roads
are empty. No one moves;
each is locked forever

in a dream.

The Obsession

It seemed so childish
to you

that I should want to stay
so desperately.

But there are things
you were not aware of;
dark, shapeless things
moving
through the twilight pools
beneath the surface:

swift bullets flying
without warning;
the inscrutable constellations
turning;
the silence.

How much like death
to sleep alone.

You called it
an irrational obsession.

The Traveler

for Betsy Hastedt

All winter long
I watched you prepare:
one by one
your leaves turning pale,
curling, brown at the edges;
each silent morning
another lying on the windowsill.

The others say you are dying.

I knew all along
you were only passing through.

When you reach the end,
tell the one who sent you
I was kind.

Granddad

I Remember only a table,
Fig Newtons and a lap
on the porch of a house
in Asbury Park, New Jersey.
You don't even have a face then;
I found it later
in pictures.

Grandmother says you were crazy:
building railroads
and going wherever you pleased;
one job here,
another one there,
footloose half your life;
and always the opera,
and Verdi; and later,
teaching your children Italian.

She never has used
the word love
when she speaks of you.
But in spite of herself,
rumpled old Eastern Shore Scots-Irish,
she speaks with respect,
and I know she loved you.

She says I'm a lot like you.
I grow silent inside
to think of it—as though,
if I'm quiet,
I'll hear you moving
in my veins.

To the Asian Victors

The great miscalculation
refuses to be covered over.
I have tried every solution,
yet the paint always begins to peel
even before it is dry,
and the bare room comes back
again.

This last time
it returned as yellow frightened faces
spilling from the bellies of birds,
like splinters from old wounds
that will not heal.

In school, as a child,
I learned about Redcoats—
I studied myself,
though I did not know it at the time.
The lesson remains;
only the teacher has changed.

Looking back
at the pale shadow forever
calling at dusk from the forest,
I remember the dead, I
remember the dying.

But I cannot ever quite remember
what I went looking for,
or what it was I lost
in that alien land that became
more I
than my own can ever be again.

The Fool

Irregular motion
in the regular jostle
of the rush-hour street barely
catches the eye—
but does,
and I turn:

just another man
almost
like me.

But a withered arm
and a withered leg
have left him with the palsied
gait of one

forever walking
into the wind.

Eyeing, like me,
fresh girls in fresh summer dresses,
he shuffles by,

and I turn away, ashamed,
knowing what kind of fool suffers,
being whole,
a moment's loneliness.

Geese

When you went away,
the leaves began to fall;
the blue sky scattered before clouds
like flustered pigeons in the plaza,
and the geese by the river,
thinking winter had come,
cried out and fled.

All that day the colors
slowly drained from the world
like sand slipping through small
invisible holes in the earth.
The people lost their faces,
appearing only as bland shapes
at the ends of long tunnels.

Back home I discovered
a new silence
clinging to the walls like frost.
Later the wind came around to the north,
beating at the windows,
writing your name on the rattling glass,
and I could not sleep.

All this was a long time ago,
but the wind still blows from the north
and the frost on the walls remains.
The colors have not returned, nor the leaves
nor the faces nor the blue sky.

And I do not wonder any longer
when they will;

I only wonder how the geese knew.

Bicentennial

It was a hard winter,
and a harder march
before you finally rested.

The city you fled that fall
others later fled.
Still others remain—
some, like those who drove you out,
by choice; most
because they are crippled.

Our Fathers too are gone.
Imposters wear their faces.
They are clever—
many do not know the difference;
those that do
seem not to care anymore.

The clever ones
dress their sons and policies
in red coats.
They arm the world,
and ride their brothers everywhere.

Up north, the tide
has long since washed the tea
from Boston harbor.
Now we have votes
which are empty.

Looking down from your encampment,
the lush green hills
give way
to belching black industrial cavities
and stark concrete gouges.
They were built
by those who line their pockets

with your blood.
They remain
because your people lack the will
to staunch your bleeding.

Rebel, it was you
who made the Revolution happen.

If you could see
what has happened to the Revolution,
would you still be willing
to bear the long cold winter of Valley Forge
to cross the icy Delaware
to Trenton
and your death?

Money in the Bank

for Alfred Starr Hamilton

Sixty-one years
of your life are gone and I
have never heard of you
until today.

I understand the poems
simply grow
beneath your pillow as you sleep
in your cheap boardinghouse room,
and you only have to rise
and type them in the morning,
ten at a crack before lunch
and the daily paper you read
at the Montclair Public Library
because you cannot afford your own,
like the cigarettes
you pick up from the street.

Sixty-one years old,
and I have never heard of you
because you are not taught in school
and your poems do not appear in *Poetry*
and your only book was not reviewed

because we have no use for poets
who have no use
for us.

Well, Mr. Hamilton,
now I have heard of you,
and tomorrow the mailman
will give you this
(along perhaps with another summons
from the Garden State
because they say you are a vagrant),
and you'll open it and find
some person that you do not know
has sent you money.

I'd like to say I sent you this
because I simply care
about another human being.

But the truth is, Mr. Hamilton,
this money you receive
is for myself,
and for the future,

and I send it out of fear.

Shadows

You came back
almost in a dream.
I didn't even notice the door opening;
only your shadow on the floor
made me look up.

And there you were,
wearing the same white dress you wore
the last time I saw you,
wearing that smile
in your eyes
and chestnut hair.

And even after all those nights
I'd practiced every word,
I couldn't speak;

my joy, my tears,
your radiance reducing all my words
to mumbled guttural knots.

I only wanted to touch you,
but as I did,
you fell into your shadow.
Then I fell into your shadow.
Then your shadow fell into my lap.

When I held the shadow to the light,
it was empty,
except for the eyes in it,
which were yours,
and blind.

Making the Children Behave

Do they think of me now
in those strange Asian villages
where nothing ever seemed
quite human
but myself
and my few grim friends
moving through them
hunched
in lines?

When they tell stories to their children
of the evil
that awaits misbehavior,
is it me they conjure?

The Silent

They are the dark ones,
the black ones,
gliding
through the cold hollows
between the stars.

They are the keepers
of what we shall be

when we finally discover
who we are.

This is their home we inhabit,
like lost travelers
huddled near fires,
aware that we are intruders,
not knowing why
or how,
afraid they will tell us
You Belong.

All night their fingers clatter
softly on the windows
like the padded claws of cats,
sleek,
invisibly sure,
reminding us
it is they who command.

When morning finds them,
they are shadows
we can almost see
tucked away in alleys
and abandoned doorways
as we scurry for the shelter
of the noise of day,
knowing
they can wait.
They are only waiting.

1976

Vietnam Veterans, After All

Beginning in a dream
of America's turning
and of our yet finding
a reason,

we harnessed our terrible knowledge
and we joined the demonstrations
and became the soldiers
for peace

and we marched
and we prayed
and we marched
and we marched

till the din subsided
in one small corner of the world,

and the people all went home,

and the government returned to its business
unmolested,

and nothing remained
but an awareness,
an invisible hurt,
a gaunt energy bearing
the rags of our dream

like morningmouth
that cannot be scrubbed away.

To Those Who Have Gone Home Tired

After the streets fall silent
After the bruises and the tear-gassed eyes are healed
After the consensus has returned
After the memories of Kent and My Lai and Hiroshima
lose their power
and their connections with each other
and the sweaters labeled Made in Taiwan
After the last American dies in Canada
and the last Korean in prison
and the last Indian at Pine Ridge
After the last whale is emptied from the sea
and the last leopard emptied from its skin
and the last drop of blood refined by Exxon
After the last iron door clangs shut
behind the last conscience

and the last loaf of bread is hammered into bullets
and the bullets
scattered among the hungry

What answers will you find
What armor will protect you
when your children ask you

Why?

Going Home with the Monkeys

Another day gone;
we go home in winter twilight,
warm in our scarves and mufflers,
counting our small accomplishments
like fingers on a hand.

We did our jobs;
we were kind—
or if we were not,
tomorrow we can mend it.

It is evening;
we could rest—
except for the beggar on the corner,
a headline, a siren, a dream
of green palms in moonlight:

they rise up before us like wind,
like warnings,
and go away,
and rise up farther on.

They are the shadows of everything
except what we are
and what we have done.

And they never seem to get
any closer.

And they never leave us alone.

Ghosts

Driving north on 95, I pass
the time imagining
the ghosts who stare at me in silence
from the signs:
Delaware, Manhattan, Narragansett;
only their names remain,
stuck to the cutting-edge
like dry blood.

My fathers came from Germany
and Italy and Scotland,
their fathers from Caucasus—
each wave driven
by the one behind,
engulfed, exterminated,
or simply brushed aside.

East of the Aral Sea,
beyond the pale of time, the poets
tell tragic tales of madness
and a people who could ride the wind:
Ko Dali's daughter,
lynx-eyed raven of the Asian hills,
leads her Tajik horsemen
through the high, unbroken night;
sinewy freedom
on the Golden Road to Samarkand.

Going Down Off Columbia Bar

It seems foolish now, but at the time
this was all I had wanted: the sea,
and the steady roll of a steel deck,
and the beating engines, and stars.
I try to remember
what loneliness brought me here,
what comfort I found in quiet moonlight
dancing on water,
but this last unvoicable resignation
drowns all that might have had meaning.

My dying ship groans all around me.
Through savage rain, fever-whipped
by the smell of victory,
the sad beacon of the offshore lightship
sweeps slowly by, an eerie finger
admonishing the waves, so close
I could touch it; I could touch it,
but it would not hold me.
Smaller lights twinkle
from the houses on the cliffs.
What are those people thinking,
watching our lights bob and heave
in the black boiling cauldron below,
knowing those lights are a ship
beyond earthly salvation?
I imagine them fondly, recalling
an unquenchable longing for the sea,
never dreaming, till now,
What price she would demand in return.

To Maynard on the Long Road Home

Biking at night with no lights
and no helmet, you were struck
and hurled sixty feet,
dead on impact.
The newspapers noted the irony:
surviving the war
to die like that, alone,
on a hometown street.
I knew better.

Years before, on Christmas Day,
I met you on a road near Quang Tri,
a chance reunion of Perkasie boys
grown up together in a town
that feared God and raised sons
willing to die for their country.
"Who're you with?
Have you seen much action?
What the hell's going on here?"

All afternoon we remembered
our shared youth: the old boat
with Jeffy and the slow leak,
skipping Sunday School to read comics
and drink orange soda at Flexer's,
the covered bridge near Bryan's farm.
Though neither of us
spoke of it, we knew then
we had lost
more than our youth.

I show my poems to friends now and then,
hoping one or two might see
my idealistic bombast
in a new light:
the sharp turns of mood, anger
defying visible foundation,
inexplicable sadness.
How often they wonder aloud
how I managed to survive—
they always assume the war is over,
not daring to imagine our wounds,
or theirs, if it is not.
I think of you,
and wonder if either of us
will ever come home.

The Death of Kings

> "...tell sad stories of the death of kings."
> —Shakespeare

Giant,
sleek master of the oceans,
you alone command
the land beyond the land.
What else could Jonah have feared
more than the will of God?
Who else could have broken iron Ahab?
Even irreverent Hobbes
paid you the highest respect.

Light gets lost
trying to find you, beating
ever more faintly on your black door,
the black wall of your kingdom.

But the harpooneers wait on the surface,
patient as lean cats:
they dare not seek you in your own world,
but they know they do not have to.
In the end they will win,
and we shall have one more kingdom
empty of kings.

Colorado

All around me
sunlight plays
in fire sparkle pools of snow
still clinging
to these mountains;
silent mountains
stalking time
like patient walkers
going slowly somewhere
far beyond me.

Rootless

I have been walking all afternoon,
wondering how I have come to this day
already exhausted,
with nothing but holes in my pockets,
and only a handful of poems
to bind these twenty-seven years together,
trying to cling to small things
like the names of the flowers I know
or the crazy paths of butterflies,
but always returning to a woman
who told me once
I was a man
without roots—born

to the deck of a ship at midnight
or the soft purr of stars
or the cry of water searching for the sea,
but not to this world.

That woman and I made love,
our bodies slapping with desire—
but in the morning,
both of us naked,
she saw the desperation in my eyes,
and left me
with her words
drumming in my ears like thunder.

I used to fear death.
Now I only fear
a slow and violent death,
and even that, I know,
will be bearable.
The hot, windless afternoon
aimlessly drifts toward evening.
In the park, a man set in stone
stares at his lengthening shadow.

Letters

All these letters
disappearing through the vast
hole you tore
in my life:
messages in bottles.

I wonder where they go.
They never come back,
not even an oil slick
or a broken splinter of liferaft.
Just gone.

Cascais

for Natalie Meyers

Across the bay
from the gambling hotel

where Arabs and Americans
cast hundred-dollar chips
on games of chance,
night bells beat the black
like fists: storm warning.

In the village of Cascais,
Portuguese fishermen rise
without complaint or hesitation,
moving with the instinct
of a dozen generations.
Methodically,
they cast off mooring lines,
turning boats toward open sea
as the first deep rollers strike the shore.

They will ride this storm all night,
all day, until it passes:
skittering awash, disappearing,
bobbing up again, disappearing—
taking chance to sea
because it is the only
way to save
their only boats.

Wrapped in a robe
on a ninth-floor balcony,
I watch their fragile lights
weaving through the rain,
amazed,
stunned silent by tiny men
clinging to tiny lives
I could buy with a nod.

Jimmy

(for James J. McAdoo, Jr.,
Swarthmore College Men's
swimming coach for 34 years)

Age finally caught him from behind
like a swimmer coming on strong
in the last ten yards of the race

nobody ever really believed
would end.

We all knew it was coming, of course,
but it was hard to think of him
as an old man; somehow, he was still
just a kid, just one of us—
"French 75s" and his lost jeep on VE Day
just another campus prank. Jimmy
with his "Knock their jocks off, boys!"
and his soft eyes misting
when you'd done your best
and lost.

The last time I saw him
he was stooped and puffy, moving
with slow deliberate care—
but he went for a ride in my MG Midget,
muttered a curse in my ear,
and kissed me with an exuberant joy
ageless
as the love which binds him to us
even now.

1977

The Trial

Grandfather Ehrhart
dead of the flu in 1918,
younger than I am now,
leaving a wife and two kids
on a farm in Adams County:

fifty-four years
my grandmother labored without him,
trusting in God and living to see
four grandchildren spring from his blood
to devour her cherry pies.

Strong as a willow, that woman,
bearing the winds with a whispered grace,
and the yellow blossoms with joy.

But the night he died,
a widow of twenty-five lay down
beside his body
with the promise of a lifetime
turning cold.

Leaving the Guns Behind

for Doris & Carl Brenner
and the *Lindy Sue*

Light sails west;
night sails in across the Eastern Shore;
we sail south past Turkey Point
where colonial gunrunners anchored.

We sail south past Aberdeen,
where the modern merchants
test their latest wares;
past Georgetown, where the lady
loaded cannon with the troops;
past Baltimore, where the British navy
burst bombs in air.

We sail south past Annapolis;
past the river of the eastern Union army,
where the Pentagon squats;
past St. Michaels, where the hunters
manned their duck-blinds with artillery.

Night sails on, and we sail south
past Norfolk navy yard
toward open sea
and bellies full of Caribbean rum,
toward always-sun and always-willing
nut-brown women
Lord Cornwallis dreamed of in the night
before the morning he surrendered.

Helpless

Why didn't you tell me
    there were tears in your eyes?
I could have borrowed a rose
    from the vine.
I could have brought you a rose
    in a crystal jar.
I would have captured the moon
    and put it in your eyes.
Why didn't you tell me
    they were dreams in your eyes?

Coma

Your sister and mother and wife
coo in your ear
as though you were an infant:
they think you are here
in this hospital bed,
helpless, asleep
on the eyelash of death.

I don't believe them, uncle.
Where are you really?

Tramping the stars.
Riding the dolphins and tigers.
Kissing the wind naked
high
on the slopes of Everest.

Letter

    to a North Vietnamese soldier
whose life crossed paths with mine
    in Hue City, February 5th, 1968

Thought you killed me
with that rocket? Well, you nearly did:
splattered walls and splintered air,
knocked me cold and full of holes,
and brought the roof down on my head.

But I lived,
long enough to wonder often
how you missed, long enough
to wish too many times
you hadn't.

What's it like back there?
It's all behind us here,
and after all those years of possibility,
things are back to normal.
We just had a special birthday,
and we've found again our inspiration
by recalling where we came from
and forgetting where we've been.

Oh, we're still haggling over pieces
of the lives sticking out
beyond the margins of our latest
history books—but no one haggles
with the authors.

Do better than that
you cockeyed gunner with the brass
to send me back alive among a people
I can never feel
at ease with anymore:

remember where you've been, and why.
And then build houses; build villages,
dikes and schools, songs

and children in that green land
I blackened with my shadow
and the shadow of my flag.

Remember Ho Chi Minh
was a poet: please,
do not let it all come down
to nothing.

Portrait of Friends

What a day that was:
five thousand feet up, and the high

desert soaring away
on all sides into the mountains,
Joshua trees poking stark
incredible thumbs at the sky,
and the three of us, stoned,
chasing bewildered
coyotes out from the rocks.

Sixty degrees, though the snow
still lay in the shadows.
David and I stripped
to the waist and battled it out
with snowballs
while Diana sat laughing—
hair on the breeze, and the breeze
in the folds of her antique dress—
grand, radiant
lady of the desert.

David and I went east from there;
Diana went west. The coyotes
went on skulking through the underbrush,
nervous, listening
half afraid, half
lonely for the laughter
still dancing down the years.

After the Fire

After the fire
burns out,
and the stillness
sweeps in, we
begin to observe
small things: red
welts, slight
bruises on
pubic bones, musky
impatience of wet lace—Oh, my
face in your
breasts, and
yours in my

hair, and the
laughter
softly lapping the night
like a sea.

Desire

I want a Cadillac.

I want a green-eyed Auburn coed
sitting in the front seat of my Cadillac.

I want a cold case of beer
for the cooler in the back seat.

And a couple of twenties for gas.

Cast Out

after *Les merveilles de la nature*
(The Wonders of Nature) by Magritte

Light surf breaks beneath clouds.
On a flat rock by the beach,
two figures sit. Behind them,
in the distance, a ship
in full sail beats to windward.

Slight posture variations,
differences in size
somehow suggest
the perfect pair,

but their graceful muscled thighs,
full calves and tender bellies
startle—out of place
beneath thick-tapered heads
with thick-lipped mouths,
dorsal fins, and fins
where arms should be.

Half fish, half human,
these strangers seem
to raise their voices
in a keen
so dignified, so bottomless and pure

the sea, the ship, the clouds
all pause

forever on that single
steady cry.

Twodot, Montana

I knew that Sunday morning
only what I could see: dust
dancing in waves on a single unpaved street,
swirling in tiny plumes, unswirling,
blowing away through summer heat; two cats
asleep on a windowledge; a dog asleep
on the shade of the plank sidewalk;
squat frame buildings, half of them boarded shut.
I had followed Mac's directions perfectly;
this had to be Twodot—but I was lost.
Out of the car, I gingerly looked in windows:
peer in the barbershop-post office—nobody there;
peer in the Twodot Bar, where Saturday nights
the cowhands wash down whole weeks
of prairie dust—nobody there either.
At one end of town, the railroad station seemed
to collapse board by board as I watched, the train
coming once a year, loading cattle for slaughter.
Beyond the last buildings, a few small silver
Airstream Specials crouched, bolted to concrete
foundations against Canadian winter winds,
space between them for kitchen gardens.
A woman there answered my question:
on down the road ten more miles; Mary and Pete's
would be the Big House, the first one; the 'boy,'
Mac, lived in the Little House beyond that.
Clawing dry earth with a hoe as she talked, hair
stiff and pale as dry prairie grass, her eyes
fell back inside themselves like old volcanoes
or the insides of empty whiskey bottles,
something deep within resenting the intrusion
of people who come and go when they please.
I got in the car and left, thinking that morning,
"Perhaps because it's Sunday."

Growing Older Alone

Good morning.
Look at me smiling. Talk to me:
touch me alive, please try,
I'm only a man, and it's awkward
to ask out loud.

"Holy Mother of God, intercede for us.
Mary, Mother of God, pray for us.
Holy Mother of God, please save us"
from this poverty—

or is it still
that beautiful mild woman from Charleston
you pray to, shy as a fawn
and deaf.

It all goes on in a dream:
day after day, and nothing changes
but the slow accumulation of years
recorded in your joints,
which don't quite work
the way they used to,
and the empty bed where you sleep
growing larger.

It makes you afraid;
it's hard to remember why;
waiting for someone
to turn on the lights:
hey wake up, it's time to get up—
but no one ever does;
so you just pretend,
and get up anyway and go on

wondering when you'll finally
rape the girl next door,
or open the window and bail out,
or mentally jump ship somewhere
east of Macao, disappear
into the soft white fog
and never come back again.

Have you earned the right
to all this?
Where did you put the apricots?
Why don't you go for a walk?

The Last Prayer of Michelangelo

Eighty-six years I have labored on the scaffold.
Under my chisel, the marble fell away like rain;
But I have never found you, Lord.
In my hands remained only empty shapes—stone idols.
Though you beckoned like a rainbow there
In every flying chip, Lord, I could not find you.

Now I am old—scarred, silent, weathered
Like the marble I have hammered all my life;
Yet in my soul I know your light still burns.

How can I crack this rock that traps my soul?
With a gesture on the anvil of the earth,
Master Sculptor, you can forge the sun:
If you can still love an old sinner,
Lord, hammer me!

Adapted from the original Hungarian
by Gyorgy Faludi with translation
assistance from Anne Ferenczi

Sanctuary

This is the ancient cathedral,
lifting its stone pure spires
forever up to the sky,
holding the perfect faith
over the heads of the faithful
like magic,
the hollow space between
filled with their hymns:

Christ on the cross
dying for those who are lonely
and helpless, and afraid.

And if you believe—no matter
the grossest injustice
you suffer, the cruelest cancers
concocted by men and the fallen,
the clockwork blindness
of stars—you shall be free.

And those who are here know this
almost for what it is:
shelter, the perfect
defense, so beautiful
one could remain forever.

And they do.

Welcome

When you have ridden once too often
jostling on the El
in a crowd at dusk with no one
to talk to and no one
waiting at home,

when you have eaten your last meal
alone,

when you have said your final
hello to the grocer
in that same strange voice
like a cry,

when you have given up hope
ever of turning the next corner
to find the door
with no lock and a lamp
burning on the other side,

you will come to the door
with no lock
and no lamp,

and you will open it.

Come in;
sit down, rest, and eat.
See: we have saved you a place
at our table.

Empire

I.   Barbarian tribesmen
     stand in the light
     still on the crests of the hills.
     They shake their weapons in the air,
     gesture lewdly, and jeer
     at the soldiers in the valley
     where the watchfires
     flicker at the rising shadows.

     Down below, Roman officers
     drink wine and plan;
     soldiers tug cloaks
     more tightly around their shoulders,
     mutter about the food,
     and think of wives and lovers
     as the sentries take their posts
     around the camp: a circle of eyes
     peering into the darkness
     at the edge of the empire.

II. In Perkasie and Pittsburgh,
     North Platte, Grosse Point and Portland,
     Memorial Day crowds line the streets
     cheering for the local high school band.
     The majorettes are beautiful
     and young,
     and the solemn Legionnaires, young
     thirty years ago, fire
     fake bullets for the dead.
     Picnics follow in the afternoon,
     and all across America
     swimming pools open for the summer.

     The honored dead are white,
     or died
     trying to be white,
     red and blue: there are
     no twenty-one gun salutes
     for Crazy Horse.

On this day, in 1431,
Joan of Arc was burned to death
by the English
and the Catholic Church.
She died for France.

III.   When the dinosaurs died,
dim-witted and without complaint,
they left behind
a noble silence,
and a world
still capable of life.

IV.   The great auks
and the passenger pigeons
are gone forever;
the gorillas are in Lincoln Park Zoo.
The redwood trees, poking
into the clouds already when Christ
calmed the turbulent waters of Galilee,
are picket fences in Daly City.
The whales—greys and blues, fins
humps and pilots—breaching for air, find
only the patient harpooners' exploding barbs
while the whooping cranes sail south
each year in smaller numbers,
their nesting grounds
along the Texas Gulf of Mexico
cities now, and refineries.
The bald eagles die
unhatched in their eggs;
the dolphins die in the tunamen's nets.

V.   Toward the end, they understood
it was no use
complaining: they began to pray,
truly believing their prayers
and in the God they prayed to,
calling each other
sister and brother, sharing
what food and shelter they could find.

In the darkness when they died,
they were alone.

1978

Vietnamese-Cambodian Border War

January 1978

Stories on the six o'clock news,
familiar diagrams:
the Parrot's Beak, a black
arrow pointing west. "The same
route taken by U.S. soldiers ..."
(May 1970)—
Poker-faced, the newscasters
never fail to mention
the connection.

Like these years of silence,
the reminder too
is deliberate:
the communists
are fighting each other now.

America quietly smirks,
and orders another drink.

The Spiders' White Dream of Peace

I've had nightmares before—this
wasn't an ordinary
nightmare that jerks you awake
at the last second, startled
but free—this was something else:
it was spiders telling their
secrets in my ear, at night,
alone with them in my bed—
I wasn't even asleep.
There were hundreds of them, all

crowding around me, crawling
on top of one another,
each trying to be the one—
be the first one—to tell me
their whole plan. It was easy
to see they wanted to please
me; I couldn't understand
why. They knew what we needed—
I couldn't believe it—I
tried to wake up; I couldn't.
They were plotting the end of
the world: together they would
rise up, rise as one army
of weavers, together spin
their delicate webs back and
forth, under and over, wrap
the whole earth in a cocoon
and leave it hanging in space—
a soft white ball forever
silent, preserved, without want.

An Exorcism

"If you're a writer, you should get up
every morning and give thanks that America
is totally crazy."—Michael Anania

Suddenly the woman fell down
thrashing all around the floor
of the crowded lounge, screaming
"I've got seven devils in me!"
Not six, not eight—"Seven devils!"—
little red ones, with pitchforks.

"Whadaya expect us to do about it?"
said the paramedics to no one in particular,
scratching their heads,
fondling their fancy equipment.
The woman went on thrashing:
I've got seven devils in me!"

"Call a priest," someone said; someone did.
"Oh, seven devils," the priest intoned,
"in the name of the Lord, get out!
In the name of God,
by the body and blood of Christ,
oh, seven devils, out! Out, out!"

It worked: "Ah!"
The woman stopped thrashing.
She wiped the foam from her bleeding lips,
stood up sheepishly, straightened her dress.
"Thank you, Father," she said,
"Oh, thank you, Jesus, thank you.
America, thank you, thank you—
it's a blessing to be free."

A Confirmation

for Gerry Gaffney

Solemn Douglas firs stride slowly
down steep hills to drink
the waters of the wild Upper Umqua.
In a small clearing in the small
carved ravine of a feeder stream
we camp, pitching our tent
in the perfect stillness of the shadows
of the Klamath Indians. Far off,
almost in a dream, the logging trucks
growl west down through the mountains
toward the mills of Roseburg.

I hold the stakes, you hammer:
"Watch the fingers!"—both laughing.
Both recall, in easy conversation,
one-man poncho tents rigged
side by side in total darkness;
always you and I, in iron heat,
in the iron monsoon rains—
not like this at all; and yet,
though years have passed
and we are older by a lifetime,

a simple slip of thought, a pause,
and here: nothing's changed.

For we were never young, it seems,
not then, not ever. I couldn't even cry
the day you went down screaming, angry
jagged steel imbedded in your knee—
I knew you would live,
and I knew you wouldn't be back,
and I was glad, and a little jealous.
Two months later I went down.

We all went down eventually,
the villages aflame, the long
grim lines of soldiers, flotsam
in the vortex of a sinking illusion:
goodbye, Ginny; goodbye, John Kennedy;
goodbye, Tom Paine and high school history—
though here we are still, you and I.
We live our lives now
in a kind of awkward silence
in the perfect stillness of the shadows
of the Klamath Indians.

And I am truly happy
to be with you again. We stand
on the rocks; you point to clear
patches between white water
where the shadows of sleek fish slip,
effortless streaks of energy.
I'm clumsy: with an old, eager patience
you teach me how to cast the fly
gently, so it rides on the surface
with the current, far downstream—
till the rod bends, springs back,
bends again: strike! Your excitement
rises above the river like a wild
song the Douglas firs bend
imperceptibly to hear: shouts,
advice, encouragement, half an hour
and a fourteen-inch rainbow trout
panting hard, eyes alive, its tiny heart
beating with defiance still unbroken

though I hold the fish
helpless in my hands.

I throw the fish back
in the awkward silence, and you
slip your arm around my shoulders
gently for a moment, knowing why.

Later we eat from cans,
the rainbow flashing in the fire
reflecting in our eyes, alive:
familiar gestures—fingers burned
by hot tin lids, a mild curse, quiet
laughter, swish of a knifeblade
plunging idly deep into damp earth.
You ask do I remember the little shy
flower who always wore a white *ao dai*,
and I smile across the flames as the river
tumbles through the darkness toward the sea
that laps the shores of Asia.

The wind moves through the Douglas firs,
and in the perfect stillness of the shadows
of the Klamath Indians, we test
our bonds and find them, after all
these years, still sound—knowing
in the awkward silence we will always share
something worth clinging to
out of the permanent past of stillborn dreams:
the ancient, implacable wisdom
of ignorance shattered forever, a new
reverence we were never taught
by anyone we believed, frail hope
we gave each other, communion
made holy by our shame.

You've found religion since then,
a wife, and two children;
I write poems you admire.
The knee's still stiff, like an old
high school football wound,
and I have trouble hearing. We are
both tired, but reluctant to sleep:
both understand we will never

see each other again; once is enough.
The logging trucks have long since
left the mountains in peace;
in the perfect stillness, we can almost
hear the solemn Douglas firs drinking
the waters of the wild Upper Umqua
we have come so far to worship:
together now, in this small circle of light,
we bow our hearts to the shadows
of the Klamath Indians; now,
and always, in our need.

Driving Through Wisconsin

My beat-up old VW tumbles
down hills and around curves
and over bridges between fields
and fields of brilliant
black farmland mile on mile:
me at the center of a moving
perpetual blanket of earth.

Here and there, a farmhouse
pops up and drifts
lazily off behind me, carefully
painted and carefully kept;
a barn, a silo, a corncrib, a harvester:
symbols and signs,
a permanent creed.

What are they like, these
people on farms that dot
the black earth—rooted deep
as though they have always been here?

It doesn't really matter;
I will never meet them.
We will never exchange ideas over cups
of hot coffee in warm
kitchens or rise together before
dawn to milk the cows.

Almost suppertime:
perhaps content, perhaps

wishing they could shuck it all like
feed-corn from the cob, they
must be sitting down to eat as I pass
unnoticed through the cold
late afternoon down this
two-lane highway from somewhere
to somewhere else.

Great Horned Owl

The hunter awakes
to the last broken
pieces of light
scattered among the trees.
Silent eyes search
the forest for movement.
Rustle of leaves,
scuffle of tiny feet;
the waiting air
shivers: night rises, effortless
on terrible wings.

Eighteen Months in Chicago

And then one night I left—
just drove down Lake Shore Drive
along the Golden Mile,
crossed the river at Navy Pier,
passed Grant Park
and took the Ryan down by 22nd Street.

I stopped along the Skyway once,
looked back to see Chicago dazzling
in the night above the dark
silent waters of the lake,
and then drove on
toward Indiana and the east.

I've had a dozen homes
in half a dozen years,
a dozen jobs;

and it's a strange feeling
watching yourself in a dream saying goodbye
to friends you've come to love and places
that have come to seem familiar
while you wonder
if the place you're going to will be
half as kind—

and I don't know why I always go,
for everywhere I am
it's always where I've been
that I remember.

Waking Alone in Darkness

It's only the wind, mothers
tell their children in the night
when upturned leaves rattle on the windowpanes,
furious and black;

only the wind
when night cries in children's dreams,
and children cry out
in the darkness.

Peary & Henson Reach the North Pole

Donaldo, Stephen and I
started out at dusk as light
snow fell from scudding clouds
in the middle of the coldest
winter in the history of Chicago.

Along the lake, mounds of ice
obscured the shoreline; we trudged
in silence where it should have been,
across those wind-carved crests frozen
in the final act of breaking.

North and east, through failing light,
great jagged dragons' teeth of ice
reared up in broken rows,

and farther out, the white
horizon lumbered into night.

We could have walked through
falling snow and glowing darkness
over ice all the way to Mackinac
had we been bold enough,
equipped, and slightly mad,

but we turned back finally
because Kathleen was waiting
with hot rum in a warm apartment,
because our jobs were waiting in the morning,

and because, for most of us,
it is enough to feel the blind
brute hammer of the earth
beating at the limits of endurance
only for a moment.

The Teacher

for my students at Sandy Spring
Friends School, September 1978

A cold moon hangs
cold fire among the clouds,
and I remember colder nights
in hell when men died
in such pale light as this
of fire swift
and deadly as a heart of ice.

Hardly older then
than you are now,
I hunched down shaking
like an old man
alone in an empty cave
among the rocks of ignorance
and malice honorable men
call truth.

Out of that cave I carried
anger like a torch

to keep my heart from freezing,
and a strange new thing called
love
to keep me sane.

A dozen years ago,
before I ever knew you,
beneath a moon not unlike
this moon tonight,
I swore an oath to teach you
all I know—
and I know things
worth knowing.

It is a desperate future
I cling to,
and it is yours.
All that I have lived for
since that cold moon long ago
hangs in the balance—
and I keep fumbling for words,
but this clip-clapper tongue
won't do.

I am afraid;
I do not want to fail:

I need your hands to steady me;
I need your hearts to give me courage;
I need you to walk with me
until I find a voice
that speaks the language
that you speak.

Turning Thirty

It isn't that I fear
growing older—such things as fear,
reluctance or desire
play no part at all
except as light and shadow sweep a hillside
on a Sunday afternoon,
astonishing the eye but passing on

at sunset with the land
still unchanged: the same rocks,
the same trees, tall grass gently drifting—
merely that I do not understand
how my age has come to me
or what it means.

It's almost like some small
forest creature one might find
outside the door some frosty autumn morning,
tired, lame, uncomprehending,
almost calm.
You want to stroke its fur,
pick it up, mend the leg and send it
scampering away—but something
in its eyes says, "No,
this is how I live, and how I die."
And so, a little sad, you let it be.
Later when you look,
the thing is gone.

And just like that these
thirty years have come and gone,
and I do not understand at all
why I see a man
inside the mirror when a small
boy still lives inside this body
wondering
what causes laughter, why
nations go to war, who paints the startling
colors of the rainbow on a gray vaulted sky,
and when I will be old enough
to know.

Again, Rehoboth

I have stood by this bay before.
I have watched the light from the moon
dance in the eyes of friends
while the moon danced on black water,
wanting to know where you were,
exactly what you were thinking.

There was a time when I thought
a man could suffocate
in the dark abscess of want,
a time when I didn't believe
tomorrow would come
except in the shape I gave it.

You belong to that time—you
and the tears that fell in the wake
of the false peace of October
when it still seemed possible
to wield light like a sword.

I am a teacher now;
I live alone.
I am anchored to this world
by all cold necessity
holds sacred: water, salt,
the labored rhythms of breathing.

I cherish my friends,
whose thin threads spread like glowing wires
out from the center, bending away
over the four horizons
in smooth unbroken lines,
and the quiet slap of the water
kissing the land.

When did the recognition come—
the slow submission of dreams; the wind
turning to blow down the years
like a steady silence—
things seem hardly to have changed
at all: these hands; this head
with its wild brown mane;
this heart still beating.

Evening approaches; already
the first star burns in the east.
There will be no moon tonight.
Out on the bay, the boats beat home
to the seagulls' plaintive cries,
their smooth bending sails
blood-red from a fire sun.

Companions

Older than ancient, you shadow me
like some puzzled persistent companion.
Wherever I go, whatever I do,
you are there gazing over my shoulder
wide-eyed, bent forward from the hips,
your broad brows furrowed in thought,
long arms gently swaying.

The simplest things amaze you:
when I eat with a fork, your hands
open and close in clumsy imitation;
when I pull on my boots, you
paw at them softly, rocking
back on your haunches, wide lips
stretched in a kind of grin;
you ride in the back seat of my car
terrified, cowering down in a corner.

Yet you swing from the branches of trees
graceful and light as a cat, scampering
over the earth swiftly, agile, alert
to every sound and odor on the wind.
You understand fire, pointing in awe
to the thin flames of hot light,
prodding the coals with a stick,
chattering explanations in your
strange guttural tongue.

You mourn for the dead;
I have heard your heartbroken howl
piercing the night beneath the new moon.
You know what it means to be lonely.

Feeling the undefinable pull
of the dark centuries rising between us
like tides, you huddle inside your cave
with the small fire leaping against the walls
and the glowing eyes of jackals
dotting the black mouth like stars.
The young burrow deeply into your fur.
On the threshold of sleep, you peer
far into the night, awaiting the first

signs of light in the eastern sky—
and I am the bright gleam leaping
deep in your eyes.

Last of the Hard-hearted Ladies

I was always afraid of you—
other grandmothers lovingly
baked pies for grandchildren;
you kicked my ass
for leaving socks on the floor:
it made no sense—

until that day, fifteen,
and no one home but you,
I asked you for a cigarette,
and you said yes,
and talked with me all afternoon
as though I were a man,
and never told a soul.

Years later, I understood
you'd simply always seen the man
leaving socks on the floor
and coats on chairs, and all
you'd ever asked
is that I see it too.

Oh, you bitched about my hair
and my moustache, never liked
my politics: that socialistic crap—
but you grinned like the devil
when I held my ground.

I didn't say a word today
when Dad and Uncle Merv
read that stuff from the Bible
you'd scoffed at all your life,
remembering the times we'd sat
listening to the hymns in church
next door, smoking cigarettes:

they think their faith will help you,
and maybe it will, and anyway

it can't hurt—and the grief,
at least, is real.

So don't be angry with me, Grandma:
if I'd had it our way,
I'd have lit up another cigarette
and passed it to you.

1979

Fog

Snow all night, and then the temperature
up fifteen degrees before dawn:
white slush, wet sludge beneath,
not fit for anything—not even children;
and the fog curtaining up from the ground
luminous, so thick you have to part it
as you walk, and duck quickly
under branches out of nowhere.
You know today the sun is shining
somewhere, but it isn't here.

Here, the day is wrapped tightly
in a white shroud shivering thoughts
out of places no one ever visits
on an ordinary day, though admission price
is cheap and never varies:
see yourself the way you really are—
the way, at least, light bent through fog
makes you seem when all reassurances
are gone, it's Sunday, you live alone,
and even the telephone won't ring. Funny

how the good seems nebulous as fog.
Wrong ways, wrong words, wrong decisions
hammer like a blacksmith on an anvil:
people you will never see again come back

real as people you will have to face tomorrow—
and if you've done it wrong, you've done it
wrong so many times it hurts to be alone
on days like this with thirty years of flaws
and nothing in the house but bourbon.

A long, a very long day. Well,
it's good bourbon in any case, and it's
evening now. Snow and mud are freezing,
fog is lifting: clear sky, perhaps,
by morning. So you go to sleep
listening to the silence broken
only by the hammer, waiting
for an ordinary day to set you straight.

Another Way of Seeing

January, heavy snow
followed by rain; a bad day
for thinking: the damp seeps
clean to the bone, and joints ache
like bruises; thoughts turn
gray as old snow.

We buried my grandmother two months ago:
at fourteen a wife, fifteen a mother,
six kids, a husband dead, her last
twenty years two dozen afghans,
eulogized in a church she
never entered while alive.
What did her life amount to?

And someone waved a flag,
and someone beat the drum,
and I fought in a war that cost
the lives of millions—dozens alone
at my own hand. And what
did their lives amount to?
And what did I gain?

Cold rain falls toward evening.
Somewhere, sirens wake
from dreams and heavy equipment
levels a block of old homes;

old nightmares raise the small
hairs on the back of my neck,
and a bear I used to sleep with
lies in some old attic, one-eyed,
torn, with no fur. I am told I'm

far too serious. What does one tell
the dead? The broken-hearted? Hungry
lost creatures, staring, dumb?
Bird on a wire in January rain,
bare tree clinging to earth
like a claw,
woman, child, friend,
teach me I'm wrong.

The Grim Art of Teaching

Don't look at me
with those woman's eyes
and that burgeoning womanhood bursting
out of clothes just made
for walking into classrooms:
Stop the show! Who cares
about Shakespeare, anyway?

Don't smile, don't stare, don't
tell me I'm cute, and don't make jokes
about meeting after school
that don't sound funny.

I'm damned near old enough
to be your father;
you're damned near old enough
to be my lover;
this is one damned dangerous way
to make a living—
and the Devil is the headmaster.

The Dancers

for Arlene Horowitz

The audience knows
only what it sees:

dancers
gliding over the floor to music,
the beat of a drum, silence—
turning arching melting whirling
starburst forms: tears
where hands should be,
love in a graceful
parabolic curve.

Beads of sweat
dropping from the temples,
hearts knocking, pulses on fire
can't be seen—nor the hours,
nor the days, nor the months,
nor the fear, nor the knowledge
that it's never good enough,
never finished: every bone, every fiber,
every gesture of the dancers
straining
in the unforgiving moment of performance
to achieve the illusion of ease.

The audience only knows
what it sees.

Lost at Sea

Green Turtle Cay, Bahamas

In the language of people,
there is no word for this moment:
as you lie sleeping, the sun breaks
over the rim of the New World,
and an east wind shimmers the sea
white over a dozen shades of blue.
Offshore, where the waves break
over the reefs, the broken hulls
of old ships lie crusted with coral.

Watching the rhythm of life
beating beneath soft breasts falling
and rising through the stillness
of your dreams, I imagine
men on the deck of a ship

within sight of trees on a white beach
after the long passage west.

Will we ever return
to the safety of familiar places
where channels are marked by lights
and bells signal shoal water?
Did the men whose bones lie
there beneath the sea beyond the window
cry out loud in the last moment
as the ship went down?

The sun pours color over your face,
and I stroke your tangled hair,
feeling the pull of warm lands
beyond familiar northern seas, knowing
at least a few of those sailors
went down in silence, content.

Afraid of the Dark

She was rude, obnoxious, slovenly,
parading through the hotel lobby
blouse untucked,
empty glass in hand.

All she wanted was a drink.
She embarrassed me.
"Beat it," I said,
and she disappeared.

All she wanted
was a friend.

Like a ghost after a small boy
caught outside on a black night,
a terrible honesty
chases me down the years.

The Dream

I'm at this party. We're all having fun—dancing and drinking and smok-
ing joints, talking and laughing, bumping into each other the way you do at

a party when it's very crowded and everyone is feeling loose. We're in a nice apartment, a basement apartment fixed up very modern. The livingroom is full of dancers. People are crowding around a keg in the laundryroom while others are making mixed drinks in the kitchen. The hallway is jammed with animation, dozens of conversations piling on top of each other. The bedroom is piled with coats, and there are people sitting on the coats and on the floor.

The only strange thing is the people: there's nothing wrong with them; it's just that there are friends from high school and friends from college and friends I've known from all over. They couldn't possibly all know each other or be here together like this—but here they are. Maybe it's a party for me; I don't know. Anyway, I'm having too much fun to worry about it. I feel great.

All of a sudden the door bursts open. No, it's been kicked in; it's all splintered around the latch. Eight or ten men in combat gear swagger in. They're wearing green jungle utility uniforms, flak jackets, and helmets. It's a squad of Marines. Hey, what is this?

They barge into the livingroom, knocking people out of the way with their fists and rifle butts. Wayne Gregg—I think it must be his apartment—starts for the lead man, his arms outstretched as if to say, "What are you doing?" But before he can open his mouth, the Marine opens fire full automatic with his M-16, and Wayne is blown back against the wall where he slumps down dead.

People start screaming. Other Marines are already beyond the livingroom. I can hear shouts, gunfire, and screaming coming from the back of the apartment. The Marines still in the livingroom begin shooting and bayoneting people at random. Jesus Christ! I can't believe what I'm seeing. I beg them to stop, but they don't seem to notice me. The whole place is screaming and shouting and filling up with the acrid sting of burnt gunpowder. People are trampling each other; there's nowhere to run. Mark Halley is slumped in a chair staring vaguely at his own guts which he's holding in his hands. A Marine bashes his skull in with a rifle butt. Another Marine has just climbed off Linda Titus. She's lying on the floor, naked from the waist down. He drives a bayonet through her throat and her eyes pop wide open. I can't believe it. The inside of my head feels like it's going to explode. I can't see the faces of the Marines. I keep trying to, but I can't see their faces. The apartment is full of dead and dying people now. They are lying helter-skelter everywhere, wherever they've fallen. People are whimpering and cowering in corners and behind overturned furniture, begging hysterically. Their eyes are vacant and glassy. The Marines go on shooting and stabbing. They are working methodically now, almost casually. There is blood everywhere. They don't seem to notice me at all. I don't understand why they don't shoot me. I beg them to stop. Please, please, stop, this is insane. Mary Jane Farrell is doubled over in the hallway; she's been raped and shot in the stomach. She's crying for help.

I bend down to her and try to stop the bleeding. A Marine pokes a rifle barrel past my shoulder from behind and blows the top of her head off. I scream. He doesn't even notice me. I can't understand it. Why don't they notice me?!

I run down the hall crying, but something catches my eye, and I stop abruptly. I'm standing in front of a full-length mirror. I'm dressed in combat gear. There is a black M-16 rifle in my hands. The barrel is smoking.

Driving into the Future

We never did talk much.
Perhaps, after all, we had nothing to say.
But I think now of a hundred questions
I forgot to ask you, and a hundred more
I didn't forget, but never asked:
I was always content
simply to share the silence.

I hear you are happy in New Orleans.
Believe me, I would have it
no other way. Do they still play jazz
in the streets, dance and sing their syncopated
celebration of farewell lifting souls
all the long way to paradise, skipping notes
like good flat stones between the tugs
and barges hooting the Mississippi River
through those lazy southern nights—those
Black musicians of the city jazz made
magic? Do you ever stop to listen?

Already the autumn wind carries the weight
of a hard northern emptiness onto the plains.

Your postcard blossomed with flowers;
out here, pale yellow grass
stubbornly clings to the earth.

I drive slumped behind the wheel,
counting the white hypnotic streaks
tracing a straight line west; in the mirror,
I can see them sliding into the past.

Imagine a time when buffalo herds
covered this land from rim to rim

like dry rolling thunder. Imagine the sound
of laughter; give it a voice that sounds
like mine, and put it in your pocket.
By tomorrow, I should reach the mountains;
it is a long way, but it's all downhill
from the Continental Divide to the Pacific.

Sunset

Dresden Nuclear Power Station
Morris, Illinois

Late afternoon: in the stillness
before evening, a car on the road
between cornfields surrounding
Dresden Station raises a plume
of dust, and a light wind
settles the dust over the corn.
Power lines over the cornfields
audibly sing the power of cities
beyond sight, where neon lights flash
tomorrow, laughter and dreams.
Deep within Dresden Station,
human beings tamper with atoms.

Dresden: say it, and the air
fills with the wail of sirens,
thin fingers of light
frantically probing the clouds,
red bursting anger, black thunder,
steel drone of the heavy bombers,
dry bones rattle of falling bombs:
    deliver us from fire;
    deliver us from the flames;
    Lord, have mercy upon us.
135,000 human beings
died in the flames of Dresden.

The air to the west is on fire.
The lake to the west burns red
with the sun's descending fire.
The sky rises out of the lake gold
to copper to deep blue, falling

gently away, black, to the east.
Deep within Dresden Station,
human beings tamper with atoms.
Light wind rustles the cornstalks,
the sound like the rustle of skirts
on young graceful women.

1980

The Farmer

Each day I go into the fields
to see what is growing
and what remains to be done.
It is always the same thing: nothing
is growing; everything needs to be done.
Plow, harrow, disc, water, pray
till my bones ache and hands rub
blood-raw with honest labor—
all that grows is the slow
intransigent intensity of need.
I have sown my seed on soil
guaranteed by poverty to fail.

But I don't complain—except
to passersby who ask me why
I work such barren earth.
They would not understand me
if I stooped to lift a rock
and hold it like a child, or laughed,
or told them it is their poverty
I labor to relieve. For them,
I complain. A farmer of dreams
knows how to pretend. A farmer of dreams
knows what it means to be patient.
Each day I go into the fields.

Near-sighted

Christy is eighteen.
She is learning to master
the knowledge of generations
to make dreams
a three-dimensional living future
of wood, and steel, and pure light on brilliant
white stone surfaces soft as human skin.
The dreams are hers—
they come in the night,
and keep her awake for hours;
in the morning she goes to class
sleepy, and eager. The energy

     is awesome:
she is every child; she dreams all vibrant
possible dreams; some of them are mine.
She doesn't understand the hollow stalker
war—the skeleton, the bandit;
she doesn't see the scarred carcasses
of salmon floating in still pools
along the banks of gray foam-speckled rivers;
she doesn't hear the starving angry
voices shouting for bread. She believes
in tomorrow; I believe
          she is important:
when the rage rises, I want to beat
my fists upon the blind
heads of governments, the money kings,
the scientists and soldiers: "Why
are you stealing Christy's dreams? Are you all
without children of your own?"

     Sometimes,
I am unfit to live with.
It is hard to remember—
if we blow ourselves to hell,
or choke, or starve to death,
the pages of my books fluttering
in the wind pouring in between
the cracked bricks of Christy's buildings,
all the yellowed bones of obsolete humanity

strewn like old cars in fields beside roads,
the unborn generations permanently blind—
something will survive:
dolphins, perhaps, opossums,
the scuttling, clicking crabs,
those iron-plated roaches we forever crack
jokes about, as though our nervous laughter
could hold true progress
in check.

Something will survive—
if only a dark cold lump
whirling through the silence
between the stars, the stars,
the billions on billions
of stars.

Channel Fever

When I cast off in my small boat
with its one sail white and yellow
brilliant in the sunlight, I thought
I heard the sea calling in a soft song
sweet as any mermaid sings to sailors
in their dreams. I disappeared after it
into that vastness searching, searching.

I have caught fish to feed myself,
throwing the offal and bones to the sharks,
eating the meat raw, washing it down
with rainwater collected in a tin cup.

I never imagined it would be so lonely.
At times I have been delirious:
tearing the tattered remnants of my clothes,
shouting at stars, fighting to keep
from pitching myself headlong into the sea.

The dolphins, at least, were real; sometimes
on bright days they paced my small boat,
breasting the waves, laughing—or at night,
their sleek gray bodies luminescent green
in phosphorescent moonlight. For awhile,

I thought it was their song I followed—
but the wind blew too steady for that;
the wind drove my small boat always
over the next wave, and over the next wave.

When I first smelled land, I didn't believe it.
"Is this what it means to be mad?" I thought.
But my small boat surged suddenly forward,
and the seabirds riding the waves suddenly
surged up screaming and whirling in great
wheeling circles of excitement—and I know now,
as any sailor does even before the long voyage

is over, all along it was your
invisible hand on the tiller, your
breath beating my small boat steadily on
toward the harbor shaped like a heart.
It was you.
It is your song I heard.

The World As It Is

I am tired of philosophy,
of causes and high purpose
and constantly searching the mirror
for some small flaw marking the start
of the long final surrender to all
that is wrong with the world.
I resign my commission
in the regiment of poets.

Give me a desk in the City Room
with a typewriter, telephone, chair,
three frantic editors, news—
hard news in short
hard paragraphs tight as fists,
and easy to swallow as pills.

The Hatboro-Horsham Joint
Water and Sewer Authority,
the New Hope-Solebury School Board,
the Hilltown Township Planning Commission—
it makes no difference to me.

Who, what, where, when and how;
it's all the same story:
today's news
is tomorrow's blanket
for a frozen fish—
but every other week I get a paycheck.

The Vision

It can happen anywhere:
on a bus, on the street,
on a soft afternoon standing
by an old spring the first Maryland
Quakers quenched their thirst at
after a hard day in the fields;
at work—often at work—in the midst
of the dull ache of moving
from day to day; over a beer;
in the arms of the person you love.

Maybe a flower will trigger it off—
its fiery petals, yellow and orange,
dancing the breeze like cobweb;
or a girl's shy smile and hesitant
sparkling eyes; an aroma
that conjures a memory;
or the snatch of a song,
a touch, or a word, or silence—

and the heart leaps up
like the first glimpse of the cloudless
moonless night sky above New Mexico,
and you suddenly stare
into the infinite power
of how things could be
if the dreams you live on
came true.

Only a flash,
a single terrible instant,
lifting and swift as lightning,
an explosion of joy—

and then it is gone,
and only the vision remains.

And the longing.

The Eruption of Mount St. Helens

for Nimimosha of the Bear Tribe Medicine Society

"Ash fallout is the hot news here."
Too far away to feel or hear the blast,
Nimimosha watched the gray-brown cloud
rising and advancing east
until the land and all living things
lay blanketed in ash, and her daughter's
infant eyes burned red with grit,
then she went inside.

"If it rains lightly now," she writes,
"the ash will turn to caustic paste
and harden to dissolve slowly,
burning the earth as it goes.
We're concerned about the fish"—
jellied mud on surfaces of ponds
and lakes, blocking oxygen exchange;
"the cows are eating ash-coated grass,
drinking ash-coated water,
blinking ash-coated eyes.
Then there are the horses...."

"We must stay inside.
The highways all around Spokane
are blocked; telephones are down;
everything is closed. We're thankful

"things are not too bad; even though
the day turned black at noon, the world
continues, and we're all still here.
The feeling here is powerful.
Walk in balance on Mother Earth."

My ash-coated heart soars
to where she is—as if desire alone
could lift the burden of her hardship,

clean the water, feed the cows, wipe
the burning grit from Yarroe's eyes—
and yet I cannot cry:

Nature's fury lacks the malice
of seashore wildlife sanctuaries
smothering in oil from sinking tankers,
or an Indochinese village disappearing
in an orange ball of napalm, or a lake
dying from the mills in Buffalo,
or the slums of Baltimore.

I will not cry for Nimimosha:
St. Helens is the throat of Mother Earth,
and the violence is Her song—
and there is no sadness in it.

Matters of the Heart

for Thomas McGrath & James Cooney

Old Tom, your rasping low voice
is so soft it's hard to imagine machinegun
bullets among the strikers in New Orleans
or the hard clubs on soft round heads
by the docks in New York City;
Jim, shuffling along with your walking stick
like an angry shepherd, kind as a good Samaritan,
first American printer of Miller and Nin:

"The deepest part of a man is his sense
of essential truth, essential honour, essential
justice: they hated him because he was free,
because he wasn't cowed as they were ..."

"Wild talk, and easy enough now to laugh.
That's not the point and never was the point:
What was real was the generosity, expectant hope,
The open and true desire to create the good."

You rascals. What am I supposed to do?
Storm the White House? Picket Chase Manhattan?
What? I've tried it all, believe me; nothing
works. Everyone's asleep, or much too busy.

The point is: things are different now.
In the age of the MX missile and the Trident
nuclear submarine and the 20-megaton bomb
multiplied by a couple of thousand or so,
what are the odds I'll ever see
the same age you are now?

Did it seem so bleak in 1940
in that awful twilight when half the world
plunged headlong into darkness
out of the decade of comradeship and hope
while the other half stood poised to follow?

Four more decades have passed since then,
and you're still at it. The Pole Star's gone;
even the dreams we steered by only ten years ago
are gone. Where do you get your strength?

I'm tired of being swatted like a bothersome fly:
pariah, voice in the wilderness. My friends
look at me with pity in their eyes.
I want to own a house, raise a family,
draw a steady paycheck. What, after all, can I do
to change the course of a whole mad world?
I'm only a man; I want to forget for awhile
and be happy …

                                    … and yet your lives,
your words, your breath, your beating
old tired fighters' unbowed hearts
boom through the stillness of excuses
like a stuck clock forever tolling:

"Don't give in. Go on. Keep on.
Resist. Keep on. Go on."

Briana

                    for CJ, in memory of Jill

Death comes knocking and the silence descends
like a black bird alighting on the windowledge
on a black night with no candles.

Yet everything continues: bottle time,
nap time, play time, bath time, story time,

bed time—only a brief confusion:
for a few days you asked for mommy;
then you stopped asking.

You can't know the black bird will sit
for a lifetime in your father's heart.
I watch him with you now:
the tall slender frame
bending over your crib like a willow;
the large hands hesitantly poised—
wanting to touch,
not wanting to wake you;
the soft searching eyes permanently puzzling
an incomprehensible absence
he will never let you feel
if he can help it.

Years will pass before you understand
the secret tremble when your father holds you,
just how much such a small child weighs—
but that's okay;
                    don't trouble your dreams
with wondering. Be what you are:
your mother's daughter. Be a candle.

Light the awful silence with your laughter.

1981

Gifts

for Anne Gulick Ehrhart

I give you the worst gift first
as a warning: the sullen silence
awakening in the morning; the self-
centered dolt too blunt sometimes
to button his own trousers;
the quick tongue slashing;

the perpetual anger at being
perpetually mortal.

The second gift I give you
of necessity: the come-what-may;
the kiss on the cheek on the way
out the door, real and mindless
as superstition; rumpled clothes,
broken dishes, grocery bills;
the guarantee of disagreements;
the mundane goings and comings
of daily routine.

But the third gift is a promise,
and I give it also to you: a warm
heart constantly beating;
a companion; warm arms, warm lips,
laughter brighter than mountain fire,
tears as wild as the sea;
the unrelenting desire to please;
an unrelenting struggle to know;
unrepentant exuberant love
for as long as we share this earth.

27 June 1981

Sound Advice

Remember the time Jerry Doughty
beat you up for no good reason
on the ice at Sellersville while all
the other kids stood around and laughed?
You skated home alone that day, swearing
you would find a way to even up the score.
But you never did: years passed,
he moved away, your adolescent pride
still tucked beneath his belt like a trophy.

Or one year later, in the fifth grade,
when Margie Strawser told the teacher
you had hit her with a bean-shooter?
Nothing you protested mattered:
the shooter and the beans were in your desk.

You got paddled as the whole class watched,
and Margie got an A in citizenship.

You should have learned something
growing up. Instead, you volunteered.
And when you found your war as rotten
as the rotting corpses of the dead
peasants lying in the green rice
they would never harvest, you were shocked
that nothing you protested mattered.
Thirteen years have passed since then,
and still your anger rises at the way people
turn away from what you have to say.

Who taught you to believe in words?
Listen: injustice is a fact.
Like dust rising when the wind blows.
Like heat when the fire rises.
A natural thing. The white space
between the lines of every history
book you've ever read. The back side
of the Golden Rule. The one unbroken law.

And yet you've quit a half a dozen jobs
on principle: point of order! Point of order—
as though you think it matters more than bread.
Everywhere you go, the blade of your contempt
draws blood. No wonder people hate you.
Listen, friend: don't make us so uncomfortable.
We don't like it any more than you do,
but the world is what it is. You can't change it.
Face it. Learn to bend. We have.

Continuity

Because I love my wife, I've traveled
six hundred miles to stand for fifteen minutes
by a cold stone standing in a grove of pines
in West Tisbury, Martha's Vineyard, Massachusetts.
What are you to me? A name. A few
silent photographs I've seen in albums.
Second-hand stories. I never even met you.

The taxi idles by the graveyard gate;
a cold Atlantic wind whips the pines.
Your daughter grips my arm—once, twice, hard:
"My mother died!" she cries, as though the news
had just arrived, the tears standing for a moment
in her eyes before they topple down her face.
I think of mothers, think of death, and love

and all at once my throat constricts
in startled grief; my own tears rise:
mother of my wife, your living soul
breathes in every gesture of your daughter,
and your daughter is the touchstone of my life.
Because I love my wife, I've traveled
six hundred miles to discover that I miss you,
and to thank you for the splendid child you raised.

New Jersey Pine Barrens

Sixty miles away, in New York City,
herds of cars stampede down avenues,
animated lumps of steel and fumes.
Thirty miles away, in Philadelphia,
a mugger steals a purse in broad daylight
from a screaming old woman on Broad Street.
Here, I wake to whippoorwills and bullfrogs.

Swamp cedar, scrub oak, stunted maple
whisper as I ready the canoes
beside the beaver dam on Batsto River.
The children on the school camping trip
are still asleep. A beaver tail slaps.
I urinate beside a blueberry bush,
notice white violet and lady slipper,
pickerel gliding through the quiet pond.

Soon the children will awake, all energy.
Alien and graceless in their sleek canoes,
they will spend this day ricocheting
off sunken stumps and overhanging trees,
heaping angry blame for faulty navigation
on anyone but self, their adolescent

piping shrieks splitting the awesome
silence with a day-long jagged gash.

Too young to understand, their thoughts
are all of who-rammed-who, and the hot-faced
shame of looking clumsy. I cup my hand,
dip it in the beaver pond and drink
the majesty of wilderness, wondering
how much longer will it be
before children like these will have to learn
the majesty of wilderness
from books.

Pagan

for the people of El Salvador

In the heart of the night
that beats in the heart of the people,
something is waking
out of the half-sleep
of centuries.
Beckoned alive
by the endless nightmare of priests,
viceroys and chains,
the pestilence of toil
and submission,
where nothing has ever been sacred
but gold,
greed,
and the lash,
it rears its slow black head
and blinks its eyes open.
Its wings unfold
like the slow seepage of blood
from a festering wound:
thunder and clouds
are among the stars.
Slowly it rises
on the rising wind,
the hard white tips
of its fangs
catching the moon.

Deer

Two white-tailed deer stood still
on George School's South Lawn
not fifty yards away from where we jogged.
My wife said, "Look," and as she did,
they both looked too, then bounded off
across the lawn, white tails flying.
We jogged on in silence, thinking
of their quick flight at our approach,
their perfect strides, their grace.

Two nights later, my wife came home
in tears—a rainy night, unseasonably
warm, foggy—she'd almost struck a deer
already lying on the highway,
had stopped the car just in time
and gotten out to find it
not yet dead: at her approach,
it kicked its mangled legs, convulsed,
and tried to rise as if to run, fell back,
tried again, and fell, and tried, and fell.

I thought of the deer on South Lawn:
their perfect strides, their grace;
their quick flight at our approach,
as if they thought we meant
to do them harm.

A Warning to My Students

George School
November 1981

The B-1 bomber
is going to be built
after all: not scrapped, after all
our resistance; just postponed.
"Necessity requires...,"
yet another president insists;
the secretary of state discusses
limited nuclear war
as if it were sane;

and in El Salvador, another
petty upper-class junta
needs American aid
to fight the communists.

What happened
to the last twenty years?

If I were young again,
I could do it all
differently: go to college,
go to Canada, live underground
on the lam in basement apartments
in strange cities—anything
but kill
somebody else's enemies
for somebody else's reasons.

And now I see it all
coming
one more time; one
by one, all the old flags
resurrected
and ready
for the rockets' red glare
still another time—
and I wake up nights, afraid,
and I have to reach out
and touch my wife,
just to make sure.

Sometimes she wakes up, too.
"It's all right," she says;
she strokes my head;
"It's just a dream."

And she's right, too:
these days, for me
it's just a dream

because the next time they come looking
for soldiers, they won't come looking
for me. I'm too old;
I know too much.

The next time they come looking
for soldiers, they'll come looking
for you.

1982

Surviving the Bomb One More Day

For three days, iron cold gripped
the earth in a blue fist:
mucus froze in nostrils, lungs
ached with the weight of breathing,
cheeks turned red with pain.

Is this how we would finally end?
Not in fire, not consumed
in mushroom orange heat,
but laid out stiff and hard
like fish in a peddler's cart?

After all those nights of waking up
to thunder, sweating, thinking, "Christ,
we've finally done it," and waiting
in the eerie fog of half-awake
for the final slap of the blast.

On the third day, it began to snow.
Into the night the snow fell,
and by morning the earth was white.

But by afternoon, the wind
was tailing off, and a warming sun
foretold another night
of waiting for the fire.

The Blizzard of Sixty-six

Snow came early here, and hard:
roads treacherous; wires down.

School authorities should have cancelled
the annual high school Christmas dance:
two couples died on the way home.
"Tragedy!" the local papers declared,
but the snow kept falling.

Somewhere in a folder in a file
is a photograph of me in a uniform:
one stripe for PFC; girl in a yellow gown.
I took her home through the falling snow,
kissed goodnight, and left for Asia.

All through that long year, snow
fell and fell on the green rice,
on gray buffalo, thatched huts, green
patrols, and the mounting yellow dead.

Randy, class of '65, died
in terminal cold in the Mekong Delta;
Kenny, class of '66, died in a blizzard
of lead in the Central Highlands;
I came home with permanent chills,
the yellow nameless dead of Asia
crammed into my seabag, and all of us
looking for a reason.

We never found one. Presidents
come and go away like snowdrifts
in driveways; generals come and go;
the earth goes on silently turning
and turning through its seasons,
and the snow keeps falling.

Letter to the Survivors

To any who find this,
understand:

year by year, we could see it
approaching—the tensions
mounting, the missiles
mounting, the bombers
rising, the submarines slipping
down their long thin launch-ramp rails,

the warheads, and multiple warheads.
We knew it,
but we were afraid.
We were ordinary people, only
the work-a-day Marys and Joes.
Our leaders insisted
they were striving for peace.
What could we do
but believe them?
We had only our one vote each,
only our small voices,
and it was a crime to refuse
to serve, and a crime
to refuse to pay.
We did not want to lose our friends;
we did not want to lose our jobs;
we did not want to lose our homes—

and we didn't really believe
it could happen.

Everett Dirksen, His Wife, You & Me

I read once that Everett Dirksen,
United States Senator, never slept
a night without his wife of fifty years.
One can almost see them, near the end:
two doddering old white-haired giggling
lovers climbing into bed, the undimmed
passion still glowing steadily from within—
enough to light the darkness one more night.

And yet I think that light was raised
against a darker darkness both, perhaps,
saw approaching years before the end.
I see it coming, too—saw it years
before I met you; it scared me then,
and still does, and you're the only one
who's ever made me feel the weight
a little less. We giggle, too, sometimes.

One might marvel at the long-enduring
passion of that husband and his wife:

fifty years without a night alone;
marvelous, indeed—
but it's other couples who amaze me:
their ignorance, their faith, their sheer
bravado. Whether we shall be together
or alone in death, I have no way of knowing;

but I know the weight, and how it feels
to pass the night without you.

High Country

Brad pitched the tent beside the creek
among the hummingbirds below the beaver
dam where the water flowed swiftly,
and whenever we wanted we could dip
our tin cups into the creek and drink.
For three days we lived on rainbow trout,
and at night the stars were so close
we climbed the Milky Way with our dreams
and stalked the Bear with Orion.

We were twenty-three. The world
6000 feet below swept out across
the compass points like a storm.
Our Asian war staggered on; calculating
men in three-piece suits and uniforms
with stars called firestorms down upon
the heads of people with conical hats
and spoke of Peace with Honor.
But up in the high country, life
went on with only a brief intrusion,
once, of contrails knifing the sky.

Time since then has driven a wedge
of ten years and 2000 miles between us.
Brad's a surgeon in Madison; I teach
in a Quaker boarding school in the east.
Calculating men in three-piece suits
and uniforms with stars are calling down
firestorms upon the heads of peasants
in Central America now. I often think

of plunging into the icy creek at dawn,
of the water rushing among the rocks,
and over our bodies, and on.

Cowgirls, Teachers & Dreams

for Betsy in Montana

That day we fished Coyote Creek
from Pete's ranch to the upper barn,
dry pale prairie grass rippled
pastures mile on mile to mountains
shouldering sky. Cattle grazed the high
plateaus where men in winter still
go mad from loneliness and snow. Hard
land, its beauty self-composed; a long
way from anywhere. We shared one rod.
You showed me where the best spots were,
parted bushes—"Shhh," you said, "don't
scare the fish"—coached my clumsy casts.
It didn't help: you caught twenty; I
caught none. It didn't matter. Seven
hours working up the creek through
morning into afternoon toward evening.
Words passed softly back and forth
like dry prairie grass in wind. Magic
how that hot dry day in summer in Montana
passed so gently. At the upper barn,
we cleaned the fish: you deftly lopped
off heads and tails, taught me how
to slit their bellies, poke my finger
down the spines to clear the guts in one
swift stroke. How was I to tell you
I was squeamish? Biting flesh inside
my mouth, I did as I was shown. "It's late,"
you said, "we'd better take the horse."
How was I to tell you I was scared
of horses, hadn't ridden since that day
when I was ten and rode four wild miles
on a horse that wasn't stable-broken?
I climbed up behind you: no saddle,
nothing but your slender waist to hold—

a stalk of prairie grass in wind—and you
went straight for every ditch you saw,
jumping, laughing: "Hang on tight!"—stopping
only when you saw the mother antelope
and fauns, babies still with spots, all
three staring, undecided. Maybe next time
bobcats or wolves instead of riders.
The cook got fired while we fished.
Drinking on the job. A hard life in Big
Sky Country. I was only passing through;
I've never seen you since. Not that I
would have a reason: you were eight, and I
was twenty-two. The friends I stopped
to see were only summer help—married now,
a lawyer and a teacher in the East.
I'm a teacher, too. So were you.
And in my mind, you'll always catch
the fattest trout and ride the swiftest
horse, always stop to gaze at fauns,
and never lose your innocence or courage
in that lonely hard land you offered
to a stranger like a treasure,
like a blessing.

Canoeing the Potomac

As rivers go, this one isn't much.
It doesn't drain a continent; it doesn't
flow through wilderness; it isn't wild,
or wide, or deep. Between Antietam
and the Shenandoah, only scattered
mild rapids interrupt its calm.
What makes this river awesome
is its sadness: along these gentle
tree-lined banks, in 1861, a nation
shattered like a brittle stone.

Up ahead, at Harpers Ferry, abolitionist
John Brown captures the federal arsenal
for freedom, but he in turn is captured
by a West Point colonel, Robert E. Lee.
Behind us, nearly three years later,

Lee's Confederate Grays are met
by George McClellan's Union Blues.
Cannon shot and bugles blare
the ranks of razored bayonets across
the fields littered with the cost
of John Brown's Glory.

The Union was preserved, of course,
but the sadness remains. Our sleek
canoes move in silence through the gap
between the violence of those years
and the violence we've inherited.
Moral people, principled and kind as Lee,
still apply their talents to the sword,
and people mad as John Brown still insist
their service to the noblest ends.
Saddest of all, Blues and Grays, Browns, Blacks,
Yellows, Reds and Whites are still in chains
that bind us to the deadly past
out of which we seem this summer day
to glide with such apparent ease.

"…the light that cannot fade…"

Suzie, you picked a hell of a time
to teach me about mortality.
I was in North Carolina then,
talking tough, eating from cans,
wearing my helmet John Wayne style—
and you were suddenly dead:
a crushed skull on a pre-dawn road
just two weeks shy of college,
and me about to leave for Vietnam.

I wanted you and me alive;
I wanted out.
That night I cried till dawn.

Funny, how I managed to survive
that war, how the years have passed,
how I'm thirty-four and getting on,
and how your death
bestowed upon my life a permanence

I never would have had
if you had lived:

you'd have gone to college,
married some good man from Illinois,
and disappeared like all the other
friends I had back then who meant
so much and whom I haven't
thought about in years.

But as it is, I think of you
whenever dancers flow across a stage
or graceful gymnasts balance on the beam.
And every time I think of you,
you're young.

(for Carolyn Sue Brenner, 1948–1966)

The Outer Banks

1.

Hysterical seagulls dart and soar
through evening's rising calm. Some alight
and strut like tiny generals among the children
chasing spindly ghost crabs on the beach.
Here, a fisherman. There, two lovers sharing secrets.
And there a kite, riding a stiff sea breeze
that makes the dune grass ripple and toss
like slow green rollers just before they burst,
exploding phosphorescent white on dark wet sand.
A half-mile south, Cape Hatteras light, its tower
spiraled black and white, begins to flash
in deepening twilight. Stars appear.
The flash atop Cape Hatteras light becomes a soft
revolving beam casting silver light on rooftops,
dune tops, sand and surf, then skittering over waves
and out to sea.
Returning.
Gone again.
And back.
And gone.
A perpetual circle of moving light.
An all-night silent song.

2.

Here, between Cape Henry and Cape Fear,
the Gulf Stream and the Labrador Current
collide: the turbulence of opposites,
the centuries of wind and tide
have built the Outer Banks,
a slender stalk of weathered land,
two hundred narrow miles of low-slung sand
between deep water and the Carolina coast.
Behind them lie the sounds: Currituck
and Albamarle, Pamlico and Core:
rippling sheets of shallow pale green.
To seaward lie the shoals: Wimble, Diamond,
Frying Pan and Lookout: restless nightmares
shifting, ever shifting, like the tentacles
of an octopus, like grinding dragons' teeth.
Exposed, and hunched against the seasons,
the banks are shifting, too:
northeasters scrape the beaches raw;
gales uproot what little that remains of forests;
hurricanes tear gaping holes from sea to sound,
and overnight, grain by infinite grain,
old inlets disappear; roads and houses
disappear, docks, dunes, ponds and marshes.
Wind on sand, sea on sand, sand on sand;
a thousand years, five thousand years:
still the banks endure.

3.

Verrazano thought the banks an isthmus;
the sounds beyond, the legendary oriental sea.
Amadas and Barlowe, sailing under Raleigh,
claimed the banks for England and the Queen.
"The people of the countrey," Barlowe wrote,
"are very handsome, and a goodly people,
in their behavior mannerly, and civill,
gentle, loving, void of guile and treason."
Croatoans on the banks; along the sounds,
Poteskeets and Machapungas, Woccons,
Neuse and Corees: fisherpeople, gatherers
of wild grapes and melons, deer hunters.

"I think in all the world," wrote Barlowe,
"the like aboundance is not to be found."
Elizabeth, impressed, issued Letters Patent.
Three successive settlements on Roanoke failed—
the last, shrouded in mysterious disaster.
Still the English dreamed, and finally,
farther north, Jamestown closed the cover
on the ancient book of tribes,
and wrote the names of Indians on maps.

4.

From the sounds and inlets of the Outer Banks, nimble
English privateers raided Spanish treasure fleets.
Later came the runaways and fugitives:
indentured servants, Africans and outlaws,
pirates from the Caribbean, shipwrecked seamen.
Some came and went; others stayed
beyond the reach of warrants, writs, and masters.
Cold to strangers, clannish, making do with two-room
shacks in sheltered sound-side woods and marshes,
those early Bankers hunted, fished and farmed
survival, combing beaches in the wake of storms,
stripping stranded ships for salvage,
rendering the carcasses of whales: rooting,
clinging, holding on like stubborn dune grass.
Scarbroughs, Midgetts, Gaskills, Dixons, Grays.
Names on gravestones; names on the rolls
of the lighthouse keepers and surfboat rescue crews;
names on tackle shops, restaurants, homes and stores:
children and children of children's children
live and grow old and bequeath to their children
the will to adapt to a shifting world
defined by weather, sand, and tides.

5.

Milestones:
Virginia Dare born at Roanoke, 1587.
First permanent English settlement on the banks, 1664.
Blackbeard killed and beheaded at Ocracoke, 1718.
First public tavern on the banks, 1757.
Profession of pilot closed to Blacks, 1773.
First U.S. Marines on the banks, 1778.

First lighthouse on the Carolina coast, Cape Fear, 1783.
Last known reference to Native Americans on the banks, 1788.
First attempt to mark Diamond Shoals fails, 1823.
Steamer *Home*, carrying 135 passengers and two lifejackets, wrecked
    off Hatteras with the loss of 90 lives, 1837.
Whaling gun introduced to the banks, 1875.
Rasmus Midgett, unassisted, rescues all ten people from the
    Barkentine *Priscilla* during a hurricane, 1899.
Orville Wright: "We came down here for wind and sand, and we have
    got them," Kitty Hawk, 1900.
Audubon Society gains protection for egrets and terns, nearly extinct
    by the turn of the century, 1903.
First paved highway on the banks, 18 miles, 1931.
The Lost Colony first performed at Roanoke, 1937.
Anne & Bill Ehrhart honeymoon at Buxton, Hatteras, 1981.

6.

Sea bass, striped bass, bluefish and butter fish,
carp and croakers, eel, herring,
Spanish mackerel, menhaden and mullet,
shad, sharks, spot and sturgeon,
northern and southern weakfish,
clams, crabs, oysters, scallops and shrimp;
porpoises and whales;
diamondback terrapin and loggerhead turtles.

7.

Near rushes in a marshy pond in Buxton Woods,
an egret, like a solemn elder of the realm,
stands alone knee-deep in water. The posture
of the bird suggests a kind of wisdom,
or a perfect inner calm. Behind the bird,
beyond the woods, the black and white spiral
of the lighthouse rises. Bird and lighthouse;
blue sky; the silence of the whispered afternoon.
An old road, a rutted double sand-track
long overgrown, passes by the pond and disappears
through loblolly pines toward old abandoned houses.
A bare breath of wind disturbs the rushes:
the black beak turns; the stilt-like legs
take two steps forward; the slow broad wings
unfold. The great bird flies.

8.

St₂ nd on the beach at night at Cape Hatteras
looking east across the water. Keep watching:
there! Flash. Flash.
That's the beacon on the Texas Tower
marking the outer edge of Diamond Shoals.

The buoys placed on Diamond Shoals
washed away in a storm.
The lightship stationed on the shoals
broke loose and wrecked in a storm.
The floating bell beacon disappeared.
More buoys washed away.
The Diamond Shoals lighthouse project
ended in a storm before completion.
Another lightship stationed on the shoals
broke loose and wrecked in a storm.
A German U-boat sank another.

Look again at the flashing light.
Look at the darkness between the flashes.
Look at the waiting sea.

9.

Barks and barkentines,
brigs and brigantines,
battleships, barges and yachts;
flyboats and pilot boats,
gunboats and fishing boats,
ironclads, trawlers and tugs;
transports and tankers,
surfboats and schooners,
submarines, steamers and sloops;
liners and lightships,
cutters and clipperships
broken and wrecked on the banks.

10.

The sea breeze gently rubs the dunes. The sky
is clear. The beach is empty now of children,
fishers, fires, and kites. Only the lovers,
huddled down for shelter in the hollow of a dune,

stay to watch the light revolving, listening
to its song. What secrets do they share
as night moves on toward dawn? Ageless secrets.
Timeless secrets. Listen to their muffled giggles
drifting on the air. This is how it always is
because all lovers think themselves
immortal. How else could we go on?
Cape Hatteras light casts silver light on rooftops,
dunetops, sand and surf, skittering over waves
and out to sea.
Returning.
Gone again.
And back.
And gone.

The Suicide

That winter the woman hurled herself
under the Bethlehem Local,
I was ten. Understand: in Perkasie,
no one had died for years
of anything but old age and heart attacks,
maybe an auto accident now and then,
sensible causes even a child could grasp.

That winter I walked the tracks a dozen times
looking for clues:
dried blood, shredded clothing, flesh,
trying hard to imagine screaming
steel wheels clawing at steel rails
and the inconceivable thump
of deliberate death.

1983

Climbing to Heaven

for Brady Shea

That evening you and I and Daniel
climbed to the peak of a barn
on a soybean farm in Payne, Ohio,

only pride compelled me
not to climb back down.

"God, this land is flat!" you shouted,
standing up abruptly, six-foot frame
astride the peak as if to climb
still higher. 'Sit down," I said,
"You make me nervous." You laughed,
but out of kindness sat back down.

"See those lights?" you asked.
"Fort Wayne. Thirty miles away,
and not a thing between us
higher than a railroad overpass."

How trapped you must have felt
in Payne, Ohio.

Later I heard you'd gone to Idaho.

Later still, Daniel's letter
said you fell from a mountain in Colorado—
but I know you must have reached the peak
and climbed straight up from there.

Moments When the World Consents

Atlantic waves roil over reefs beyond the cut
between Tooloo and Elbow Cays, boom
and boom on jagged coral, disintegrating
skyward in repeating crystal spray.
A quarter-mile away, behind the windward cays,
Abaco Sound lies blue on gently rippling
blue, and in the islands' lees, wild peas
and bougainvillea blossom under Caribbean pines.

You lie face down; I watch the water
in the shallow sheltered cove we've come to share.
Warm wind in coconut palms along the beach
seems to set the broad green leaves to talking
softly: "Stay awhile, you two, be still;
this hour, this afternoon, this day; be
jealous of the moments when the world

consents to give you to each other
undistracted. You may not find another place
or time to smell good air blown all the way
from Africa or Spain, or lie on sand so
smooth and white and warm and meant
for you."

I let my fingers fall across your hips.
You turn, and open like a flower.
Love, like sun-warmed swirling tiny pearl waves
on satin water, laps our naked thighs.

Letter from an Old Lover

After all these years, how strange
to find your letter in the mail.
The year I spent at sea, I stood for hours
on the fantail, leaning on the rail,
the gnawing ache like cancer
of the heart, the lights of California
luminescent in the darkness. Beyond
the lights, the dark shadows
of the coastal range. Beyond the mountains,
three thousand miles of darkened continent.
Then the pilot boat, the tugs, and bells
clanging in the engine room; half ahead, dead
slow; Long Beach, home port, perhaps a letter
this time.

Now, ten years later, here it is at last:
the missing letter, re-routed back and forth
across three thousand solitary dreams.
I'm married now, and you're a relic
from an old life that's long since past.
The letter lies unopened on my desk.
Alone, I sit and study the address,
the postmark, the flowing script.
I don't regret a moment—then or now.
I only wonder what you have to say
that couldn't have been said
long ago.

Appearances

in honor of DB at GS

The deceiver
slithers into its chair
and coils its heavy body
into a lump, its head raised
and weaving slowly over the desk,
the forked tongue darting
out of a kind of sleepy
half-smile, testing the air.
Another day.

Two signs hang on the wall:
"Right" and "Left."
The right sign hangs on the left;
the left one hangs on the right.
The mahogany desktop gleams
like the cold eyes of a snake.
Where are the mice?

A knock at the door:
an imperceptible flashing
of razored fangs.
"Come in," says the man
seated behind the desk,
"Tell me the nature of things."

Responsibility

The Congress shall have power to lay
and collect taxes ... to ... provide for
the common defense and general welfare
of the United States.
                    —Article I, Section 8, Paragraph 1,
                    United States Constitution

The sun taps on the kitchen table;
coffee boils. As birds awaken
trees beyond the window, I think of you
upstairs: your naked body curled
around a pillow, your gentle face

an easy dream of last night's love.
It's Friday; summer.

Somewhere
in another country to the south,
government troops are stalking
through a nightmare; a naked body
in the dusty street behind them
sprawls in rubbish, and a woman
in a house with the door kicked in
pounds fists on empty walls. There,
the news is always bad, the soldiers
always armed, the people
always waiting for the sound
of boots splintering wood.

What if you and I were wrenched from sleep
by soldiers, and they dragged me out
and shot me? Just like that; just
the way it happens every day:
the life we share,
all the years ahead we savor
like the rich taste of good imported coffee,
vanished
in a single bloody hole between the eyes.

Would you fix the door and go on living?
Or would the soldiers rape and shoot you, too?
Idle thoughts. Things like that don't happen
in America. The sun climbs;
the coffee's gone; time to leave for work.
Friday, payday, security:
money in my pocket for the weekend;
money for my government;
money for the soldiers of El Salvador,
fifty bullets to the box.

The Reason Why

In Russia, everyone drinks vodka.
They all wear furry hats, and worship
at the tomb of Lenin. Godless,
every last one of them, and hell-bent

on conquering the world. Yesterday
Afghanistan, today Nicaragua, tomorrow
New Jersey. Atlantic City! Sweet
Jesus, all those elegant casinos
in the hands of Reds. That's why
we need missiles. MX missiles.
Cruise missiles. Pershing missiles.
Let 'em try to take the Boardwalk;
we'll blow their godless hats off.

The Invasion of Grenada

I didn't want a monument,
not even one as sober as that
vast black wall of broken lives.
I didn't want a postage stamp.
I didn't want a road beside the Delaware
River with a sign proclaiming:
"Vietnam Veterans Memorial Highway."

What I wanted was a simple recognition
of the limits of our power as a nation
to inflict our will on others.
What I wanted was an understanding
that the world is neither black-and-white
nor ours.

What I wanted
was an end to monuments.

1984

On the Right to Vote

Believe in a raw wind scraping over the land.
Believe in the crackle of fire.
Believe me, nothing you have ever possessed
is yours. The makers of wind and fire

care nothing
for dreams that are not their own.
They care nothing for you—
not even enough to hate you.

You think I am lying.
I am not lying. I know
how swiftly the wind piles clouds into the sky,
how the fire suddenly rises,
how the rain falls into the open eyes of the dead,
how the dead lie silent, forever,
astonished.

Listen: a machinegun clacks
like rain on a tin roof;
someone is moaning in darkness.
It is your brother. It is your sister.
Even as you sleep, someone's finger twitches
on the trigger.

1985

Winter Bells

In the dark breath of February,
how your voice lightly rises
over clouds, cold rain, the first
flat gray of early dawn,
lifting me into another day.
Small miracle, such magic.

I almost died in February,
Hue City, 1968; and once I drove
non-stop for twenty-two hours
all the way to Coconut Grove
just to escape the cold,
such fear I have of cold

and the aching emptiness like cold;
February, so empty of dreams,

so like the life I labored through
season by slow season.
Who would have thought a single
voice could change the natural world

or my unnatural fear
of short days and a long life?
Woman with voice like a carillon
pealing the cold from my bones.

Parade

New York City
May 7th, 1985

Ten years after the last rooftop
chopper out of Saigon.

Ten, fifteen, twenty years
too late for kids not twenty
years old and dead in ricefields;
brain-dead, soul-dead, half-dead
in wheelchairs. Even the unmarked
forever Absent Without Leave.

You'd think that any self-respecting
vet would give the middle finger
to the folks who thought of it
ten years and more too late—

yet there they were: the sad
survivors, balding, overweight
and full of beer, weeping, grateful
for their hour come round at last.

I saw one man in camouflaged utilities;
a boy, his son, dressed like dad;
both proudly marching.

How many wounded generations,
touched with fire, have offered up
their children to the gods of fire?
Even now, new flames are burning,
and the gods of fire call for more,
and the new recruits keep coming.

What fire will burn that small
boy marching with his father?
What parade will heal
his father's wounds?

POW/MIA

I.   In the jungle of years,
     lost voices are calling. Long
     are the memories,
     bitterly long the waiting,
     and the names of the missing and dead
     wander
     disembodied
     through a green tangle
     of rumors and lies,
     gliding like shadows among vines.

II. Somewhere, so the rumors go,
     men still live in jungle prisons.
     Somewhere in Hanoi, the true believers
     know,
     the bodies of four hundred servicemen
     lie on slabs of cold
     communist hate.

III. Mothers, fathers,
     wives and lovers,
     sons and daughters,
     touch your empty fingers to your lips
     and rejoice
     in your sacrifice and pain:
     your loved ones' cause
     was noble,
     says the state.

IV. In March of 1985, the wreckage
     of a plane was found in Laos.
     Little remained of the dead:
     rings, bone chips, burned
     bits of leather and cloth;
     for thirteen families,
     twenty years of hope

and rumors
turned acid on the soul
by a single chance discovery.

V.   Our enemies are legion,
     says the state;
     let bugles blare
     and bang the drum slowly,
     bang the drum.

VI. God forgive me, but I've seen
     that triple-canopied green
     nightmare of a jungle
     where a man in a plane could go down
     unseen, and never be found
     by anyone.
     Not ever.
     There are facts,
     and there are facts:
     when the first missing man
     walks alive out of that green tangle
     of rumors and lies,
     I shall lie
     down silent as a jungle shadow,
     and dream the sound of insects
     gnawing bones.

1986

Apples

for Tran Kinh Chi
Hanoi, December 1985

"Can you guess what it is?" you ask,
handing me the small green fruit.

I take a bite: it's good;
crisp and tart.
"An apple," I reply.

"Our apples in Vietnam,"
you say, "are not so big
as the apples in your country."

"Bigger isn't always better," I reply.

A slow smile spreads,
a thoughtful nod,

then you laugh,
and I laugh,
and our eyes meet,

and I wonder if we're both laughing
at the same joke.

For Mrs. Na

Cu Chi District
December 1985

I always told myself,
if I ever got the chance to go back,
I'd never say "I'm sorry"
to anyone. Christ,

those guys I saw on television once:
sitting in Hanoi, the cameras rolling,
crying, blubbering
all over the place. Sure,

I'm sorry. I never meant
to do the things I did.
But that was nearly twenty years ago:
enough's enough.

If I ever go back,
I always told myself,
I'll hold my head steady
and look them in the eye.

But here I am at last—
and here you are.
And you lost five sons in the war.
And you haven't any left.

And I'm staring at my hands
and eating tears,
trying to think of something else to say
besides "I'm sorry."

The Ducks on Wissahickon Creek

It's never as simple as this, of course.
Most of the time, hard questions

gnaw at the brain like rats,
and it's hard to imagine a life

that isn't forever perplexing.
But today, with last night's snow

still undisturbed and slowly turning
wet and heavy under February sun,

a pair of mallards followed
by a pair of perfect wakes paddled

side by side through quiet water,
so sure of where they were going.

Twice Betrayed

for Nguyen Thi My Huong
Ho Chi Minh City
December 1985

Some American soldier
came to your mother for love,
or lust, a moment's respite from loneliness,
and you happened. Fourteen years later,
I meet you on the street at night
in the city that was once called Saigon,
and you are almost a woman,
barefooted, dressed in dirty clothes,
beautiful with your one shy dimple.

It doesn't really matter who won;
either way, you were always destined
to be one of the losers:

if he wasn't killed, your father left
for the place we used to call The World
years before the revolution's tanks
crushed the gates of the old regime forever.

Now we sit on a bench in a crowded park
burdened by history. It isn't easy
being here again after all these years.
I marvel at your serenity—but of course,
you can't possibly know who I am,
or how far I have come to be here.
You only know that I look like you,
that together we are outcasts.

And so we converse in gestures and signs
and the few words we can both understand,
and for now it almost seems enough
just to discover ways to make you smile.

But it isn't, and I have no way
to tell you that I cannot stay here
and I cannot take you with me.
I will tell my wife about you.
I will put your photograph on my desk.
I will dream you are my own daughter.
But none of that will matter
when you come here tomorrow
and I'm gone.

Water

A dry spring after an April
that promised better: funny, the way
the weather seems to be drier now
than what we always remember.
We draw the Delaware River down
to cover the difference, build a new
power plant, cover our pastures
with houses, wonder whatever
became of summer evenings
on porches with thunderstorms.
The radio says it may rain today
every day for a week, but the sky

gives up nothing but blank blue
space from here to the moon.
Men have walked on the moon,
but the salt line on the Delaware
inches its way north year by year.
We believe the earth will go on
giving forever, and we don't believe
what we can see with our own eyes:
dust devils, withering violets—all
we need is a little rain.
We turn on the radio, gaze
up at the sky, and wait.

Adoquinas

                              for the old man

I never thought I'd see the day
Samoza would be gone. But God
helps those who help themselves.
Somoza helped us, too.
Oh, yes. That's the best part.
After the earthquake, Somoza decreed
all the streets and roads
be paved with *adoquinas.* Somoza
owned the *adoquina* factory.
He made a fortune
selling *adoquinas* to himself.
So after we had finally
had enough, we tore the streets
and roads apart and used
Somoza's *adoquinas* for our barricades.
These we used to stop Somoza's
armored cars. We did this here,
in Masaya, in this very street.
Then our fighters killed Somoza's
Guardsmen with their homemade bombs.
We had nothing, but we won.
And I'll tell you why:
look at the belltower.
You think those holes are bulletholes,
but they're the wounds of Christ.
I've even seen them bleed.

Heather

for Frances Tomelty

The afternoon we walked among
the churchyard's weathered
tilting gravestones, heather
tumbled wild and purple on the barren
moor surrounding Haworth, slate-green
and solemn under threatening clouds.

You picked a sprig of heather for me,
saying it would bring good luck,
then told me of your childhood
in Belfast, of that bloody civil war,
English exile, and your broken marriage.

Your letters hadn't ever quite conveyed
the private heart where sorrow lies
the way your eyes revealed that afternoon
what words refused to say: even as you spoke,
you tried to spare me that particular burden.

Were you thinking I would turn away?

I know there's little I can do for Ireland
or you

except to care. Here:
this sprig of heather is for you.

1987

The Beech Tree

My neighbor leans across the fence
and gestures upward grandly, making
with his two arms a tiny human

imitation of a beech tree lifting
two hundred years of sprawling growth.
"Quite a tree you've got!" he says,
"By God, I wish I owned it."

But though it lives in my backyard,
this tree belongs to the squirrels
leaping branches just beyond my window.
"You'd like to catch us, but you can't,"
they seem to scold the tabby cat
that crouches daily with a patience
too dim to comprehend the squirrels
own this tree and will not fall.

It belongs to the robins that nested
last year in a high sheltered fork.

It belongs to the insects burrowing
beneath its aging bark like miners.

I'm just the janitor: raking leaves,
pruning limbs to keep them from collapsing
the garage roof next door or climbing
into bed beside my wife and me.

Possession is a curious thing:
some things are not for owning,
and I don't mind caring for a tree
that isn't mine. I take my pay
in April re-awakening and summer shade.
Just now, I'm watching snow
collecting in the upper branches,
waiting for the robins to come home.

Some Other World

Was there ever a moment
more perfect than this?
The house all dark, the wind
at the windows, the warmth
of your body against my chest,
and you asleep in my arms.

I thought for awhile
you would never stop crying:
the knife-edged howl, the sucking gasp
for breath, the quivering lower lip—
but I'm learning what troubles
an infant's dreams can be soothed
with patience and time.

Once, before you were born,
I watched for a moment
an egret ascend from a pond
with the grace of a whisper.
And once I dreamed a man
with a rifle refused to take aim;
I awoke to a sadness
deeper than dreams.

And I'm wishing this moment
could last forever; I'm wishing
the things that trouble my dreams
could be kept outside like the wind.

Nicaragua Libre

for Flavio Galo
August 1986

When they dragged me out of sleep
that night and took me to their prison,
I was eighteen. They kept me chained
for twenty days, and when I left, my scrotum
and my fingernails were burnt and blistered.
I had organized a strike of public workers
and they wanted names. I gave them
nothing, but they took my youth.

I'd like to say they all stank fat
and jelly-soft with opulent corruption,
but some of them were lean and sharp
as steel blades. I'd like to say
they all laughed happy and content
with what they did to me,
but some of them had eyes that never
seemed to see enough and never laughed.

They should have killed me. I gave up
organizing strikes and started organizing
armed resistance. Call it revolution,
if you like; I call it freedom.

Let them try to take my country back again.

[In 1994, after the Reagan Wars restored
the anti–Sandinista forces to power, Galo was murdered
in a roadside robbery, leaving a wife and daughter.]

Why I Don't Mind Rocking Leela to Sleep

Sitting at night on the porch
with my daughter asleep in my arms,
I thought I heard a rifle shot—
that singular crack
with no past
and a future chiseled in stone.

It was only a car,
but the memory of bullets
shivered a cold hole tunneling
half the distance to dawn.

*

Once, when I was a boy,
standing alone in my father's church
amid the rows of polished pews,
ponderous oak beams pushing
the darkened ceiling aloft, a Jesus
larger than life knocking softly
at the door to the heart
of the stained-glass window
lit by a distant streetlamp,
I heard a voice,
and I thought it was God.
It terrified me home to fitful sleep.

*

Strange God, to sing such a voice
in the heart of a small child.
But the world is a strange creation,

and now my own small child
cries out in her sleep,
and I wonder what she is dreaming
and what she has heard.

*

What hurts most
is the plodding sameness
of cruelty, a circular world
impervious to change,
the grinding erosion of hope
stripping the soul.
These days, it almost seems enough
just to accomplish the household chores
and still be ready for work.

*

What I want for my daughter
she shall never have:
a world without war, a life
untouched by bigotry or hate,
a mind free to carry a thought
up to the light of pure possibility.

She should be young forever.
I could hold her here in my arms
and offer her comfort,
a place to rest,
the illusion, at least, of shelter.
I don't want her
ever to be alone in a world
with the Gentle Shepherd
frozen in glass and the voice
of a pitiless, idiot god
chasing her down the years.

The Trouble with Poets

So after I had read my poems,
the man who'd promised two hundred dollars
"payable the night of the Poetry Reading"
gave me this soft-shoe song-and-dance shuffle

about hard times in Poetryville and a guy
named Dwight who'd split for DC
on short notice—and the short of it was
I only got eighty-five bucks.

If you owe the bank two hundred dollars
and you only pay them eighty-five,
two guys in trench coats and dark glasses
come and take your car away.

But I'm not the bank,
and this was only a bar in South Philadelphia.

I was just about to go away angry
when a man at the bar called me over.
"Hey, listen, Mac," he said, "People get
messed with and short-changed and fucked over,
glad-handed, back-handed, brass-knuckled,
bludgeoned, bullied, beat up and knocked down
day in and day out all over the world.
That's life, Mac. That's the trouble
with poets: you guys refuse
to accept it."

What Keeps Me Going

Pressed down by the weight
of despair, I could sit for hours
idly searching the ashes
from my cigarette, the darkness
of silos, the convoluted paths
we have followed into this morass
of disasters just waiting to happen,

but my daughter needs to sleep
and wants me near. She knows
nothing of my thoughts. Not one
missile mars her questioning
inspection of my eyes; she wants
only the assurance of my smile,
the familiar placed just so:

Brown Bear, Thumper Bunny, Clown.
These are the circumference

of her world. She sucks her thumb,
rubs her face hard against the mattress,
and begins again
the long night dreaming
darkness into light.

Small Song for Daddy

It isn't like my daughter
to awake at one a.m.—
but here she is.

She pulls the hairs on my chest
idly, wiggles her toes, sighs
almost as if in meditation,
and begins to sing softly,

the language hers alone,
the voice clear and fragile
as water striking stone.

New in a world where new
is all she knows, she sings
for each new wonder
she discovers—as if those

curtains, the chair, that
box of Kleenex were created
solely to delight her.

And they do. And she sings,
not knowing she is singing
for a father much in need
of her particular song.

The Storm

Midnight, and a rain falls black,
October cold, the wind obstreperous,
stinging.
                        You wait on the unlit
platform, soaked and shivering,
thinking the years at once

too far gone and far too many
to carry.
                        At last, the last
train to anywhere comes
out of the darkness, your dark
wet coat too perfectly black
until the train is almost past:

the engineer brakes to a stop
far down the tracks.
The conductor opens the rear door,
motions for you to run.

But you are where you belong,
it is raining and cold,
and what is a world or a life
without principles?
                        The engineer,
the conductor, are wrong.

You hold your ground. The conductor
signals the engineer, the train
hesitates,
                        then moves on,
                        leaving you
standing alone,
heart filled with obscenities
cold and black like the rain.

Starting Over

for Nguyen Thi Kim Thanh

You were eight years old when you hunched
in your home during Tet. Saigon. Gunfire
rattled the ritual table your father set
with incense, moon cakes, photographs
of the family's ancestors, praying for their
spirits' safe return. The family all together,
fireworks and dragons were to celebrate
the New Year. But not that year,

nor any year to come. The war persisted
like a slow tide advancing and receding

and advancing yet again, the old regime
rotting like a corpse from the inside out,
the end, when it came, coming swiftly, the cost
of privilege, even modest privilege, steep.
You left because a stranger in a foreign land
seemed better than a stranger in your own.

World enough and time now for second thoughts,
alone, you struggle with a second tongue,
snow and ice of Boston, and the effort to create
a life from nothing you remember but the smell
of incense and your father's prayers at Tet
when Tet meant time for calling family spirits
safely home, the family all together, each heart
renewed, forgiving, full of hope.

Second Thoughts

for Nguyen Van Hung

You watch with admiration as I roll
a cigarette from papers and tobacco.
Hanoi. The Rising Dragon. 1985.
You can't do what I can do
because it takes two hands

and you have only one, the other
lost years ago somewhere near Laos.
I roll another one for you. You smile,
then shrug, as if deformity from war
were just a minor inconvenience.

Together we discover what we share:
Hue City. Tet. 1968.
Sipping *Lua Moi*, we walk again
familiar ground when you were whole
and I was whole and everything around us

lay in ruins, dead or burning.
But not us. Not you and I. We're partners
in that ugly dance of men
who do the killing and the dying
and survive.

Now you run a factory; I teach and write.
You lost your arm, but have no
second thoughts about the war you fought.
I lost a piece of my humanity,
it's absence heavy as a severed arm—

but there I go again: those second thoughts
I carry always like an empty sleeve
when you are happy just to share
a cigarette and *Lua Moi*, the simple joy
of being with an old friend.

1988

Lost Years

I still remember bicycle rides
along the Susquehanna: me on the bar
on a pillow, holding tight, you pedaling,
John and Bob just old enough to ride
on their own. We were a family then.
I even remember you singing me to sleep.

None of the years between
matter now. Now I love you
as I did then: fiercely, from the gut,
without having to pause first and think,
without the confusion of all those times
one of us failed—you, or I—whatever it was

that drove us apart but kept us
paired like clumsy dancers at a prom,
at arms' length, ill at ease. Lost years

are better forgotten.
You are here now. In a hospital bed.
Hooked up to a tangle of wires and tubes.
I remember the feel of your hands
on the handlebar, the gurgle of moving water,
the old rusting steamshovel at Red Rock.

I am singing a song
you taught me.

Chasing Locomotives

Tonight I pull a plastic locomotive
while my daughter wobbles after it.
Just learning to walk, she careens
down the hall like a small
drunken sailor on a rolling deck,
a tiny comedy. How many times
I've missed the obvious:

a world full of children, each child
a world in itself.
How can anyone so misconstrue
duty, honor, country,
he could make himself believe
some other parent's child
worth the cost?

Leela stamps her feet and shrieks and
off we go again. I'm tired. I would like
to let myself enjoy my daughter's laughter;
I would like to let myself forget
that mutilated child in its mother's arms,
a house amid dry paddy fields
crushed by heavy guns—

but it's little enough
my daughter has to keep her
from a world full of men
like me
who can't imagine any world
except the one they think
belongs to them.

Secrets

Each room except the room you're in
is empty. No need to check.
How many times in forty-five years
did you wish for such a silence,
just a moment to collect yourself

amid the chaos of a life too full
with other people's needs?

And now you've got more silence
than you'll ever need, more time
than anyone should ever have
alone, each memory another moment
in a world where time holds
nothing but the past
and someone else's future.

What do you dream of?
What do you fear each time
you turn to hear Dad stirring
and you realize that what you hear
is just the silence of an empty house,
an absence permanent as stone?

Surely such a silence turns
the heart back in upon itself.
Do you find your husband there?
Four sons and four grandchildren?
Some little Brooklyn girl
in pigtails skipping rope
that once was you?

Mother, does it all come down
to empty rooms and half-imagined sounds
of someone familiar? So many hopes
and disappointments make a life.
What were yours? I'd like to know.

Lenin

Managua, Nicaragua
July 1986

The remarkable thing
was not her age; my grandmother
bore a child at fifteen.

It was not her shyness,
as if I might not see that sweet
brown breast she offered to her son
if she didn't meet my gaze.

It wasn't the quiet incongruity
of dark rich hair framing
dark eyes hollow as an empty room,

nor the poverty of cardboard and tin
that was her home.

It was the cheap red bracelet
on her wrist, the profile of a man
dangling on a plastic disk.

I asked her who he was.

She didn't know.

Keeping My Distance

The ambush lasted only seconds:
caught in the open, mid-thought,
they fell like ducks, wings
useless, feathers fluttering.
Dead, the four men sprawled
beneath a squinting moon.

All of them were armed
for once: bodies with weapons—
a rare thing where women
carried rice for soldiers, children
threw grenades in jeeps, and even
elephants were strafed and counted.

I was elated, blood pumping
through my temples, nostrils flared:
one of those rifles was mine.
A custom ancient as the art of war.
Proof. What men need
to substitute for strength.

I kept that rifle
long enough to understand
I hope to God I never
have to find myself

in need of one again,
and one too close at hand.

Just for Laughs

When I was ten, I thought that I
would live forever, I could kill
whatever I pleased, I was all
that mattered. How else
can one explain the firecrackers
stuffed down throats of frogs and lit:
hop, hop, boom! A lot of laughs.

Once we found a plump snake
sunning itself beside the creek.
Sluggish in the early morning
chill, it only raised its head
and turned two diamond-black eyes
to see four small boys with sticks.

It didn't understand until we
started beating on its flanks
that we were dangerous
and it was trapped.
Our sticks were too light
and we too timid to inflict
anything but fury, so we
started throwing stones.

Small gashes ripped that snake's
fat thrashing sides until it
finally tired, though it couldn't
run and wouldn't die. It only
lay there heaving as the stones
fell faster—till a miracle
of birth—a miracle of birth
began so strangely even we
were brought up short and stood
there for a moment dumbly watching:

out of those gashes crawled a dozen
baby watersnakes, a dozen more,
small wriggling slivers of their

mother's flesh; some were bleeding,
some had broken backs and dragged
limp tails sideways through the dust.

Premature, even the ones uninjured
that we carried home and put in jars
all died. But it didn't matter.
We had frogs and painted turtles,
salamanders, and a praying mantis.
Years later, I volunteered for war,
still oblivious to what I'd done,
or what I was about to do, or why.

The Next World War

A man with his hand on a trigger
waits for a sign from the gods.

He stands. He moves.
He begins to dance.

He dances on flames.
He takes the flames in his hands,

into his lungs, his eyes
burning, his hair, on fire.

He lifts his burning arms
to the gods.

Not Your Problem

Avoid this place.

Here time travels in tiny circles
like the hands of a clock.

Here dust rises like smoke
until it rains;
then we lie down in mud
and dream of dust.

Here our children will never learn
to read or write; their teeth
will rot from their heads;
they will join the army, or die
like us beneath foreign bombs.

Here men with guns at night
make sleeping people in houses
disappear.

Here voters are branded with ink,
and those unmarked are found
days later in trash dumps.

Here being poor is a crime
unless we are also quiet;
almost everyone is poor,
and we can hear a bullet
being chambered a mile away.

We will change all this.

You won't want to be here
when we do.

For Anne, Approaching Thirty-five

Alone in the basement, sorting clothes,
I found that pair of panties I like
(the beige ones with the lacy waist).

I meant to put them in the washer—
but they felt so smooth, so soft, I
just stood there getting hard. Woman,

never mind the crows' feet and creeping slack.
For me, you'll always be sultry,
mysterious, ready for anything.

1989

For a Coming Extinction

Vietnam. Not a day goes by
without that word on my lips.
I hear the rattle of small-arms fire

when I tuck my daughter in,
think of the stillborn dreams of other men
when I make love to my wife,
sharp snap of a flag in high wind—
blood, stars, an ocean of ignorance.
Sometimes I mumble the word to myself
like a bad dream, or a prayer:
Vietnam, Vietnam. Already
it's become what it never was:
heroic, a noble cause. Opportunity
squandered, chance to learn turned
inside out by cheap politicians
and *China Beach*. So many so eager
so soon for others to die,
and the time's fast arriving
when Vietnam means only a distant
spot on the globe, only a name
on a dusty map, when no one alive
will understand what was or is,
what might have been and was lost.

What You Gave Me

for Jeff Apple

Even when we were nine,
you were what I wanted to be:
the brave one plunging into the creek's
green slime barefooted, catching snakes
barehanded with a careless skill
and courage I could only dream of.

I swam in your wake,
sat on the bench while you became
State Champ, watched you lift my weight
in solid iron as the years passed.

You bought the motorcycle,
always waited for the girls to call,
and the phone was always ringing.
I got the grades, but who puts grades
in the family den like trophies?

What teenaged girl ever yearned
to be kissed by a straight-A student?

Once, much later, we were twenty-two,
some girl you liked had dumped you.
We were sitting in your kitchen.
"I feel so blue," you said, "I wish
I knew a way to say it like you can."

I'd never realized you might envy me,
that being held back in school
had bothered you. Your silence
always seemed so strong,
not the cowed shyness of a boy
well-meaning grown-ups had convinced
that he was dumb.

Every time I get a student
who's a little slow with words,
I remember that you never seemed
to notice how I waded in the creek
with sneakers on, the snakes each time
somehow just barely out of reach,
that you knew but didn't care
I wet the bed till I was nearly twelve,

that kids who can't articulate the blues
are songbirds locked in small cages
alone in darkened rooms.

The Origins of Passion

I am eight years old and naked
in my mother's bedroom: lipsticks,
brushes, combs and stockings fragrant
with her blessing hands, the vanity
an altar, I her secret acolyte.
A white lace slip drapes carelessly
across a chair; I take it in my hands,
press my face too deeply in its folds,
lift my trembling arms and drop it
over me, aching with desire
I can't articulate or understand,
immersed in her, burning with loss.

In all the years to come, I will
make love to women smelling softly
of lavender and talc, blessing me
with hands adept at rituals I want
to share but don't know how or why:
lipsticks, brushes, combs and stockings.
I will beg my wife to leave
her slip on; I will press my face
between her breasts and thighs and buttocks
too deeply, burning
to immerse myself in what I love,
still inarticulate, uncomprehending.

America Enters the 1990s

The lies lie
greasy and cold,
thicker than old gravy.

But you're hungry.
You are still hungry.
You were born
all belly and mouth.

It's not your fault
saliva speckles your lips
and your white eyes bulge
at anything
even remotely edible.

So you tuck the past
under your chin,
imagine silver candelabras,
fine china, delicate wine,
lick the platter clean,
and reach for more.

The Way Light Bends

A kind of blindness, that's what's needed now.
Better not to know. Better to notice
the way light bends through trees in winter dusk.

What, after all, does knowledge bring? Cold rage,
the magnitude of history, despair.
A kind of blindness, that's what's needed now

because it's hard enough to pay the bills.
So long as you can still appreciate
the way light bends through trees in winter dusk,

what's possible, what is, what can't be changed
is better left to dreamers, fools, and God.
A kind of blindness, that's what's needed now,

the wisdom not to think about what waits
in dark holes beneath the earth. Marvel at
the way light bends through trees in winter dusk

and don't imagine how the light will bend
the way light bends through trees in winter dusk
and burst forever when the missiles fly.
A kind of blindness, that's what's needed now.

The Poet as Athlete

for Lou McKee

One look at him induces adjectives:
gargantuan, Brobdingnagian, humongous;
what manatees might look like
if they put on clothes. Somewhere under
all that vast expanse like open ocean
must be something solid, but no imagination
could be vast enough to conjure even
flaccid muscles, bones like coral atolls
in that briny, rolling sea.

Against the tide of gravity, he struggles
to the podium like someone swimming,
takes a drink of water, and begins:
a poem about the powerful intoxication
of his first car, a poem about
the expectation of a first teenaged love,
a poem about a son he doesn't have.

Surely he must know what we are thinking.
Surely he must swim through every day

against a tide of gravity and ridicule,
but in a sure voice steady as the tides,
he draws us to the heart
of what we share.

Not one word about his own affliction.
Consider poetry, how good poems
offer us the world with eyes renewed.
Now see the swimmer I am watching:
all discipline, all muscle, lean and hard.

In the Valley of the Shadow

Something made us bolt upright,
all zombie eyes, all ears and nerves.
Something out there in the dark
came breathing, stalking, waiting.

Our fathers, who bequeathed to us
this rotten patch of earth, this fate.
Satan. God. The government.
No matter: it was there and deadly.

All night we hunched in what we wore
like turtles, like the frightened kids
we were and were not anymore,
silent, lost, half-crazed, and deadly,

wanting women, girlfriends, mothers
to protect us, to descend in fire
on angels' wings, torch the darkness,
pluck us from this sad mistake.

No one came. Something stayed there
just beyond our range of vision,
just a shadow on our hearts,
and no one willing to admit

we'd rape our mothers, shoot our fathers,
overthrow the government and swear
our innocence to God or Satan
for a single drop of sun.

Something left us slack-jawed, staring
at our own reflections in the dark:

what we were, what we are, and will be.
Bent, we drag it with us like a cross.

How I Live

for Leela
who gave me the first line

I bumped my head on the setting sun.
The night had only just begun
and I was dizzy already, reeling
like a drunk walking on the ceiling
of a world turned upside down.

A steady star burned above the town
I thought I lived in, but I couldn't
find it, and a voice said I shouldn't
even bother, what with the wind
rising, clouds piling, tide coming in.

What was I supposed to do?
Jump ship? Run amok in Fortescue?
Abandon mother, wife and daughter
to the lunatics and pimps? Slaughter
common sense and go to sleep?

I couldn't stop thinking of the sheep,
the wolves, pigs, rifles, missiles
and a diesel east of Barstow, whistle
howling through the empty desert night
as if it were a soul in headlong flight.

Maybe I was only dreaming
all the lies, the calculated scheming,
computating, calibrating. Maybe not.
It never seems to end, I thought,
the dizziness, the mocking darkness.

Then an owl swooped low, the starkness
of its beating wings against the air
too savage, too beautiful to care.
Then a stillness, and a man alone
calling: Is it here? Is this my home?

The Facts of Life

Winter, and a gray storm sea
behaved as if we didn't matter,
driving the main deck under water,
breaking over the flying bridge,
leaving the catwalks slick with ice.
Even our tanker seemed to ignore
its own despair, wallowing
steadily north like floating brick.

For a night and day we didn't eat
or sleep or change our filthy clothes,
staring into a sky the color of ash,
trying to will the weather to break,
even the old salts studying clouds,
reluctant to meet each other's gaze.
And the freezing rain blown horizontal,
sweeping the decks like shotgun blasts.

Bells down in the engineroom.
The slow finger of moving light
from the lightship off Columbia Bar
barely able to bore a hole
in the smothering darkness. Christ,
why did we ever come to sea?
Where are the whales and porpoises,
the thousand mermaids singing?

Then the ship turned east, Astoria,
the shelter of the river, still
invisible across that deadly patch
of turbulence, the criss-cross waves,
the shifting sandbars just beneath
the surface, tossing steel like cork,
and all of us in life preservers,
hatches battened, portholes battened.

Maybe we would make it over.
Maybe by tomorrow we'd be drinking
beer in bars in downtown Portland.
Maybe we would sail again. Or maybe
we would finally prove what any sailor

understands, the scientists be damned:
the earth is flat, you reach the edge,
fall off, and don't come back.

The Heart of the Poem

Split the ribcage open
with a heavy-bladed knife,
a hatchet or an axe.
Be careful with an axe;
it can do more damage than you need.

Grasp the ribs and pry them back.
They won't want to give at first:
pull hard and steadily;
keep pulling till they snap.

Forget about the skin;
it'll tear when the ribs give way.

After that, it's easy:
push the other guts aside,
let your fingers dig until the heart
seats firmly in your palm
like a baseball or a grapefruit,
then jerk it out.

Get rid of it.
Sentiment's for suckers.
Give us poetry.

What We're Buying

November 16th, 1989

Impossibly sprawled
as only the dead are capable of,
they have all been shot at close range:

six priests, their cook, her daughter.
The men have had their skulls bashed in,
their brains scooped out.

Like ice cream. Only the blessed rich
eat ice cream in El Salvador.
The poor eat silence, tears and dust.

The brains deliberately piled
beside these bodies are a warning:
fuck with how it is and die.

Ten years of war and taxes
and it still comes down to this:
Priests. Cooks. Children.

1990

A Scientific Treatise for My Wife

The ancients thought the world is flat
and rides upon a turtle's back,
or that the planets, sun and stars
revolve around the earth in crystal spheres.

Thus they defined the universe
till Galileo burst simplicity
by gazing at the heavens with a glass,
confirming Kepler and Copernicus.

All hell broke loose,
churchmen apoplectic, and the renaissance,
and finally Newton to explain it all,
a scientific substitute for Adam's fall.

Not exactly simple, but it worked
till Einstein stumbled on some quirks
in Newton's logic, and explicable
at last evolved incomprehensible.

Not good enough, said Stephen Hawking,
who proceeded to apply his daunting
intellect to postulating ways
black holes disfigure time and space.

He's got a Cambridge Ph.D.;
he's looking for a unifying theory,
and he's covered acres with equations.
Amazing. Centuries of speculation.

Okay, I'm not a physicist.
But even geniuses can miss the obvious,
and I don't need a Ph.D. to know
the universe begins and ends with you.

Song for Leela, Bobby & Me

for Robert Ross

The day you flew to Tam Ky, I was green
with envy. Not that lifeless washed-out
green of sun-bleached dusty jungle utes.
I was rice shoot green, teenage green.
This wasn't going to be just one more
chickenshit guerrilla fight:
farmers, women, boobytraps and snipers,
dead Marines, and not a Viet Cong in sight.
This was hardcore NVA, a regiment at least.
But someone had to stay behind,
man the bunker, plot the H&I.

I have friends who wonder why I can't
just let the past lie where it lies,
why I'm still so angry.
As if there's something wrong with me.
As if the life you might have lived
were just a fiction, just a dream.
As if those California dawns
were just as promising without you.
As if the rest of us can get along
just as well without you.

Since you've been gone, they've taken boys
like you and me and killed them in Grenada,
Lebanon, the Persian Gulf, and Panama,
Afghanistan, Somalia, Iraq.
And yet I'm told I'm living in the past.
Maybe that's the trouble: we're a nation
with no sense of history, no sense at all.

I still have that photo of you
standing by the bunker door, smiling shyly,
rifle, helmet, cigarette, green uniform

you hadn't been there long enough to fade
somewhere in an album I don't
have to look at any more. I already know
you just keep getting younger. In the middle
of this poem, my daughter woke up crying.
I lay down beside her, softly singing;
soon she drifted back to sleep.
But I kept singing anyway.
I wanted you to hear.

The Old Soldiers

The old soldiers imagine themselves warriors.
They remember the benediction of duty,
the future of women and pride.
They remember the beautiful weapons,
and always the beautiful dead.

They are wearing their colored ribbons.
They are watching the years march by.
They are full of a glorious sadness,
believing themselves important
and cheated of what they have earned.

Love in an Evil Time

for Diana Bedell

There was a woman I knew.
There was a candle, an altar,
a window, soft curves and shadows.
Miracles stirred in her eyes:

that she could raise the dead;
that she could see through the darkness;
that I could fall into those eyes
and just keep falling forever.

I hadn't known the gun was loaded.
I hadn't known how far I was from home.
I didn't believe I deserved it.
I didn't know what to do.

Trees lifted the moon into the sky.
In the moonlight, ordinary men
tore flesh from a broken corpse;
they grinned like dogs at a banquet.

No one explained this to me.
The woman sat beside me
singing of tea and oranges.
I wanted to slide into her.

I wanted her to kiss my wounds.
She kissed me on the mouth,
then blew the candle out
and left without another word.

Somebody cried, but it wasn't me.
Somebody burned the trees and the moon.
Somebody died of a dirty needle.
The dogs left nothing but bones.

A Small Romance

Suddenly, to your surprise,
I plucked two sapphires from your eyes
and held them to the fading light
like two blue burning stars. Night

was hard upon us, and the snow
fell in sheets beyond the window,
but we were warm in your small bed
and on your pillow, around your head,

a soft blue light seemed to dance.
I held you tight, a small romance
of sleepy child and sleepy father
singing sapphire songs together

in gentle darkness burning blue
until your breath came deep and you
were sleeping, and to my surprise,
I plucked two sapphires from my eyes.

The Children of Hanoi

June 1990

There in that place the Americans bombed,
where the children were sent to the hills
away from their mothers and fathers,
taking their laughter with them,
leaving their city in darkness,

in the market among the bicycles,
baskets of spices and fruit,
beer and cigarettes, burlap bags
and people singing their words
in a language forty centuries old,

in a toystore cluttered with orange
inflatable fish and wind-up monkeys
and dolls: two identical warplanes,
flight leader and wingman,
"U.S. Air Force" stenciled on the sides.

And the children touch them without fear,
pick them up with their hands,
put them into the sky
and pretend they are flying;
nothing but now in their eyes.

Who Did What to Whom

Hue, Vietnam

Because this street was washed with fire,
because I nearly drowned in fire,
I have come here again to sift the ashes.

How did I ever find myself
stumbling through Asia
dropping lighted matches like a fool?
"Okay, fool, you want some trouble?"
And they lit me up but good.

I have walked this street each day
ever since; each day the fire startles,
boys beside me go down screaming

or in silence, rise like smoke,
and I can't find a reason
that doesn't leave me burning.

But there are no ashes here, nothing
I can touch. Just some buildings
I recall; just the ghosts of soldiers.
These people don't remember me.
Curious, they only smile and stare.

Whatever might have hurt me here
is far away in quiet rooms
poring over maps and plotting fire.

The Lotus Cutters of Hồ Tây

The lotus cutters gather morning
into their small reed boats.

Graceful as egrets, they weave
through mist so fine it curls

them into its gossamer arms
like a woman holding a child.

One turns to catch a ball
of sunshine balanced on a stalk.

Who would come ten thousand miles
to bomb them?

What have they ever done
but keep the sun from falling?

Guns

Again we pass that field
green artillery piece squatting
by the Legion Post on Chelten Avenue,
its ugly little pointed snout
ranged against my daughter's school.

"Did you ever use a gun
like that?" my daughter asks,

and I say, "No, but others did.
I used a smaller gun. A rifle."
She knows I've been to war.

"That's dumb," she says,
and I say, "Yes," and nod
because it was, and nod again
because she doesn't know.
How do you tell a four-year-old

what steel can do to flesh?
How vivid do you dare to get?
How explain a world where men
kill other men deliberately
and call it love of country?

Just eighteen, I killed
a ten-year-old. I didn't know.
He spins across the marketplace
all shattered chest, all eyes and arms.
Do I tell her that? Not yet,

though one day I will have
no choice except to tell her
or to send her into the world
wide-eyed and ignorant.
The boy spins across the years

till he lands in a heap
in another war in another place
where yet another generation
is rudely about to discover
what their fathers never told them.

Singing Hymns in Church

My mother loved to sing,
but couldn't sing to save her life.
My childhood passed from week to week,
counted out in Sunday mornings
I would have to sit beside her
in the first pew, pretending I was
far away and she was not my mother
while she bellowed out the hymns

so loud and badly I was sure
God or Mr. Hoot would silence her
with lightning or a sharp word
and look at me as if to say,
"Why don't you keep her quiet?"

At home, she couldn't sing out loud.
Her husband and her sons were quick
to say what God and Mr. Hoot
were too polite to tell her.
All those many hurts she carried
in the stillness of her heart
we never thought of, being men
too conscious only of ourselves,
too ignorant to understand the beauty
of the Christian Church where once a week
my mother sang for God and me,
and all the angels sang along,
and what she heard was joy.

1991

The Cradle of Civilization

Where the Tigris and Euphrates meet,
human beings planted seeds and stayed
long enough to harvest them
on common ground.
This is where the world we know began.

How far we've come
that we should come to such a place
not with gratitude and wonder

but with bombs and guns,
that we should not find this odd,
that we should so believe our otherness
that we would rather kill and die
than search for common ground.

Finding My Old Battalion Command Post

What we came here to find
was never ours. After the miles
we've traveled, after the years
we've dreamed if only we could touch
the wound again, we could be whole,
no small wonder to discover
only a lethal past between us,
what we thought a brotherhood
only a mutual recollection of fear.

Something was lost, but it wasn't ours,
and if not here, we'd only have lost it
somewhere else. The young always do.
That is why we remember the young
who die too soon to lose
anything but their lives.
That is why we envy them.
They will always believe the world
is simple, and they only die once.

This is not what I intended,
but it won't stay down: nobody
wants a fool for a lover, a fool
for a father, a foolish friend.
Nobody wants excuses. Still,
there are stars that burn with no light;
there are things too evil for words,
too evil for silence.
Even a fool needs a friend.

But only the dead are permanent,
so we've come to this place to find—
what? Lost innocence? Our true selves?
What we think we were before we learned
to recognize incoming enemy mortars
in our sleep? What you've found is just
how frail I am. Now you think I can't
be trusted to my buttons. Grunt to grunt,
you say, it's all that matters.

Nevermind particulars. This is just
between the two of us: "Heave ho,

into the lake you go with all
the other alewife scuz and foamy
harbor scum. But isn't it a pity."
Yes, a pity, though I've long since learned
that losses are the way things are.
And look, I've found a village where I once
thought nothing green would ever grow.

The Simple Lives of Cats

Cold spring rain drums hollow rhythms
on the windowpanes. Two a.m. The house
so dark and empty even the kittens
lie mesmerized by the echoing patter,
heads raised, ears twitching, eyes wide,
tiny noses sniffing the air for danger.

But the only danger here is me.
Once again I've lost it, temper flaring,
patience at a too-quick end, my daughter
crying, and my wife's heart sinking
in the sadness of another good day gone bad.
If sorry has a name, it must be mine.

The kittens don't suspect a thing.
One turns her head to lick my hand.
The other, having satisfied herself
this new sound filling up the night
is just another harmless curiosity,
stirs once, then settles in my lap.

Tonight my wife and child are sleeping
somewhere else. I've done this to myself
often enough to wonder just how many
chances I've got left. I stroke the cats,
who purr like engines; happy to be near,
they see no need for my improvement.

After the Latest Victory

I call the sea. The wind calls back.
No seagulls' cries, no sailors' ghosts,

not mermaids, God, nor any human voice
disturbs the silence closing hard behind
the last reverberations of that solitary cry.

Does sound just die? Or does the universe
reverberate with cries from Planet Earth?
Novenas, speeches, shouts, whole supplications
striking Jupiter, careening off the stars
like frozen screams or unsaid thoughts?

Only the wind, and the waves' dull roar,
the dune grass dancing for the moon.
Behind me lies a continent asleep,
drunk with martial glory and an empire's pride,
though each is transient as sand.

This continent was called the New Jerusalem.
So much hope and expectation carried
in the hearts of men and women brave
enough to hazard all in search of this.
Look what we have made of it.

In Fairmount Park, a girl is raped.
Her father is a soldier in the Middle East.
Her brother cannot read or write.
The rapist wants a pair of sneakers
like the ones he's seen in Reebok ads.

The moon's wide river rides the swells
from breakers to the dark horizon.
Above me, like a dignified procession,
the stars turn slowly through the night,
indifferent to our helplessness.

A Vietnamese Bidding Farewell
to the Remains of an American

Was your plane on fire, or did you die
of bullet wounds, or fall down exhausted?
Just so you died in the forest, alone.

Only the two of us, a woodcutter and his wife,
dug this grave for you, burned joss sticks,
prayed for you to rest in peace.

How could we know there'd be such a meeting,
you and I, once separated by an ocean,
by the color of our skin, by language?

But destiny bound our lives together.
And today, by destiny's grace,
you are finally going home.

I believe your American sky
is as blue as the sky above this country
where you've rested twenty years.

Is it too late to love each other?
Between us now, the ocean seems so small.
How close are our two continents.

I wish a tranquil heaven for your soul,
gemmed with twinkling stars and shining moon.
May you rest forever in the soil of your home.

From the original Vietnamese poem
by Tran Thi My Nhung, translated by
Phan Thao Chi and adapted by W. D. Ehrhart

Star Light, Star Bright

Under stars in late October cold
you asked, if stars are suns,
why is ours much bigger than the rest.
I said, because they're far away.
As far away as Grammy's house, you asked.
Farther still, I said, much farther.
Where is Grammy now, you asked.
Her body's in the ground, I said,
but maybe what she really was
is up there somewhere shining down
like starlight you and I can feel
all around us on a night like this.
You stood in silence for awhile,
gazing up, one thoughtful hand
resting lightly on my shoulder,
one stretched out and turned palm up
as if to catch the starlight.
Then you said, almost singing,

what a pretty feeling
to be a little star,
white, and beautiful.
I could feel the whole heart of you
lifting dreams beyond the reach
of earthbound limitations and I
love you more than you will know
until I'm starlight and you understand
how each of us needs little stars
to lift our dreams beyond ourselves,
and I was hers, and you were mine.

More Than You Ever Imagined

You wake to a pain in your right side,
the left shoulder always stiff,
knees aching. Age advances
one sore muscle at a time,
hair on the head of the face
in the mirror peppered with gray.
But you still can't shave without bleeding.

On the radio news, nothing but war.
American planes are bombing Baghdad.
Knicked in three places, you remember
the nameless dead you carried home.
You remember you promised to bury them.
You thought you could. You didn't know
there'd be more than you ever imagined.

America in the Late 20th Century

He's giving up his paper route.
Only ten, and here he's written up
already in the Boston *Globe*:
held hostage by a customer who
shot him with a bow and arrow.
A hunting arrow, for Chrissake,
the sharp steel tip meant to kill.

What would cause a man to shoot
a boy like that? Ten years old.
Innocent enough to want to work
instead of splitting people's heads

or lifting people's wallets.
I used to carry papers as a kid.
No one ever took a shot at me.

I broke the Van Leers' window
once, put the Wilsons' Wednesday
late edition through their door.
Neither family even made me pay.
I didn't like the Morgan's dog
or Jimmy Whiteneck, but the things
I feared a kid should rightly fear.

These days a kid must learn to fear
crazed customers with hunting bows
and random gunfire in the street
that killed a boy six blocks from here.
What an age to come of age:
better to sell cocaine than news—
fewer surprises, and you die rich.

The Exercise of Power

Say it's the way things are.
Respectable men, for the greater good,
nod their heads as if at the edge
of a grave. Confronted with facts,
they are all agreed. The choice is
hard
but obvious:

do it. Done,

they gather papers,
head for home and solace,
other decisions and pressing affairs.

Like lumbering fire,
they move into the night.

Like slow deliberate stars they burn
whatever they touch: the millions of souls
caught in the darkness,
far from home,
at the mercy of nothing kind.

The Open Door

The door was opened just enough
to let the wind inside the house
and curl itself from room to room
like mist, or like a bony finger calling:
Here. Come here. I've come for you.

I didn't even know the door was open
till I felt those quiet words, a tingling
in my spine, like flakes of ice on bare skin.
I shivered once, twice, turned, saw nothing
but a fleeting shadow and the door ajar.

So, I thought, and listened hard.
The old house groaned, as old houses do.
No other sound disturbed the night.
And yet I'd seen a shadow, and a chill
settled on my heart and softly shook it.

Afraid, I tiptoed to my daughter's room,
but she was sleeping, and the cat beside her
didn't stir. Down the hall, my wife slept too.
I checked each room, each closet, the attic
and the basement. Nothing was amiss.

Sleep, I thought, but I couldn't sleep.
I hadn't left the door ajar. I know
I saw a shadow, just a passing breath
but real as cold or love or sorrow
or the loss of dreams we hold too dear.

Governor Rhodes Keeps His Word

Kent State University
May 4th, 1970

The girl kneels in the parking lot,
her face uplifted, mouth so twisted
she appears to be hysterical.
She has turned her outstretched hands
palm up, her arms extended down
as if to lift the body at her feet

out of the photograph into a place
where none of this would be happening,
where May would still be springtime
flowers, Frisbees, marijuana, love,
not soldiers, not these loaded rifles,
not the nightmare war that's finally come
to fill her unbelieving eyes with this
boy who will not rise again.
His blood coagulates on dusty asphalt.
She thinks some great injustice done.
She thinks the pain too great to bear.
She doesn't understand
the gray-haired men who've done this
or the millions more who think
the dead boy at her feet has gotten
just what he has asked for and deserves.

1992

The Distance We Travel

Hue, Vietnam, 1990

The strange American steps out of the night
into the flickering light of candles and small
fires and open stoves cooking evening meals,
families and neighbors clustered together,
moving like birds on the wings of words.

Discreetly their eyes follow the man,
bowls and chopsticks rising, pausing,
gracefully rising, so subtle a gesture
he wonders if he has imagined it.

In silence he passes among them
nodding agreeably, nodding in wonder,
nodding at what he remembers was here,
wanting to gather the heart of this place
into himself, to make it forgive him.

He is sure the older faces remember:
"Why are you here? Who are you?"
Questions alive in thick summer air,
a suggestion of posture.

But he has no answers to give them.
His explanation lies on his tongue
like bird with a broken wing.
Only the fact of the lives around him.
Only the need to be near.

Two girls too young to remember
are playing badminton without a net.
They turn to look, then giggle and stop.
One offers a racquet and shuttlecock.

In the dim street, he begins to play.
He marvels at his ineptitude,
their simple delight with his laughter,
how they have taken him into their game
as if he were not a stranger.

From out of the shadows a stool appears,
a cool drink. The girls' mother gestures
for him to sit. Unsure of himself,
he takes from his wallet a photograph.

"My daughter," he says, "Li-La."
He touches his heart with his open hand.
He writes the name in Vietnamese.
She touches the picture. The father appears,
another daughter, a nephew and son.

The father is reticent. Finally the stranger
touches the scars on his neck and says, "VC."
He points to the opposite bank of the river.
"Over there," he says, "*Tet Mau Than.*"

The father lifts his shirt to reveal
a scar on his chest. "VC," he says, then
drops his shirt and lights a cigarette,
offers one to the stranger. Together
they smoke the quiet smoke of memory.

Seven years the father spent in a camp
for prisoners of war. The wife
lightly touches her husband's knee.
Lightly his hand goes to hers.

The stranger considers the years he has spent
wearing the weight of what he has done,
thinking his tiny part important.
The father points to the gap-toothed bridge
the VC dropped in the river, long repaired.

The children are playing badminton again.
The shuttlecock lands in the stranger's lap.
"Li-La," the father softly says, touching
the stranger's heart with his open hand.

What War Does

It's like when you see something ugly and it shakes you up. A vividly gruesome roadkill perhaps, the skin broken and the fresh red meat just beginning to cook in the sun.

Or those two big dogs bounding through the woods along the Baltimore-Washington Parkway, a shepherd and a retriever, their glossy coats shining, having the time of their lives until they suddenly veer into the path of a BMW and *thump thump*, they are lying helpless beneath the wheels of other drivers with reflexes no quicker than those of the driver who crippled them, a confusion of cries almost human above the whine of tires and the muffled engines for a split second before you are by them and all you can see are cars veering this way and that in the rearview mirror, and then even that is gone.

The blink of an eye and years ago, but you still remember. Some little thing you're not expecting—the squeal of tires, the yelp of a dog, the hot smell of rubber—and you suddenly have to blink your eyes and swallow a sour bile rising in your throat.

It's like that.

Only you don't blow by in the blink of an eye, and the roadkills are human, and it isn't just once. It happens day after day, hour after hour, minute by minute. It's as if time is standing still. You are held hostage by time, forced to look and look and look till what you are seeing is burned into your retinas, until it is tattooed on your soul. And what you are seeing is the bottom line, the cold butchery upon which civilization is built. And when you close your eyes, you see it there, too.

You don't forget such things. When you look at your daughter, you see the child dead in its mother's arms, its skin blue, its small body turning rigid. When you look at your wife, you see the mother keening softly, rocking the child as if to sleep, unaware of the armed men staring down at her, unaware of her own fatal wounds, lost in a mother's grief that nothing will ever set right.

You remember the people who sent you to do this. You remember their words, how they made it sound like something worth doing, how they said they would always be grateful, how they called you a hero, invoking necessity, honor, and God. They have long since dusted off the wreckage of history, shucking it off like a bad dream, brushing their teeth and washing their hands and going on with their lives, leaving the pain of clarity, the burden of truth, to you.

But not to you.

To me. To my friends. To the straightleg grunts and boonie rats. The triggermen. The bloody survivors who never sleep without fire. And you wonder what is wrong with me. You might instead do well to marvel at the generosity of spirit that compels me to refrain from grabbing you by the scruff of your neck and pushing your face into the cesspool of sorrow and misery for which you with your gentle lives and two cars and four telephones are in no small measure responsible. What you don't know is evil.

You don't believe that, of course. If you did, it would make your life untenable. You would never again be able to let those you love out of your sight, even for a moment, without a fear so deep and stark it leaves you paralyzed, as if you could actually see the bullets violating their bodies, sending them sprawling like wounded dogs, their skulls smashed open, their brains leaking into the ground.

I have told you one lie. If I thought you would understand, I would push your face down into that cesspool and put my foot on the back of your neck and hold you there until you die of the stink and the shit and the blood in your lungs. I would not hesitate to suffocate you in the filth you refuse to see. It's what you deserve. You with your willful ignorance. You with your gentle lives. If I thought it would help.

Pray that I never do.

Sleeping with General Chi

The old general wants me to sleep.
He pats the bed and points to my shoes.
His voice tells me this is a man
accustomed to being obeyed.

After the ride to Tay Ninh
in a sheetmetal box with two flat tires,
the red laterite dust in our lungs
so thick you could hear it bubble,

after the commissar's welcoming speech:
so many wounded, so many homeless,
so many dead—even the general
falling asleep in his chair,

I wanted to walk to the river
to sit in the shade and wash my lungs
with the cool breath of a graceful land
of buffalo boys and herons,

but the guard at the gate spoke
only Vietnamese, and I did not.
Only a boy, he held his weapon
at port arms and tried to smile.

Years ago, in another life,
I had killed young men like him
and they had tried to kill me.
But not today. I'm tired of fighting.

So I turn away and find
the general under a fan in tropical heat.
I want to explain what's happened,
but the general wants me to sleep.

I've never slept with a general before.
Men don't sleep with their officers
and don't take naps together in bed
in the afternoon in my country.

But this is not my country.
The general pats my arm and dozes off,
serene as any aging man content
to have his grandchild sleeping near.

Making Love in the Garden

I have never seen you naked before.
Not like this: nothing at all
but sunlight, sky and skin
here in the garden
where you and your mother used to play,
the garden rapidly going to seed,
the house sold and awaiting settlement.

Nothing can bring your mother back.
Missing the ferry, losing the key,
up all night with intestinal flu,
getting a ticket while driving to see
your mother's grave for the last time:
God has been telling you all week long
what you remember is what you have.

That, and a garden empty of all but us.
The sun reflects the whiteness of skin,
the ocean breeze cool as grass,
two brown nipples, swaying breasts,
two white thighs across my hips,
hairs intertwined like the lives
that lie before us, yours and mine.

Once in awhile, love should be
with nothing between a man and a woman
and the universe they've chosen to share
but good clean air and no regrets,
your eyes half-closed,
the wetness of you,
pelvis a passionate blur.

What I Know About Myself

for Gloria Emerson

I always have to wash my hands
before my wife and I make love.
She likes the feel of clean hands
and I the feel of soapy hands,
so warm, so slick, so like

the secret places that we'll
soon be sharing.

A friend told me a story once
about a woman who planted a bomb
in a French café in Algiers.
The woman, Algerian, hadn't wanted
to do it. The men had told her
she must, it was her duty.
A hand, a French woman's hand,
had landed at her feet.

"Men," my friend had said, "love war.
Women endure it, but men love it.
You were there. You know.
Say you deny it, I don't care."

She reached for a book of photographs
from Vietnam. She'd been there, too.
"Look at the woman's face," she said,
"Look at them all. Those women
never looked at you. How could they
look at men with rifles
pointing at them? Look how young
you are. How innocent. How evil."

She knew I knew what she meant,
and she was right.
"Our hands will never be clean,"
she said, "but we must try."

And so I do, washing my hands
again and again of the filth
I've touched and never want
to touch my wife.
I want clean hands
to make her sigh and spread
and share those secret places
what I know about myself
can't find.

On Any Given Day

When the creep who was different
opened his mouth, we knocked him down

and kicked him until he stopped
moving, walked away high on adrenalin.

We didn't tell you this, but what
we think is a punch in the face, a knife
from the crotch to the throat.

What did you expect?
Him being different like that.

Guatemala

for Kari

Like a large cat rising out of a sleep
after a good kill is fully digested,
its stomach beginning to ask for more,
the General grins in the woman's face,
pulls the top of her dress aside,
cups a breast in his hand and pinches
the nipple hard, like a bullet.
She winces. American, twenty-six,
she's come to bring the joy of Jesus
to the children of the city dump:
thousands of families, thousands
of children, living on trash.
She runs a kitchen and school,
begs for what she gets and thanks
the Lord, but wants to know
why the General and his friends
feed steak to family dogs while
families starve. He rubs her breast.
He rubs his groin against her hip.
"There will always be poor," he says.
"The ones in the dump would find you.
Your embassy would send me a letter.
Nothing more would be done."

Long Shot O'Leary Ain't Dead Yet

to the Memory of Tom McGrath

The hell it's not class war.
Them that's got want more

and have the means
to get it, never mind
the rules, they're made
by them that's got
to keep us good
and scared of niggers,
feminists and queers,
name your poison,
they'll invent it.
Ask Rebecca Nurse, Joe
Hill, Fred Hampton—Hey,
what's a little violence
now and then. You've got
enough to think you've got
too much to lose to listen
to a flake like me,
right? "Take a hike,"
you're thinking.
All in single syllables.
About your speed.

Midnight at the Vietnam Veterans Memorial

Fifty-eight thousand American dead,
average age: nineteen years, six months.
Get a driver's license,
graduate from high school,
die.
All that's left of them
we've turned to stone.
What they never got to be
grows dimmer by the year.

But in the moon's dim light
when no one's here,
the names rise up, step down
and start the long procession home
to what they left undone,
to what they loved, to anywhere
that's not this silent
wall of kids, this
smell of rotting dreams.

The Last Time I Dreamed About the War

Ruth and I were sitting in the kitchen
ten years after Vietnam. She was six-feet-two
and carried every inch of it with style,
didn't care a fig that I was seven
inches shorter. "You've got seven inches
where it counts," she'd laugh, then lift her chin
and smile as if the sun had just come out.

But she didn't want to hear about the war.
I heard the sound of breaking glass
coming from my bedroom, went to look:
VC rats were jumping through the window.
They looked like rats, but they were Viet Cong.
Don't ask me how I knew. You don't forget
what tried to kill you.

I tried to tell her, but she wouldn't listen.
"Now look, Ruth!" I said so loud the woman
sleeping next to me woke up and did
what Ruthie in my dream refused to do:
she listened to me call the name
of someone she had never heard of,
anger in my voice, my body hard.

The woman I was sleeping with
would be my wife, but wasn't yet. I was
still a stranger with a stranger's secrets
and a tattoo on my arm. She'd never known a man
who'd fought in Vietnam, put naked women on
the wall, smoked marijuana, drank whiskey straight.
And here I was in bed with her,
calling someone else's name in anger.

She wanted to run, she told me later,
but she didn't. She married me instead.
Don't ask me why. I only know
you never know what's going to save you
and I've never dreamed again about the war.

1993

Small Talk

In the town of Freiburg, Germany,
cathedral shadows creep across the square
to where an American writer sits
admiring a scholar. "Doctor Ebel"
she had always signed her letters,
sounding just a little musty,
not vivacious, thirty-six, and unattached.
It must be nice to be a student
in a class of hers, he thinks,
wonders why she wears no wedding ring.

She asks about his wife and child.
He shows her recent photographs,
tells her how he calls them every day,
how glad he is he'll soon be going home.

"I envy you," she says, then looks away.

And then looks back and says, "One night
in World War Two, we Germans bombed
this town by accident. Tourist pamphlets
never mention that." Her voice a little hollow.

"You've been to war. I don't envy you for that,
but I envy you your wife and daughter,
how you wait impatiently for time
to reunite you. I was married once.
My husband left me for another woman.

"I was thinking how it must be nice
to look ahead and count the days
between you getting smaller by the hour.

"Days I count are always looking back."

How It All Comes Back

The bullet entered between the eyes,
a hole like a punctuation mark

from an AK-47 or M-16,
white at the edges but glistening black,
a tunnel straight to the brain.
That's what I saw when I picked her up

before crushed veins reopened, blood
began to cover my shirt, reflex
covered the hole with my hand,
and I started calling for help.

It was only a child's fall on a rock;
it only took three stitches to close,
but I couldn't look at my daughter
for months without seeing that hole:
I'd seen holes like that before,
but never on someone alive.

Purple Heart

for Dave Connolly

The wraith of a shadow shivered the air
the way whatever was green around us
always went silent
just before the bullets arrived.

I never got used to the terror
of sudden beginnings
or sudden conclusions,
the random ways people die,
so I knew what I felt this afternoon
was a fact.
And I knew what was coming.

But this time nothing happened.
Only that barely perceptible shiver,
and the world going on as before.

Spooky, I thought.
Then Lisa called
to tell me you'd had a heart attack.

Which of us could have imagined
middle-aged men with failing hearts
when we were young and strong and afraid

to imagine we'd see tomorrow?
Who could have told us
the terrors still to come?

But the shiver I felt was no coincidence.
Rise from your bed and live, my friend,
for the world is still a dangerous place
and I need the few friends I can trust.

Red-tailed Hawks

Mill Grove
Audubon, Pennsylvania

These chattering children fill the woods
with so much raw exuberance one wonders
what's the point of coming here
when any local playground would suffice.

Their teacher twice tells Michael and James,
"Don't throw acorns, please," to no effect:
they start again the moment she turns
to remind Adrienne, "Stay on the path."

Leela's worried she'll fall in the creek.
Chelsea and Ben are pushing each other
when someone, one of the children, shouts,
"There's a hawk!" and points.

"There's another!" "There!" "Another!"
other children cry: four red-tailed hawks
lazily circling, gliding, whirling, wheeling,
riding an unseen thermal up so high

the children tip their heads straight back
and still the hawks rise higher, higher still,
until they're only four black dots
of elemental joy against white clouds,

the children, even Michael and James,
so intent, so silent one can almost hear
wings they want to lift them
where the hawks have gone.

Mostly Nothing Happens

East Mt. Airy,
Philadelphia

Walking home on Upsal Street,
I saw a group of young black men
gathered on the sidewalk up ahead.
What now, I thought, heartbeat
rising in a heartbeat, eyes
instantly attempting to assess
intentions, weapons, routes of egress,
do I just keep walking, do I
take a detour to avoid them, if I—
Shame arrived before an answer:
what would Harris think, I thought,
what would Harris think of me
for fearing who when we were young
was him?

Harris's girlfriend was pregnant
when we were young, and every night
the two of us would read her letters,
flashlights pressed against the floor.
God help us if our drill instructors
caught us, but gentleness was rare
and we were very much in need
of gentleness on Parris Island,
so together we would read
those gentle letters.

She'd write about the baby's kicking,
how she'd guess what sex it was,
and if it was a boy they'd name him John.
"That's my name," he'd say each time.
"I know," I'd say, too embarrassed
to admit I didn't know a thing.
I'd touched a girl's secrets only twice,
and only with my hand,
and here's a guy who's really done it—
done it and she's pregnant, and he's
neither married nor abandoned her!

All of this a wonder to a small town kid
who'd never heard sex talked about

in proper conversation, get a girl pregnant
and you marry her, no questions, no debate.
Furthermore, a town where Negroes didn't live,
and terms like jungle bunny, nigger, coon,
if seldom heard in proper conversation,
were seldom far from lips.

But I was scared to death
of drill instructors huge as houses,
mean as pit bulls, psychopathic maniacs
out to keep the Viet Cong from killing me
by killing me themselves, so I thought.
Who at seventeen could understand
how terrifying war would be,
how much more obscene? This place
was worse than any place I'd ever been.
I thought I'd never leave alive.

To my surprise, so did Harris.
Urban, street-smart, soon-to-be-a-father
Harris, just as scared as I was.
And his voice so soft, his hand
upon my wrist when we were reading
softer still, a heart so big
I thought that mine would burst.
Through all those lonely southern nights,
through all that frightened Carolina summer,
those two boys from Perkasie and Baltimore
stuck together and survived.

Harris is the reason why I'm here:
I chose an integrated neighborhood
because I didn't want a child of mine
to reach the age of seventeen
with no one in her life
who isn't white.

But something isn't working right:
the neighborhood's got crack cocaine
and dirty needles lying in the gutter,
muggings, robberies, burglaries,
guns more prevalent than basketballs
and people willing to use them.
Two teenaged kids, a couple on a date,

were shot two blocks from here
for two dollars, and just last week
a man was taken from his car
at gunpoint, shot, and left for dead
a football field's length from my front door.
How much longer will it be before
the victim's me, my wife or daughter?
And if and when it happens,
odds are high the perpetrator's
going to be a young black man.

I hate to say those words out loud.
I hate the world that's made them true.
I hate distrusting men
before I even know their names, and so
I chose to trust those men on Upsal Street,
and this time got away with it.
But every time I trust a stranger
just might be the time I'm wrong.
What then?

What would Harris do, I thought,
what would Harris tell me I should do?
Why not find him? Why not ask?

You'd think it would be hard to find a friend
you haven't seen in twenty-seven years,
but I found him faster than I ever dreamed
or ever cared to: Panel 26E, Line 105.
John Lee Harris, Jr., born September 12th, 1947,
killed in Vietnam September 21st, 1967.

Damn.

You'd think that on the day he died,
an angel might have come to me.
A heron, or a raven.
But no. Only the day came
and went away again like other days
in Vietnam, and then my tiny piece of that
obscenity was over, so I thought,
and I too went away, wanting to forget.

I didn't think of Harris for a long time,
but I never forgot what he taught me,

and now I want to pound my fists
against that stupid granite wall:
"Come out of there, John Harris!
I need to know if what I am is cautious
or hysterical, a realist or just a racist,
how the world is, how am I to live in it.
I need answers," but instead
I get that war again,
still taking friends and giving only
wounds that never heal.

And now I've got this other war as well.
Last summer someone tried to force
my daughter's bedroom window open.
This was on a Tuesday afternoon.
Did Harris and his girlfriend ever marry?
Did they have a son and name him John?
Or did they have, like me, a baby girl?
And did he get to hold his child
and wonder at the tiny life he'd made
before he went away and died, fighting
yellow people in a white man's war?
Would he understand I'm not afraid for me?

That son of his would be a man
about the age of the men I passed
on Upsal Street last week,
the pounding in my chest so loud,
surely they could hear it.
I don't want to leave this neighborhood.
I want to think we'll be okay
if only we can touch the best
in others and ourselves.
I still don't keep a gun around
because I'm through with guns,
but every day is like a day at war:
mostly nothing happens,
but you never know what's waiting
when or where or how.
The first black friend I ever had
died one day when something happened.
Every day I'm always on patrol.

1994

Beautiful Wreckage

What if I didn't shoot the old lady
running away from our patrol,
or the old man in the back of the head,
or the boy in the marketplace?

Or what if the boy—but he didn't
have a grenade, and the woman in Hue
didn't lie in the rain in a mortar pit
with seven Marines just for food.

Gaffney didn't get hit in the knee,
Ames didn't die in the river, Ski
didn't die in a medevac chopper
between Con Thien and Da Nang.

In Vietnamese, Con Thien means
place of angels. What if it really was
instead of the place of rotting sandbags,
incoming heavy artillery, rats and mud.

What if the angels were Ames and Ski,
or the lady, the man, and the boy,
and they lifted Gaffney out of the mud
and healed his shattered knee?

What if none of it happened the way I said?
Would it all be a lie?
Would the wreckage be suddenly beautiful?
Would the dead rise up and walk?

Strangers

In the photograph, my mother's slim,
almost petite. Her white dress
reaches barely to her knees, revealing
slender legs on white high heels.
My father wears a three-piece suit,
dark brown or blue, dark tie, white shirt,

dark shoes with white tops, 1940s-style.
Each with an arm around the other's back,
they face the camera, and they're smiling.

She's twenty-three, he's twenty-four,
and nothing in the photograph suggests
that by the time they reach the age
that I am as I sit here staring
at the two of them together,
she'll be sliding toward obesity,
a sad and stoic woman married
to a man who's burning slowly inward
like a star collapsing on itself
for reasons neither he nor she nor
all the well-intentioned doctors
who applied electrodes to his brain
and took his money in exchange for drugs
ever did explain or ever could.

I stare and stare, trying to remember,
but the people in this photograph
are strangers. Nothing looks familiar
but the fraying, ragged edges
of the paper, and the crack that seems
to tear them both apart.

Not for You

The man with your name and your life
isn't you.
                Well, yes, it's your name,
and yes it's your life, okay,
but he can't be you.
                His hair's turning gray,
his wife's turning the corner on her way to work,
and he's going nowhere.
                                Not
in all your nightmares did you ever imagine
you would come to this: a small life,
a few friends, a lot of dreams
that came and went: an ordinary life.

You always knew an ordinary life
wasn't for you.

Oh, not for you with the wind
at your heart and the ache in your soul
about to take wing like a bird.

This can't be you. There's some mistake.

Prayer for My Enemies

"Love thine enemies."
—Jesus of Nazareth

Because I love you, I wish for you
to listen all your waking hours to homilies
and sermons by the Pope, and when you sleep,
to sleep with the smell of rendering plants
stuffing your nostrils until you puke.
May your car keys and credits cards
come to the hands of unscrupulous teens
who know your street, the house where you live.
May your lights go out on Broadway,
may your toilets forever be clogged,
may all your vegetables be overcooked.

You think it's a joke, but it's not.
Because I love you, I wish for you
an end to all that's good in your life,
each little thing, no matter how small,
how seemingly simple or unimportant.
May your every moment become a desert
and everyone you care about fall silent.
May even the earth refuse your body,
may large animals tear your flesh,
may the buzzards pick your carcass clean,
scatter your bones to the wind.

Suffer the Little Children

Oh, how we wanted to be good.
We brought our nickels every week, our
pennies earned collecting bottles,

doing chores, and put them in the jar.
We were saving for a heifer

for a village in darkest Africa.
We didn't know where Africa was,
but lions and gorillas lived in Africa,
and Mrs. Kugler told us Jesus
loved the little children of the world,

and there were children in this village.
In slides that Mrs. Kugler showed,
the Africans were singing in a crude
bare church of grass and local timber
with a plain wooden cross for a steeple

while a missionary family beamed.
But the Africans were very poor,
their children needed milk, and only
we, the six-year-olds of Mrs. Kugler's
Sunday School class in Lewisburg in 1954,

could help them. We could save them.
We could buy a heifer for their village
if only we could fill the heifer jar.
But the jar was big, our coins so small,
and as the weeks and months passed by,

it seemed we'd never fill that jar.
We were six years old, the fate of Africa
was in our hands, the weight of it so heavy,
but we didn't want to disappoint
our teacher. Or the Africans. Or Jesus.

Sarajevo

Smoke from a single rifle shot
dissipates so quickly it's impossible
to track where the bullet came from
in a place like this: so many buildings,
so many shadows, so much hate,
and a man whose 14-year-old son
died last month of fragmentation wounds
from no one knows whose mortar round

reaches for an onion by the window,
gets instead a bullet in the neck.

Maybe he will live. Maybe not.

Another winter falls upon this city
like a large dead thing, a body
stiff and lifeless, only weight,
and nothing in the city left to burn.

The wounded man's wife
cries out to God, as if she thought
the universe should answer
for the misery of their lives.

Dropping Leela Off at School

My daughter's reached an age
where daddy kissing her
in public just won't do.
In second grade, she's too
self-conscious, too grown up.
And so I only watch
her run across the play-
ground, leap a wall, top a
hill to stand triumphant
in her independence.

But as I turn to go,
she glances quickly left
and right to see who's there,
raises hand to lips, and
quickly throws a kiss a-
cross the space between us,
as if to say she knows
already just how hard
the world can be, how hard
it is, how little she
enjoys pretending
not to need me.

After the Winter of 1994

When the first storm struck, we didn't complain.
We thought: *Okay, we can handle this.*
It's winter. You shovel. It's no big deal.
But the second storm brought freezing rain,
leaving four inches of glittering ice
snapping trees, dropping wires,
paralyzing the world. The third storm
covered the ice with thirteen inches of snow,
then the fourth storm dumped more ice,
and as pipes burst and furnaces failed,
we dug through the attic for extra clothes
and swore we would never survive.
By the time the fifth storm hit, our minds
were as empty as rooms in a house
for sale, our hearts bereft of even
the memory of hope, refusing to quit
only for reasons we couldn't explain.

When the first snowdrops popped from the earth,
we didn't believe them, didn't believe
the crocuses. "This won't last," we said,
and knowingly nodded, hunkering down
to receive whatever was coming.
But the dogwoods bloomed, the azaleas
started to bud, and the grass and trees
turned that exuberant shade of green
that proclaims the arrival of spring
no matter what winter has tried to do
to eradicate joy from the world.
All day we've bathed in the warmth of the sun
and tonight we swim through a river of dreams,
the moon alive, the forsythias
glowing with ambient light so yellow
it almost hurts our eyes—but don't for a
moment think we're complaining. Not us.

1995

Drought

Perkasie, Pennsylvania, 1957

I had never before seen anything die.
Maybe a squirrel struck by a car,
or a bird caught by a cat, but nothing
so vivid, so slow, so thorough as this,

so little changing from day to day
we hardly noticed the thickening
algae, the yellowy-green of it sick
for weeks with the absence of water,

till we suddenly found ourselves walking
where always only water ever had been.
Only the holes held water now, and the holes
grew smaller, the holes grew crowded,

the fish grew frantic until they could
only lie on their sides in the mud
gulping at water that wasn't there,
and even the mud in the deepest holes

would be brittle tomorrow, the fish
encrusted with blue bottle flies, each fly
as big as a thumbnail, hungry, the only
sounds our feet on the creek bed snapping

like rivets in iron heat, and the buzzsaw
buzzing of tens of thousands of flies
feasting on death, even our memories
of water too cruel to be spoken aloud.

Variations on Squam Lake

I

Night comes down to a loon calling
and finds two herons at water's edge,
the lake so still, the stars fall in,

the trees bend down and scoop them out,
lift them back to the sky.

II

Night comes down to a loon calling
and finds an errant star falling

into a lake so still it seems
made only of gossamer dreams

until a great blue heron's wake
disturbs the surface of the lake

for a moment or two before
the stillness settles in once more

and the moon rises and the loon
calls out again, greeting the moon.

The Perversion of Faith

Saigon/HCMC
June 1990

The riverside banquet, extravagance
served by women in flowing *ao dais*,
might be explained as a lapse in judgement,
a clumsy desire to please and impress,

but the women were no mistake:
young enough to be our daughters,
girls procured by a former Viet Cong.
One took my hand and placed it on her lap.

I thought of an evening years before,
of a frail old soldier, Mr. Giai,
and of what the war had cost him:
thirty years, three fingers, his oldest son.

I thought of how the Saigon River
so serenely slapped the pilings, how
his voice had sounded like a tiny bird
beating back a sadness with its wings.

Mr. Giai had once met Ho Chi Minh.

Reading Out Loud

I hated it. That inescapable
moment each day my turn would come
and I would have no choice except to read
what David, Karen, Jimmy and Suzanne
read as if they were sliding on glass,
not crashing through it, lurching, stumbling,
every step a public demonstration
of stupidity, each sentence hours,
the teacher's cardboard smile and tapping foot,
rustling in the chairs around me, giggles
of the other kids Miss Connie used
to punish me, pretending not to hear.

1996

Christmas Miracles

Leaving the party she takes my hand,
slips on icy sidewalk, squeezes
my hand to steady herself, laughs
a child's laugh. She tells me she hopes
I'll like the present she's made.
She imagines the presents she'll get.

Hand in hand we go through crackling
cold December night, her voice so bright
like moonlight on a field of snow,
so happy. As if she's forgotten
how scary an angry father can be,
how scary the brooding silences.

But tonight I'm a man who knows
what he's got. And tonight is Christmas Eve:
presents are waiting beneath the tree,
each one to my daughter a dream,
a desire, a wish, a new beginning.
Tonight she takes her father's hand
like a child who's not afraid.

The First French Kiss

I've forgotten the pain
of being fifteen and alone
with fiery-haired Ann Broderick,
girl I'd adorned all year,
who suddenly found me attractive
in the back seat of Max Hunsicker's car
parked in a lane off Hilltown Pike,
me with mush for a brain and a heart
beating to bust my ribs.

I've forgotten how we came
to an end because I couldn't
stop asking myself why
she wanted me now
when not before,
me the same kid as before:
taller, thinner, more
a young man than a boy,
but the same kid still
in the place where the pain lives.

But I've forgotten all that.
I've forgotten everything
except the way her tongue was in my mouth,
the warmth of it, the wetness of it,
promise of what I hardly dared
imagine, the woman's smell of her,
me with my too tight jeans
and my hands in all that hair.

Visiting My Parents' Graves

If you had told me thirty years ago
I'd miss this town, I'd have told you
—well, you know what I'd have said,
so smug it was, so self-content,
its point of view so narrow one could
get a better field of vision peering

through the barrel of a shotgun.
I, at seventeen, could see that much
and so much more I couldn't wait
to leave. It didn't help, of course,
that I was who I was:
the preacher's and the teacher's son,
blow my nose the whole town knew,
anonymous a word I used
to stare at in the dictionary,
wishing it were me. Yet here I am,
thirty years later, back again.

I've come at night because I know
in daylight I could walk these streets
from dawn to dusk, meeting no one
who would know my name, or even yours.
Peter Shelly's house lies buried under
Nockamixon Lake, the Bryan's dairy farm's
a shopping mall, tract housing's crowded
out the sledding run near Callowhill;
Jeff Apple's gone to Melbourne Beach,
Larry Rush went schizophrenic
paranoid, and just about the only
thing that hasn't changed is Larry's mom,
who's still convinced he'll come out right

if only he'll repent and turn to God.

Me, I'm pretty well convinced that she's
the reason Larry's nuts, but that's
the only thing I'm sure of anymore.
I've been to the other side of world,
said what I've thought, hedged no bets, had
no use for comfortable hypocrisies
or delicate interpretations
meant to keep the world the way it is.
I've quit every job I've ever had
for something else, for this or that, or else
because someone's always screwing someone
else, and silence to injustice
large or small is simply cowardice.

Which may be true, but what I've got
for all my years is unemployed
and unemployable, a dozen books
that no one reads, a wife who works
to earn what I cannot, a daughter
I have trouble looking in the eye
because I fear she'll recognize
her father for the failure he's become.
That's the worst of it: I don't trust
my own judgement anymore. What used
to seem so obvious has vanished
in the glare of consequences
prudent people manage to avoid.

So here I am: sitting by your gravestones
on a hill above this town I couldn't
wait to get as far away from
as the moon, and though I know it's only
an illusion, here's the moon just rising
over Skyline Drive so huge it looks
as if I'd only need to reach
my fingers out to touch it,
just like sitting here at night
makes the town appear like nothing's changed,
as if at any moment Jeff and Larry
might appear on bikes, wave to me, and shout,
"Let's chase the cows at Bryan's farm!"
As if the years might fall away
and let me start again.

Cycling the Rosental

for Adi Wimmer

The River Drau flows swiftly here,
and cold, and such a pale green
it whispers in a waking dream
we pedal through beneath the near

and jagged Slovene Alps, "Let go
of all that troubles you—believe
in all the world can be—I'll weave
a little spell to let you know

the song I sing is meant for you."
So it is, and so the flowers
also sing through all the hours
we ride together, sky so blue

we finally have to stop and strip,
jumping into the River Drau
like a couple of kids. And how
the icy pale water grips

us till our hearts cry out in pain
or joy, my friend, I don't know which,
nor does it matter: even if
we never pass this way again,

we'll know the river's always here,
these mountains, and the sky above
the Valley of Roses, and the love
that makes a day like this so dear.

The Rocker

Summer, winter, autumn, spring, Mrs. Ward
would rock each day on the big front porch
across the street from our house. Nothing
missed her steady gaze. Not the time
when we were eight and broke the aerials
off cars in Berger's lot to use as swords.
Not the time the plumber down the street
threw a wrench through his bedroom window,
standing in the street, shouting, "Filthy bitch!"
Not the time my parents went away
and all my brother's friends and mine
partied in the parsonage (our house),
cars parked up and down the street,
Mrs. Ward still rocking when the last
car pulled away at two a.m.
Bill and Edna Sine both died.
The plumber finally left his wife,
or she left him, I don't remember which.
The Shivers came and went; the Cressmans.
John and Evelyn Ehrhart raised four sons,
one of whom was me. I left when I was

seventeen, but came back often
just (not really, but I liked to joke)
to see if Mrs. Ward was rocking.
And of course, she was. We buried Dad,
and two years later when we buried Mom,
Mrs. Ward, older than Methuselah
by then, rocking on her big front porch, called
across the street, "I'll miss your folks."
"I will, too," I said. *And I'll miss you,*
I thought, knowing, now that Mom and Dad
were gone, I'd not be back again.
Nor have I been, but I've no doubt
Mrs. Ward is out there rocking still.

Ginger

My orange kitty is a wicked little girl,
pulling down the trash can in the kitchen.
What am I to do with a cat like that?

Half-awake, I stumble down the stairs
too late to keep her from a midnight snack.
My orange kitty is a clever little girl.

I turn the light on: there she is amid
the meat scraps, carrot peals, and cellophane.
What am I to do with a cat like that?

Especially when she looks at me with eyes
that say, "I'm not responsible for this."
My orange kitty is a shameless little girl.

I run her out, but as I'm cleaning up
she comes right back and rubs against my leg.
What am I to do with a cat like that?

Wide awake, I lie in bed wondering
what am I to do with a cat like that
while, curled up beside me fast asleep,
my orange kitty is a happy little girl.

Rehoboth, One Last Time

for Patty

I might have known trouble was coming.
How we kept it up through all these years.
How each summer but the one I spent at sea
I'd never miss the chance to visit,
even the year I had to drive
nonstop all night through driving rain.
How the moon would rise above those old
concrete submarine towers by the beach,
the moon's wide river spreading flames
across the darkness of Rehoboth Bay.
How our families grew around us.

But I might have known trouble was coming.
That last sad visit to Rehoboth Bay
everything had changed: all day those ugly
little jet skis whined like manic gnats,
and every night blaring music boomed
from newly-built nightclubs by the beach,
and I remember thinking how there's
not a place on earth so beautiful
people won't destroy it for a buck.
The day we left, I knew we'd never
be together here again. Not here,

though surely somewhere, I assumed
until your letter came, explaining
John had left you after twenty-two years.
So there you are, alone in Seaford,
you with your two teenaged daughters,
and your parttime job, and the wreckage
of the life you thought you still had coming
while John's vacationing this summer
with a woman half your age in Rome.
Just so, the things we love are lost
in ways we understand, and ways we don't.

Night Sailing

After darkness
swallows the world,

stars climb into your rigging
to trim the sails;
water caresses,
the wind possesses you,
chasing the flying white ball moon
to the far side of your dreams.

Is It Always This Hard?

I. Why I Stopped Going to Church

I was doing fine with God created heaven and earth and the spirit of God moving upon the face of the waters. And with Cain and Abel too, and Noah's Ark, and even Abraham and Isaac. Okay, it's a bit draconian, God telling Abraham to sacrifice his own son, but He doesn't actually make him do it. He's only testing Abe. And Abe's no fool. Look what happens when God speaks and you don't pay attention: no more gravy train for Adam and Eve. Lot's wife turned into a pillar of salt. Three days for Jonah in the belly of a whale. Ponder that one for a moment: like getting stuffed into a washing machine full of battery acid and shrimp. Anyway, it all makes sense to me. After all, God's the Creator and Ruler of the universe; He can do anything, so why not? But I hadn't counted on puberty, or the night I find myself lying in bed thinking about Chickie Snyder's older sister, and suddenly my right hand's wrapped around a part of my anatomy to which I had hitherto paid no considerable amount of attention, and it feels really good. I mean really good. I've never felt anything this good. I've never imagined anything feeling this good. But you want to talk about getting stuck between a rock and a hard-on? All the while I'm also thinking about that guy Onan who spills his seed on the ground, "and the thing which he did displeased the Lord: where-fore He slew him," and I don't know what'll come first, me or the wrath of God. This time I do, but I spend the rest of the night and all the next day waiting to die. And this goes on for a couple of years, me stroking it every night and every day constantly ducking and flinching and looking back over my shoulder for the Angel of the Lord. Which is undoubtedly the origin of the belief that masturbation leads to insanity. But I don't go insane, though it's touch and go for awhile there. Instead, I finally ask myself what kind of God would give a kid the equipment to make himself feel this good—to feel so heavenly, for goodness sake, to feel downright divine—and then tell him He's going to kill him if he uses it? And I never do come up with a good answer. And after awhile, I stop asking.

II. Switchblade Knife

I'm hitchhiking back to Perkasie from this party in Doylestown, and a man stops and gives me a lift. He asks me where I've been and after I tell him, he asks me if I like to party. I think that's an odd question, why would I go to a party if I didn't like to party, but I say, yeh, sure, I like to party. Then he asks me if I like girls, and I think what's this guy's story anyway, but I say sure, yeh, I like girls, who doesn't? He doesn't say anything for awhile. Then he asks me if I like boys, and my heartbeat jumps like that, like somebody goosed me, and now I'm thinking uh oh, is this guy what I think he is and trying to figure what do I do, I can't just say thanks for the lift and open the door and get out, we're driving up 313 doing fifty miles an hour. I reach into my coat pocket and wrap my hand around the knife I've got, but Jesus, I only carry the damn thing to impress the girls, I'm only fifteen years old for chrissake, I've never stuck anything in my life but apples, and I say what do you mean, do I like boys? He says, you know, to fool around with, like girls, and I say no, I don't fool around with boys, I like girls. He doesn't say anything for awhile, but I'm sweating like a stuck pig, and swearing to God just get me out of this one and I'll never lie to my parents again, I'll never sneak out to another party, I'll never hitchhike, and I'll go to church every Sunday for the rest of my life, honest. He makes the turn onto Fifth Street, but we're still four miles from town when he says he'll give me twenty dollars if I let him hold my testicles, that's all I have to do, nothing else, he just wants to touch my balls, and I'm so scared I can't talk, I can't think, I can't breathe, I pull that knife out of my pocket and press the little button and the blade clicks open with a loud *ka-thunk* and I stick it up under his nose where he can get a good look at it and I manage to say stop the car right now right here now, too afraid to wonder what am I supposed to do if he doesn't.

III. On Going All the Way

I'm in this play at school called *Papa Is All*. It's about this Amish girl who falls in love with a traveling salesman, to which Papa says no, absolutely not, a nice Amish boy with a broad-brimmed hat and a good team of horses, that's the kind of boy for you. That's what he thinks—me, actually, because I play Papa—but his daughter thinks otherwise, and finally Papa goes completely fire and brimstone and Mama has to call the police. Harry Nelson— he plays the cop—tries to cool Papa down, but Papa tries to skewer him with a pitchfork, so Harry pulls his revolver. He's supposed to say, "When I shoot, I shoot straight," but he's only standing two feet in front of me, you could blindfold him, stand him on his head, make him pull the trigger with his big toe, and he still couldn't miss. We never do get through that line without cracking up, so the night of the play I tell him just say, "Stop or I'll shoot," and he does and we don't laugh. Afterwards we go to a party at Tom Peacock's house—Tom plays Papa's son—and I end up with Carol James, who isn't in the play but who is the most beautiful girl in the universe, or at least all of Bucks County, and she's got her tongue in my ear. Then she says let's go out to your car—my parents' car, actually, a 1964 Studebaker Lark—and before you know it the windows are completely steamed up, we can't see out and nobody can see in, which is a good thing because it doesn't take much longer for her to get her skirt up around her waist and my hand down inside her panties. Pretty soon she stops kissing me and says what do you feel like doing? You'd think the answer would be obvious, but the truth is I don't know whether to fish or go blind because I've never done it before and I don't actually know how. Oh, I understand the general principle, sure, but we're suddenly not talking generalities here, or principles either, we're talking no more lockerroom braggadocio, no more kissy-kiss for a couple of hours and then go home and talk to your pillow, this girl wants it, this girl is ready, willing, and eager to go all the way—and what I say is I don't have a rubber. Which I don't. I crank up the car and turn the defroster on full blast, trying to clear the windshield enough to drive because the nearest gas station—the only prayer I have of finding a rubber machine at this hour—is over in Line Lexington, but when I get there, it's closed. So is the one next to the R&S Diner. And the one up by the Souderton Shopping Center. And by then I have to take Carol home before she gets grounded. She doesn't kiss me goodnight, and when I ask her out for next weekend, she says no. I don't know whether I'm happy or sad.

What Goes Around Comes Around

Okay, our father was a shit.
Reverend John, the darling of Perkasie,
much beloved, quick with a joke, a kind word,
time for someone else's problems.

Never time for ours, of course, though no one
ever saw that side of him but us:
the man with nothing but ugly words
or none at all for days on end,

so full of rage at God-knows-what,
so full of guilt, so self-absorbed
four sons grew up beneath his roof
without his ever knowing who we were.

So he wasn't Robert Young, okay?
In the end, at least he understood
he'd blown it. Ponder this: your own father
asks for your forgiveness on his deathbed

and you turn your back and walk away.
And now you've got a son who's stolen,
lied, and flunked his way through adolescence
while you've been making piles of money

and spending it on courting women
from Maine to Moscow; a kid who should have
gone to Harvard pumping gas instead.
You think you're not responsible for that?

Maybe not, but when it's you
with no time left except to ask
forgiveness for the man you've been,
I wonder what your son will say to you.

Because It's Important

for Leela

I know what you hear most often is me
explicating the sorry state of your room
or haven't you done your homework yet
or don't talk back to your mom,

but there's something else I need you to hear
and remember: from the day you were born
you were a wonder unfolding before me.
You are still. You always will be.

I Just Want You to Know

for Anne

I'm sorry it's not a vacation for two
in Rome or Rio or Katmandu.

I'm sorry it's not I've gotten a job
selling insurance or working for Bob

Miller at Mellon Bank, or anything
lucrative or practical, something

to make your life a little better.
Hell, even a hairbrush or a sweater

you could put to good use. What you'll do
with these few lines I haven't a clue.

I'm sorry it's only another poem
instead of a Lincoln or a new home

in an upscale suburb, but I'm still
just a poet. I love you. I always will.

The Sergeant

Alongapo, The Philippines, 1968

At night in the Seven-Eleven Club,
you watch the sailors dressed in white
fresh from the waters off Vietnam
get fleeced by the hostesses, brown
sensuous girls who dance with the sailors
for drinks containing no alcohol.

The girls can dance all night and never
get drunk, and at closing time the sailors,
who think they're about to get laid, get
shown the door and stagger back to their ships.

What do they know about loneliness,
those beautiful sailors in white,
sitting on ships on the blue beautiful sea,
launching beautiful bombers
into the beautiful sky,
firing beautiful five-inch projectiles
at places and people they'll never see.

In the morning you wake to a shabby
room in a cheap hotel with a hostess
who's charged you nothing but love,
the war in Asia, a war in America,
you in the middle, twenty years old,

cupping the breast of the only
forgiveness that makes any sense at all.

The girl awakes. She wants you inside her.
The two of you wash the night from your mouths
with slices of sour green mango.

Jogging with the Philosopher

for Joe Volpe

Descending into Valley Green is easy
because its all downhill. Gravity.
A delightful invention. Thanks to Newton,
I can take the time to notice squirrels,
the grace of trees, the blessing of wind,
sometimes even a deer with spotted fawns.
You can't beat that on a Sunday morning.

We can even talk on the way down,
though I have to admit that I
do most of the talking. The philosopher
isn't given to words. Once in awhile
he'll allude to Epictetus
or the perfect wisdom of breaking
the collarbones of graffiti artists,
a solution without the tyranny
of state-sanctioned death, but a lesson
not to be quickly forgotten.

Jogging along the creek is equally
pleasant. The water sings swiftly here
among the rocks, there pauses to reflect,
the ducks in every weather unperturbed,
as if they remember the soft scrunch
of our feet on the gravel path, as if
we were old and trusted companions.
I could jog for miles beside the creek
and we do, the philosopher
taciturn but not at all unfriendly.

It's coming back out of the valley
that always kills me. Gravity. That
dirtbag Newton. And the hill nearly

a mile long and practically vertical.
I do it just to remind myself
how truly miserable life can be.
Halfway up my lungs begin to burn
like I've swallowed fire, my legs become
like tree stumps, and my heart cries out,
"Oh, world! Oh, madness! God, oh, God!"

Right about then, the philosopher
slowly but surely accelerates.
I manage to gasp, "You bastard."
The philosopher only grins.

A Meditation on Family Geography
and a Prayer for My Daughter

Seven generations of Ehrharts
are buried in Hampton, Pennsylvania,
but I never lived there.
My father left when he was young.

There are Contis buried in Gettysburg
where my mother grew up,
but she wasn't born there
and she, too, left when she was young.

My parents are buried where I grew up
in Perkasie, Pennsylvania,
but I wasn't born there
and I left when I was young.

I have a brother in Colorado.
I have a brother in Montana.
I have a brother in Thailand.
They have a brother in Philadelphia,
but it isn't my home. It's only
a city; I only live there.

My wife's mother is buried on Martha's Vineyard,
but she wasn't born there.
She never even lived there.
She was born in Fresno, California.

She's only buried on Martha's Vineyard
because my wife's father grew up there,

but he wasn't born there either
and he left when he was young.

His mother is buried next to his wife,
but his mother's house was sold long ago
and he likely won't be buried in Massachusetts;
he's married again and living in North Carolina.

Scattered across the globe we are,
the living and dead of our two families,
and the older I get the more I wish
for the comfort of generations,
for the solace of long acquaintance with place
and people around me who care.

The worst is when I think of our child
and what she'll have when her parents are gone:
relatives scattered across the globe,
most of them nothing but names.

Mostly, even with Leela and Anne,
I feel like a mariner lost at sea
or a small cry lost among the stars.
How will Leela feel when it's only her?

God grant her a loving and faithful mate.
God grant her loving and loyal friends.
God grant my daughter a place in the world
surrounded by people who care.

1997

Cliches Become Cliches Because They're True

for Ben in Friends Hospital

You have to understand the way things are:
fire lives in this man's dreams, the way it
roils across the land like water churning,
the way it scours flesh from living bones.

That one's fine and delicate as lace
my grandmother used to make on Sunday
afternoons when she was young and people
stayed at home on Sunday afternoons.

This one's got a wife and kids afraid
they'll let him out again too soon and he'll
come home a nightmare with the family name
and nothing else familiar but their fear.

The woman by the window slashed her wrists.
And that one near the door has got a child
she tried ten years to bear and now can't bear
to hear or see or even think about.

God only knows what breaks inside the brain,
or why. You have to understand the way
things are: there's only circumstance, and chance,
and there but for the grace of God go I.

Detroit River Blues

I was jogging. It was cold.
I was wearing my hooded sweatshirt
and behind me for miles up Woodward
Avenue to Grand Circus and beyond
was a pastiche of retail shops and banks
and abandoned buildings boarded shut,
men and women in business suits
and street people and bums and the guy
in a wheelchair hawking the news:
"Scab newspapers not sold here!" he shouts—
big union town, Detroit, and a strike on.

Me, I'm living at the Downtown Y, nine
floors up and a window overlooking
rooftops and alleys and empty lots,
so I like to go jogging to clear my head,
take my mind off just how lonely I am.

But just as I get to the river,
the wind skipping across the water
like a good flat stone and smacking me
right in the face, the river all whitecaps,

a big damned ore boat, the *Walter J. Todd*,
comes plowing along on its way to who
knows where, and I think to myself
if I hijacked that ship I could
sail it up the St. Lawrence Seaway
to Newfoundland and then turn south
along the Atlantic coast to Cape May
and up the Delaware Estuary
all the way to Philadelphia.

I could dock the ship at Penn's Landing;
I could walk to where you work;
we could have lunch together.

I could be having lunch with you
instead of freezing my ass off
watching that boat disappear down
the river without me. Me without you
and the wind rising. And I think to myself
it's a hell of a day to go jogging.

Artsy Fartsy Whiskey & Girls

on the Avenue of the Arts
Philadelphia, Pennsylvania

There's nothing here to commend your
attention, I can tell you that
straight off, no joke, unless you're sure
what you want is only the fat

lady singing an aria
just before she drinks the poison
and dies and the whole area
from Chestnut Street down to Spruce on

Broad goes bonkers, everybody
calling out, cheering and clapping,
"Bravo! Bravo!"—and nobody
in his right mind needs that. Napping

on the railroad tracks is more fun
and probably healthier, too.
I know a place on Addison
with whiskey and girls. It'll do

in a pinch, and if this isn't
a pinch, I'd like to know what is.

Pabst Blue Ribbon Beer

Jeff and I were eight or nine the day
we snuck into the basement den,
opened a bottle of his father's beer.
What was this stuff his father drank?
How did it taste? Why did Dr. Apple
have a special room that seemed so full
of mystery? Mrs. Apple even drank
a Pabst Blue Ribbon now and then,
and she was everything I ever
dreamed a mother ought to be.

Jeff had it made: beautiful mom,
dependable dad. I never saw
them arguing, never heard them
raise their voices to their children.

Our basement didn't have a den.
Our basement was a dingy place
with crumbling walls and cobwebs clinging
to the pipes, and old wooden crates.

Jeff took a sip and made a face,
and then I took a sip and forty
years later I can still recall
the vile taste, so bitter, the confusion
of that moment: how could people
I'd have given anything to be
their child enjoy so foul a thing?

We poured the bottle down the sink,
never thinking that in five more years
Mrs. Apple would be diagnosed
with multiple sclerosis
that would slowly over thirty-five years
reduce her to a shriveled fetal ball
abandoned by her husband, left
to lie alone through all those years
to finally die alone in a room one
floor above where Jeff and I thought
nothing in the world could taste this bad.

The Orphan

After awhile, he gave
up waiting, rose
from beside his parents'
grave, looked once
more at the town un-
folding down below like
somebody's dream
of a perfect place
to rise above,
or leave behind,
church bells chiming
the hour of darkness,
close to home,
but home long gone.

Too long
was long enough
and longer still.

He bent to kiss the flat
brass plate that marked
his parents' grave,
said goodbye
to no one listening,
turned,
and walked away.

1998

Music Lessons

Standing where the water tumbles
down the broken beaver dam
above the old stone wall where
daffodils on slender stalks

nod beneath a seamless sky,
my daughter says, "Listen, Dad,
the creek is singing."

No use pointing out to her
the image isn't fresh.

How much she is her father's child;
how often adolescent need
to differentiate herself from me
becomes two stubborn people
butting heads.

But not today.

I'd have to be a fool to choose
this moment to instruct her
in the art of words.

And anyway, only the dead
at heart would ever argue
what we're hearing isn't
just exactly
what my daughter says it is.

1999

For My Daughter, Alone in the World

Though you stand on the edge of darkness,
the world before you
a black hole of despair,
my love will always be right in your pocket.

Whenever you want it,
you need only put your hand in your pocket
and there my love will be.

Gravestones at Oxwich Bay

St. Iltyd's Church
Gower, Wales

I.

"When the archangel's trump shall sound
And souls to bodies join,
Millions will wish their lives below
Had been so short as thine."

Sacred to the Memory of Elizabeth,
daughter of Samuel & Elizabeth Ace,
who died August 17th 1829
aged ten months

Also of Elizabeth
daughter of the above
who died December 11th 1847
aged 17 years

II.

Samuel Ace 72, died 1876
"Thy will be done"

Elizabeth,
wife of the above named
died 1879, age 74
"All her sorrow left behind
And earth exchanged for heaven."

Sins of the Fathers

Today my child came home from school in tears.
A classmate taunted her about her clothes,
and other kids joined in, enough of them
to make her feel as if the fault was hers,
as if she can't fit in no matter what.
A decent child, lovely, bright, considerate.
It breaks my heart. It makes me want someone
to pay. It makes me think—O Christ, it makes
me think of things I haven't thought about
in years. How we nicknamed Barbara Hoffman

"Barn," walked behind her through the halls and mooed
like cows. We kept this up for years, and not
for any reason I could tell you now
or even then except that it was fun.
Or seemed like fun. The nights that Barbara
must have cried herself to sleep, the days
she must have dreaded getting up for school.
Or Suzanne Heider. We called her "Spider."
And we were certain Gareth Schultz was queer
and let him know it. Now there's nothing I
can do but stand outside my daughter's door
listening to her cry herself to sleep.

2000

What Better Way to Begin

You can just keep your rockets' red glare.
And as for the bombs bursting in air,
with all that noise and fire and smoke
there has to be plenty of jagged steel
looking for someone to hit.
Ask Gaffney with his shattered knee.
Ask Ski with a hole behind his ear
the size of a fist.
So I'm not too keen on fireworks.
Call it ghosts from the past.

But it's Millennium Eve
and my daughter wants to see the biggest
fireworks show the City of Philadelphia
has ever put on—or ever will—
in my lifetime or hers.
So off we go to join the crowd
on the banks of the Delaware River.

When midnight arrives, the crowd explodes
as the barges moored in the river

open fire in a steadily rising rumble
of thumps and sparks like four-deuce mortars.
But before the first bomb bursts in air,
Leela silently takes my hand
and holds it tight through the rockets' red glare
till the last bomb's blunt concussion
fades away as if it never were.

Letting Go

The last time I saw my mother alive,
she lay in a coma, eyes closed,
almost as if she were sleeping.

This wasn't like my father's coma
eighteen months before, him a dead man
kept alive by machines, his eyes
half-open and looking nowhere,
glazed and gray like a fish on ice.

It had taken my mom four days
to tell the doctors to pull the plug—
a wonder to me, and a lesson:
depressed, mercurial, full of rage,
burning inward like a star gone mad,
my dad was a difficult man,
and though they'd been married forty-four years,
happily married didn't apply.

Not while I'd been alive. And yet
at the end it was clear she'd never
forgotten the happy-go-lucky
guy she'd fallen in love with,
and she didn't want him to die.

And now I didn't want my mother to die.
Not that I'd wanted my father dead—
I'd long since learned to forgive what he
couldn't help—but I knew I wouldn't miss him
the way I'd miss her. She knew it too, knew
how much her sons, grown and gone and
with kids of their own, depended on her still.

She was willing herself to live
in spite of the cancer that wanted her dead.
But she looked so tired lying there,
a lifetime of sorrows and all used up,
nothing inside but a mother's love.

Alone with her, I took her hand and cried.
And then I said, "It's okay, Mom.
You've done your best. Your work is done.
It's time to rest. Let go."

An hour later she died. My aunt says
she slipped away while her pastor
was saying a prayer. Maybe just chance,
but I like to think she heard what I said
and took it to heart, and did.

Sleeping with the Dead

I dreamed about you again last night.
This time, you were living in Tennessee,
on a horse farm, married, children
I think, it wasn't clear—you know
how dreams can be—but I finally
got you to see that I don't love you,
not like that: as if my world would end
without you in it.
                    O, to have been
so close, to have shared your bed, to have
felt like I'd been raised from the dead
after all those dead I slept with
every night. It almost drove me mad
to let you go.
                    But that was years ago.
You were eighteen then, and here I am
married eighteen years and sorry only
that I've never had the chance to tell you
that it's okay, that I'm okay,
that no one could have saved me then,
not you nor God, that I don't love you
anymore, but hope that someone does.

On the Eve of Destruction

The weekend Watts went up in flames,
we drove from Fullerton to Newport Beach
and down the coast as far as Oceanside,
four restless teenage boys three thousand miles
from home, Bob Dylan's rolling stones
in search of waves and girls and anyone
who'd buy us beer or point us toward the fun.
California. What a high. The Beach Boys,
freeways twelve lanes wide, palm trees everywhere.
And all the girls were blonde and wore bikinis.
I'd swear to that, and even if it wasn't true,
who cared? A smalltown kid from Perkasie,
I spent that whole long summer with my eyes
wide open and the world unfolding
like an open road, the toll booths closed,
service stations giving gas away.
What did riots in a Negro ghetto
have to do with me? What could cause
such savage rage? I didn't know
and didn't think about it much.
The Eve of Destruction was just a song.
Surf was up at Pendleton. The war in Vietnam
was still a sideshow half a world away,
a world that hadn't heard of Ia Drang or Tet,
James Earl Ray, Sirhan Sirhan, Black Panthers,
Spiro Agnew, Sandy Scheuer, Watergate.
We rode the waves 'til two MPs
with rifles chased us off the beach:
military land. "Fuck you!" we shouted
as we roared up Highway One, windows open,
surfboards sticking out in three directions,
thinking it was all just laughs, just kicks,
just a way to kill another weekend;
thinking we could pull this off forever.

The Wreckage Along the Road

A friend from college called today.
We hadn't talked in a long time
and he wanted to reminisce. He and I

both out of place at Swarthmore College:
me a sergeant straight from the Corps,
him a workingclass kid from Cleveland
whose father had carried a union card
and lived in a rented apartment
all his life. Jeff was proud of his dad,
proud of his heritage. Even after
he'd gotten an MBA from Chicago
and started working management jobs,
he always carried the Teamsters' card
he'd had since he was a teenager
working the docks beside his dad.
"If the guys I work for knew about this,
I'd be fired," he told me once
in Memphis in nineteen seventy-nine,
pulling the card from his wallet,
"but I'm still a member. It's in my blood."
Twenty-one years have passed since then,
and today he's CEO of a firm
with manufacturing operations in China.
"I had to close the plant in Oklahoma.
The cost of labor was killing me,"
he explains, "I didn't have any choice."
Then he tells me he's going to retire
in a year or two. "I've got enough money.
I've proved myself. I'm almost fifty.
Who wants to work forever?"
I think of those workers in Oklahoma
who would like to have worked another week,
wonder if Jeff still carries his union card.

2001

The Damage We Do

I don't know why I fell asleep
when I was eight at the top of the stairs
listening to my parents argue. Maybe I
thought they'd find me asleep and feel
so bad they'd learn how to get along.

I don't know why I put my fist
through the kitchen storm door glass
storming out of the house when I was ten,
but my mother had to wrap my hand
in a towel and call the doctor.
An accident, she said.

I don't know why I ran from the house
in my bare feet in February,
my father swearing, me in tears
and no clear thought but getting as far
away as a thirteen-year-old could get,
which wasn't far in a small town
where your dad's a minister, everyone
thinks he's a saint, and you're a disgrace
to be acting up the way you always do.

I don't remember a time when the house
I grew up in wasn't crackling with rage.
I don't know why. I think my father
was really a mess, but he didn't
discuss that with me, and my mother
just put up with him year after year.
You get so wired, you learn to think
that's the way life's supposed to be.

And you learn to be angry all the time.
You run away to California.
You join the Marines at seventeen.
You quit every job you don't get fired from.
After awhile you don't get hired,
and people avoid you; they think you're
out of control, and you probably are,
but it takes you most of a lifetime just
to begin to make the connections.

By then you've got a child of your own
who's angry all the time. I'd like to say
I don't know why, but I do.
I'd like to explain that it's not her fault,
but what's she supposed to do with that?
I'd like to undo the damage I've done,
but I don't know how.

September 11th

My name is Aysha Rahim.
I live in Abul Khasib
with my son Mohammed
who is helpless,
a body without a brain.

Mohammed was born in the midst
of the bombing of 1991.
He came too soon,
but I was frightened by the bombs:
night after night,
day after day;
some of them came so close.

And then my son came.
He needed an incubator and oxygen,
but we had no electricity
after the bombing began,
and my baby's brain starved.

My husband and I tried to understand.
We hated Saddam Hussein.
When your president said on the radio,
"Rise against Saddam. Now is your opportunity,"
Hassan went to Basra
and joined the rebellion.

Day after day we could see
the American planes in the air.
We knew they could see us, too.
We knew they could see
the slaughter unfolding beneath them,
but they let it go on.

In a couple of weeks it was done.
They shot my husband down like a dog.
Hassan,
and his brother,
and his three cousins,
and so many more.

I was left with Mohammed
and our older son Khalid.
Such a good boy, Khalid.
He did what he could to help.
So much to ask of a child so small,
but he never complained.

Until the day he complained
of a headache and chills.
When I put my hand to his head,
he was on fire,
as if he were burning alive
from the inside out.

I carried him all the way to the clinic.
They gave him a bed,
but they had no medicine to give him
for the fever, the diarrhea, the vomiting,
the bleeding from his anus, the delirium.
Seven days it took Khalid to die.

I have heard what happened in your country.
We have all heard, here in Abul Khasib.
How many died, did you say?

Not enough, I tell you,
not nearly enough.

But I am a patient woman.

My name is Aysha Rahim.
I live with my helpless son Mohammed
and my memories of Khalid
and my memories of Hassan.
I am going nowhere.
I can wait.

The Bombing of Afghanistan

for Anne

You must be sitting down to eat,
the evening air this time of day

just turning luminescent blue
and autumn crisp. I might wonder
what you've made for dinner,
how much homework Leela has,
the thousand mundane daily things
our lives are made of, and I do.
But mostly I am noticing
this moment how the stars above
the Gower shine more brightly here
than back at home: Orion's belt,
the Pleiades, the Little Dipper
pouring water into Swansea Bay.
Here it's midnight on a rare and
cloudless night in Wales, the kind
of night that poems are made of.
But though the darkness and a line
of trees hide the ruins of the Norman
castle overlooking Mumbles,
the jagged remnants of its massive
walls, the broken arches, ghostly
silence where the ring of laughter
and the might of lords once must have
seemed forever serve as stark
reminders of the transience
of what we think we wish for.
I used to wish to be a poet,
celebrated, emulated,
maybe win the Pulitzer Prize.
I've plied my trade for years, and all
it's gotten me is endless trips
too far from home, endless nights
like this, alone in strange hotels
and homes that aren't my own. Somewhere
in the darkness bombs are falling,
lives are ending in the time
it takes to write these words, and how
much time we've got together
who can know? I only know
those graceful palm trees by the hotel
pool last month in California,
the little chapel in Ohio
built in eighteen fifty-four,

that quiet Massachusetts dawn
jogging next to Walden Pond,
these stars above me, all the world
I'd give to be back home with you.

2002

Seminar on the Nature of Reality

I've never seen a person dance with death
so gracefully before. As if you were—
not rushing to embrace it, not enthralled,
but fascinated, ready to explore
this new phenomenon the way a boy
might wonder at a frog he's caught or stand,
head cocked, before a tree he thinks he'll climb.

Geez, you're dying, and you act like this is
just another challenge to be mastered.

Most of us fear death. Consider Hamlet
and his dread of something after death
so strong that we would rather fardels bear
than face the undiscovered country
from whose bourn no traveler returns.

Yet here you are, a twinkle in your eye,
telling me about the hospice music
therapist who sang for you today
and how next week you've got a physicist
coming here to lead a conversation
on what is real and what is not and how
when things are very large or very small
they don't behave the way we think they should.

You can hardly walk, you can hardly talk,
you can't even breathe without oxygen,
and still you're organizing seminars
you might not even be here to attend.

Maybe this is what you are: so large
a mind, so large a heart that you just
won't behave the way we think you should.

In Memoriam: Tom Deahl, 1930–2002

2003

Home Before Morning

for Lynda Van Devanter (1947–2002)

If life were fair, you'd be a millionaire,
ambassador to somewhere really cool
like St. Tropez, Tahiti, or the Ritz,

maybe the Empress of Everything—
not some female Job for all the world

Almighty God just seemed to have it
in for: pass one test of faith and here's
another. And another. Yet one more.

Suffer, suffer, die. Okay, we both learned
far too young that nothing's fair in life,

that's just the way it is, there's no use
whining. And you never did complain.
Not when your lungs were so congested

that you couldn't hold a conversation.
Not when your legs swelled up so badly

that you couldn't walk a hundred feet.
Not when your joints began to fail.
Then your kidneys, too. And all the while

you just kept hoping, struggling to go on
another day, another month, another year

with Tom and Molly. How you loved
your husband and your daughter fiercely
with the burden of the knowledge of those

far too many broken boys you had to fix
and couldn't, boys too young to have the chance

to demonstrate against the war that killed them,
to be an alcoholic, to get sober,
to be an advocate for broken souls,

a witness to the worst and best we are,
to marry, make a child, write a book,

call me late at night to say you're frightened
and you need to hear another voice who's
frightened by the posturing of presidents

and statesmen who have never heard the sound
of teenaged soldiers crying for their mothers.

Great-hearted woman, may the broken boys
you tried to fix and couldn't, find you now
and guide you safely home before morning.

[Lynda Van Devanter served as a U.S. Army nurse
in Vietnam in 1969–70. She was the author
of the memoir *Home Before Morning*.]

Breakfast with You and Emily Dickinson

for Jim Beloungy

The night Marie called home to say you'd freaked,
I almost packed my bags and headed west,
or south, or south-by-west, or who-cared-where
so long as I was miles away before
you got here with your automatic pistol
and a rage Marie had never seen before.

"Emily Dickinson, old girl," I said
to the ancient cat curled up beside me,
"you might outlast me yet." I scratched her ears
and wondered what the hell had happened,
what came loose inside your head, and what I
ought to try to do about it.
                                              After all,
I knew a thing or two about loose screws,
being one myself more often than I

cared to think about.
                         That's why I couldn't
just pack up and leave. You and Marie had
given me a home when I was jobless,
thirty-one, and trying to write a book
about the war I'd fought in. You'd taught me
how to pull the engine from my Beetle
when it ate a valve, strip it to the block,
and make it work again. You'd shared your love
of Pachelbel and Stan Rogers, chili
made with venison, Leinenkugel beer.
I've never known a man more generous
with time or thought, more willing to forgive
whatever pissant mood I might be in.
You and Marie just always seemed to see
the best in me. You said I made it easy,
but I know that wasn't true.
                         And besides,
Emily Dickinson wouldn't take her
medicine from anyone but me:
I hit the road, the cat's as good as dead.

So I just sat there for the next six hours
drifting in and out of sleep all night
while you were driving down from Michigan.
A long way to drive alone. A long night
to wait alone with a grumpy old cat.

But if Emily never understood
how I always tricked her into eating
pills she hated, she never held a grudge
beyond the meal that always magically
appeared before her as the pill went down.

Sometime after dawn, I heard the front door
lock unlocking and the door swing open
and I braced myself for what might happen
next. But nothing happened next except we
looked at one another for a moment.
Then you said, "You been waiting up all night?"
"Dozing on and off," I said, "You look tired.
Want some eggs and coffee?"

                    I might have asked
about the gun, about what should have been
just another pleasant camping trip,
but turned instead and headed for the kitchen,
suckered Emily Dickinson again,
then made a breakfast for the three of us.

Later in the day Marie got home.
I never learned what happened in the woods
of upstate Michigan that night, or how
or why or where you let the anger go.
I only know you were always a friend
I'd bet my life on. And I did. And I won.

2004

Kosovo

The boys with pistols and shotguns
are shooting her friends in the hall.
They are shooting her friends in the library.
In her homeroom. In the cafeteria.
They are killing her friends and her teachers.

It's supposed to be just a day at school,
only another day like all of her days
in all of her schoolgirl years at Columbine.
This isn't happening. This can't be real.
At any moment, she'll awake from her dream.

But it isn't a dream. It's suburban Colorado.
Or is it Louisiana? California? Kentucky?
After awhile, it's hard to keep straight.
This could be any school in America.
This could be our own child begging for mercy.

We would like to imagine she sees an angel.
We want to imagine a merciful angel
hovers above her on fluttering wings
and lifts her forever beyond the reach
of skulls in pieces and blood-spattered walls.

But the boys with the guns don't care about angels.
The boys with the guns are settling scores.
Like Stallone and Van Damme. Like Arnold.
Destruction is power. These boys have been powerless
all of their lives. But not anymore.

When the shooting stops, fifteen people are dead,
sixteen wounded, most of them teenaged kids.
"We must teach our children," the president
solemnly says, "that violence is not the answer."
This in the week he begins the bombing of Belgrade.

Manning the Walls

The day the towers came down, goggle-eyed
we stared in disbelief at death for once
so close to home we couldn't hide
our terror in the rubble of Manhattan:
complacency turned upside down and strewn
across a Pennsylvania field in burning pieces,
even Mars, our God of War, in flames.
Who'd have thought it possible? What next?

Overnight the world had changed forever,
all bets off, all the rules suspended
in the urgency to save our way of life
from lethal challenges so sinister
we need the Stars-n-Stripes in every classroom
and the FBI needs secret access
to the records of the books we're reading:
Dostoyevsky, Danielle Steele—you never
know what might be useful to a terrorist.

Well okay, I was as scared as anyone
that day, and I won't deny the world
we live in is a dangerous place.

But I remember gazing at the tiny
dot of Sputnik in the darkness
over Perkasie when I was only nine,
my country at the mercy of the Reds,
the world changed forever overnight.

I learned to Duck-n-Cover at my desk
in Mrs. Vera's room at Third Street School.
I learned to recognize the yellow signs
on public buildings reassuring us
of shelter from the Russians' atom bombs.
I learned we had a missile gap, a fail-
safe point, a hotline to the Kremlin.

That's how I grew up: Nikita Khrushchev,
Ich bin ein Berliner, Armageddon
always just a missile strike away.

One hell of a lot of good the basement
of the Bucks County Bank & Trust would do
against a thermonuclear warhead,
but anyone who tried to point this out
was either nuts, naive, or communist.

Most of us got lucky in the Cold War—
provided we ignore Korea,
Vietnam, the brushfire wars our proxies
fought around the globe for forty years,
the millions dead and maimed and dispossessed.
At least we never dropped the Big One, and
the good old USA came out on top.

No wonder our surprise on 9–11
to discover Huns outside the gates again.
Cry havoc, sound alarums, man the walls!

But any history buff can trace the rise
and fall of empires: Pax Romana,
Rule Britannia, Persia, Babylon,
Ottomans and Incas by the sword
made arrogant, and by the sword brought down.
Catastrophe is history's middle name,
and taking off our shoes in airports,
locking up librarians, inventing
threats that don't exist, I pledge allegiance
to the flag, one nation under God or not,
isn't going to save us from the Visigoths,
the Mongol hordes, Bin Laden, or ourselves.

Barbarism, communism, terrorism,
name your ism, something's always out there

in the darkness wanting in. You'd think
by now—we're talking generations here,
millenia, the whole of human time—
we'd figure out we're all in this together
and it's time to learn to share. Ask the Greeks.
Ask the Hittites. Ask the dinosaurs.

Meditations on Pedagogy

(while listening to a presentation
by a well-paid famous Learning Expert)

I. The Attention Controls

So many ways to waste one's time:
I am determined to shape a rhyme
by cognitive activation,
satisfaction guaranteed, salience
processing focal maintenance,
depth of detail in procession.

So many ways to waste the day:
sometimes mental effort is way
too energetically challenged,
consistently disallowing arousal,
alertness totally out of control
'til sleep be forever expunged.

So many ways to waste a life:
tempo control, a preview of self,
Monitor, Merrimac, inhibition,
facilitation of reinforcement,
systematic brain encasement
the frontal lobe of production.

What are the possible ramifications?
Energy processing mental production,
cognitive academic effectiveness
ever the interpersonal,
socially always behavioral,
domains of impacting success.

II. Levels of Language

1. Forty-four phonemes stuck in my craw,
    forty-four phonemes in all;

if one of those phonemes should happen to fall,
forty-three phonemes stuck in my craw.

2. A morpheme is a small detail;
   it can't really mean by itself.
   But linguistic gratification would fail
   if a morpheme were anything else.

3. Verbal precision
   builds important networking:
   college semantics.

4. Syntax, bees' wax, speckled axe, and sales tax,
   brass tacks, false facts; I could use some Ex-Lax.

5. There once was a man in the Air Force
   who could think of nothing but intercourse.
   A woman named Val
   said, "Okay, I shall—
   but not without first having discourse."

6. Metalinguistics isn't just jive;
   it reflects on how language works.
   In generous portions it's found among high-
   ly verbal learners with quirks.

7. Pragmatic influential ability;
   complex, fragile applicability;
   treatment-resistant vulnerability;
   language of social contexts.

All About Death

You don't want me to tell you about death,
but I'm going to tell you anyway:
it smells bad. It gets into your nostrils
and just sits there, stinking up everything.
It won't go away. Death creeps up on you
when you're least expecting it, even when
you can see it coming a mile away,
and rips your heart out through your throat and leaves
an empty place in your life you can't fill
with memories or exercise or wads

of sterile gauze, and walks away laughing.
Or maybe just slips out under the door
and floats away like mist dissipating
before sunlight on an autumn morning.
Death minds its own business and everyone
else's, too. Death does a little jig,
then lobs a grenade into your kitchen,
but it's only a dud. What a joker,
you think, just before it explodes. Death feels
sorry for nothing and no one. Death feels
nothing at all. Death drives an SUV
with a husband and two kids in Gladwyne,
loses control, crosses the median,
plows head-on into everyone sooner
or later, takes out a mortgage and then
skips town without paying a penny back.
Death takes a holiday, but not today.
Not tomorrow, either. Maybe next week,
but don't bank on it. My mother-in-law
died twenty-five years ago, but my wife
still cries out in her sleep for her mommy.
Sometimes my wife isn't even asleep.

All About Love

Everyone loves to hear about love,
but I don't feel like talking about that.
Gimme a break. You seen the news lately?
That missing blonde North Dakota coed
found dead in a ditch in Minnesota?
A hundred and ninety-one dead in Spain?
Thousands of pissed-off Palestinians.
Millions dying of AIDS in Africa.
Seven more soldiers dead in Fallujah—
and what are we doing there, anyway?
Where are the weapons of mass destruction?
Under a rug in a house in Peru?

Oh, don't let's talk about that, did you say?
We want to hear about love. Well okay:

I love Paris in the springtime. I love
the Broad Street Bullies and Just Saying No.

I love the way I call my bank and get
some guy in Bombay I can't understand.
I love the USA PATRIOT Act
and having to strip to my underwear
every time I try to get on a plane.
I love a Big Mac heart attack with fries,
tax incentives for those who need 'em least,
no child left behind without a handgun
or an automatic assault rifle.

Hey, that isn't what we meant, did you say?

What did you expect? Some sentimental
Hollywood romance? Go to the movies.
Why do you think they call it Tinseltown?

Golfing with My Father

My father took up golf in middle age,
the dumbest game I ever tried to play,
but it was nineteen-sixty-nine, and I
was at a loss to figure out a way
to bridge the gaping generation gap
that lay between us like an open wound:

the ex–Marine just back from Vietnam
and telling anyone who'd listen what
a crock of crap the myth of manhood was;
the minister who'd spent his life convinced
his cousin Bob had died in Germany
because my dad had never been to war.

Not a lot of common ground between us
in those bad old days of Richard Nixon,
Jimi Hendrix, burning bras, and LSD.

So the afternoon my dad invited me
to play a round, I figured what the heck,
it can't be all that hard to hit a ball
that isn't moving, and it's something he
and I can do together. Which it was.

Or wasn't. More exactly, it was something
he could do while I could only hack my

way from hole to hole like some demented
backhoe operator digging random
trenches by the dozen ten and fifteen
yards apart from here to Kingdom Come.

Dad tried to coach me, but he might as well
have tried to teach a mackerel how to dance.

Before we reached the seventh hole, with what
few shreds of sanity I still had left
I realized I'd better quit before
I killed someone: my dad, or me—or maybe
the sonofabitch a hole behind us
laughing every time another chunk of God's
green acres sailed farther than the ball.

Next time my dad suggested golf, we went
for lunch to Meg & Bill's instead. They served
a wicked cheesesteak sandwich and we ate
in silence, elbows on the counter top,
shoulders hunched, our fingers dripping grease.

2005

Coaching Winter Track in Time of War

The boys are running "suicides"
on the football field today:
ten-yard increments out to the fifty
and back again, push-ups in between.
It's thirty degrees, but they sweat
like it's summer in Baghdad,
curse like soldiers, swear to God
they'll see you burn in Hell.

You could fall in love with boys
like these: so earnest, so eager, so
ready to do whatever you ask, so
full of themselves and the world.

How do you tell them it's not that simple?
How do you tell them: question it all.
Question everything. Even a coach.
Even a president. How do you tell them:
ask the young dead soldiers coming home
each night in aluminum boxes
none of us is allowed to see,
an army of shades.

You tell the boys "good work" and call it a day,
stand alone in fading light while
memory's phantoms circle the track
like weary athletes running a race
without a finish line.

Reflections on the Papacy

April 2005

These guys who get themselves elected Pope have about as much imagination as a Chesapeake Bay oyster. The last guy could have been Pope John Paul George Ringo, but no, he has to go and use the same name as the Pope he replaced. Remember Pope John Paul I? Lasted about three weeks before the job killed him. Kind of like William Henry Harrison. Remember William Henry Harrison? Nobody else does, either. And we wouldn't remember John Paul I if it weren't for John Paul II. Imagine if the guy who replaced William Henry Harrison had called himself William Henry Harrison II. Then maybe we'd remember William Henry Harrison I. Anyway, this new guy, geez, he could have been Pope Eggs Benedict. Pope Benedict Arnold. What the heck, they can make up any name they want. Pope Benedict Arnold Schwarzenegger would've been a good one. We could've called him the Popinator. Or how about Pope Benedict Sweet XVI. Pope Benedictionary. Pope Beneficiary. Pope Fiduciary. Remember the Rumble in the Jungle? Not that that has anything to do with the Holy Father, but this guy could've been Pope Rope-a-Dope. How about that alliteration? Or Pope-on-a-Rope. That one has commercial possibilities. Even Pope-pourri has a certain class to it, and talk about clever: the Vatican could sell real potpourri in little Pope-shaped vases, make a fortune. I'll tell you what Catholicism needs: a sense of humor. I miss the days of the Spanish Inquisition. Now that was a lot of laughs. The rack. Thumb screws. Iron Maidens. Ripping the tongues out of heretics and tossing Jews from the belltower and burning virgins alive. By God, that was a man's life. We had fun in those days. But I digress. The one ray of sunshine I see in all of this is that good old Benedict XVI is, in fact, old. Long in the tooth. No spring chicken. Over the hill and on his way to Beulahland already. The College of Cardinals may get the chance to award another diploma sooner than they think, and I'm doing my best to put the siss-boom-bah back into the Sistine Chapel. I'm personally lobbying for my pal Dave Connolly. South Boston Irish Catholic. When's the last time they had an Irish Pope, anyway? Like, never. It's about time, don't you think? And Dave's got a great sense of humor. He mailed me a dead mackerel once with a note that said, "Hey, you Protestant Puke, eat this on Friday." Christ, I laughed for a week. He's not a priest or a bishop or anything like that, but so what? It's a fact that you don't have to be a priest to be the pope. Look it up if you don't believe me. You just have to get elected by the College of Cardinals. And I've sent letters to those guys. All 117 of them. Offered 'em neon red glow-in-the-dark mitres, shoes with heels that flash red when you walk. Next time, baby, things are gonna be different. I can feel it in my rosary. Pope Dave I. The Vicar of Christ. The Water of Life. God's Go-to Guy.

Oh, Canada

Big Timber, Montana
October 2005

This paper cup I'm drinking from was made
in Canada. Ontario. Brampton,
to be exact. Now this is odd, I think:
imported paper cups. French lace, perhaps,
Dutch chocolate, Russian caviar I get.
Swiss clocks. But Canadian paper cups?
What's wrong with American paper cups?
Buy American, keep our country strong,
that's what I say. And anyway, I've been
to Canada, and I can tell you this:
it's empty. Cold. No place for anyone
but hockey players, polar bears, and seals.
Even towns with names like Medicine Hat,
Moose Jaw, Pense, and Neepawa are boring.
No mounted Mounties in their bright red coats.
No dogsleds, lumberjacks, or Eskimos.
Not, at least, that I saw, and I'd driven
thirteen hundred miles west from Winnipeg:
not a thing but wheat and elevators,
two-lane highway flat and straight enough

to hypnotize or make a sane mind crack.
I stopped just long enough to buy some beer
in Moose Jaw, turned left at Medicine Hat,
and made a beeline for yippie-eye-oh-
ki-yay-where-the-deer-and-the-antelope-
play Big Sky Country, where I find myself
today, thirty-four years down the road, eyes
full of cottonwoods, silver Yellowstone,
snow-swept Absarokas, drinking coffee
from a made-in-Canada paper cup,
amazed at how much time a man can waste
on empty thoughts and stupid diatribes.

Primitive Art, or:
The Art of the Primitive

for Ben Steele

I call myself a primitive:
animal skins instead of clothes,
cowry shells, bone through the nose,
meat on the haunches roasted in fire,
shields and spears and manic midnight dancing—
that's the life for me.
So what if uptight Main Line mothers
cluck their tongues and warn their daughters
not to hang around the likes of me?
I never met a suit I liked,
never had a job that didn't make me sweat,
never liked the rules of any game
I couldn't play. Screw sophistication
and the cultured class. They couldn't find
their asses with a mirror and a map.
Give me a genuine jungle girl,
the thrusting throb of the jungle drums,
a calabash of homebrewed beer,
and a happier man you will not find
from here to Radnor to Timbuktu.

Home on the Range

With apologies to Brewster Higley and
Daniel Kelley

Oh, give me a home where the buffalo roam,
Where the beer and the whiskey run free,
Where seldom is heard an intelligent word,
And all of the cowboys love me.

Home, home on the range,
Where things are decidedly strange:
I can't explain how, but my sister's a cow,
And my mother's the sheriff in Butte.

How often at night when the mood is just right
Do I look up and gaze at the stars.
The Milky Way's mine, and Snickers is fine,
But my favorite is Three Musketeers.

Home, home where I sleep
While sheepherders shepherd their sheep,
Where you do things in life when you haven't a wife
That you'd never admit to a priest.

Oh, I love what I do, though I haven't a clue
How to lasso or whittle or shoot.
I can't ride a horse, and to my remorse,
Coyotes have stolen my boots.

Home, home way out west,
Where wildflowers sometimes get pressed,
Where prairie dogs prance, and cowgirls wear pants,
And my hamster's a square-dancing fool.

Where else can a man get a beautiful tan
Punching cattle for two bucks a week?
Where you're never alone if you've got a cell phone
Or a bunkmate who's fairly discreet.

Home, home on the plains,
Where the dogies get wet when it rains,
Where loco weed grows, and the locals all know
You can smoke it and howl at the moon.

2006

What the Fuss Is All About

One wonders what the fuss is all about.
They say the flag is blowing in the wind.
They say the wind is blowing up a storm.
They say the moon is blue, the lies are true,
the bogeyman is here, we must believe
whatever we are told. So all for one
and one for all the money he can get
his sticky fingers on, him and all his
sticky-fingered friends. So what's new?
Just the other day, K Street three-piece-suit
walks into a bar and orders a beer.
Sorry, sir, the barkeep says, we don't serve
sleaze in here; FBI man overhears,
calls the IRS: barkeep's doing time
in Lewisburg. Let that be a lesson
to us all: Miller Lite can change your life.
Super Size me, praise the Lord, and give me
purple mountains' majesty, Hollywood
commandos, and a gas-guzzling SUV
with GPS and Power Everything.
Burn, baby, burn, some angry Black man said,
but I say what's the hurry? Soon enough
we'll burn the whole damned planet down, choke it,
strip it, starve it, melt it, pave it over,
blow it up, and bury it in empty
bottled water bottles, Pampers diapers,
plastic grocery bags, and last year's cellphones.
Then we'll see which way the wind is blowing,
whose flags are blowing in the wind, whose lies
are worth a big rat's ass, who's rich enough
to buy a one-way ticket out of Hell,
whose God is on whose side, and who's left
to wonder what the fuss was all about.

Temple Poem

Amakusa, Japan

The sun comes up each morning in silence;
the moon disappears, but nobody sees.

Flowers dance by the roadside unnoticed;
birds twitter sweetly, but nobody hears.

People don't stop to consider what matters.
People work hard all their lives to achieve

a dream of success that will make them happy:
position or power, fortune or fame—

until they are old and they realize too late
that the beauty of living has passed them by

while the river travels alone to the ocean,
the wind sings alone in the tops of the trees.

From the original Japanese by Shinmin Sakamura,
translated by Kazunori Takenaga and adapted
by W. D. Ehrhart at the request of Morinobu Okabe,
31st priest of the Zen Buddhist Temple of Tokoji

Down and Out in Darfur

What do you do when the blows keep coming?
What do you do when you're down on your knees
with your teeth kicked in and your mouth bleeding?
Where do you turn when there's nowhere to turn
and nothing and no one to turn to?

Somebody said you get up and go on.
Somebody said that you never give in,
that you turn your face to the rising sun,
that you see things through to a better end.
Somebody's always blowing smoke up your ass.

Sometimes you get to the end of your rope.
Sometimes you come to the end of the line.
Even a cat has only nine lives,
and you're not nearly so lucky as that.
You're not lucky at all. And nobody cares.

2007

The Work of Love

for Dale Ritterbusch

Here I was in Budapest, alone
upon a bridge above the Danube
on an evening so seductive
anyone might fall in love
as easily as falling off a log,

even me: gray-haired, half-deaf,
overweight, bad eyes and all.
The falling sun suffused the air
with fire, clouds aglow, the buildings
and the river, and the whole wide sky

slowly fading into pastel pink
and pale orange of poetry and dreams.
I didn't even notice her approach
until she touched my arm and asked
if I enjoyed what I was seeing.

I said yes, then turned and saw—
how shall I explain—a woman
half my age and lovely, maybe younger,
soft as baby's breath, eyes alive
with every possibility

an aging man's imagination
could conceive: faery princess,
Magyar goddess, Eve before the Fall
until she murmured in my ear,
"You may have me, if you wish."

The Bodies Beneath the Table

Hue City, 1968
(or was it Fallujah,
Stalingrad, or Ur?)

The bodies beneath the table
had been lying there for days.
Long enough to obliterate their faces,
the nature of their wounds.
Or maybe whatever killed them
ruined their faces, too.
Impossible now to tell.
Only the putrefying bodies
bloated like Macy's Parade balloons,
only unrecognizable lumps on
shoulders where heads should be.

The two of them seemed to be a couple:
husband and wife, lovers perhaps,
maybe brother and sister—impossible
now to tell—but they'd pulled the table
into a corner away from the windows,
their only protection against
the fighting raging around them,
crawled beneath it—the table, I mean—
half sitting, bent at the waist,
close together, terrified, almost
certainly terrified, nothing but noise,
only each other, only each other,
any moment their last.

All these years I've wondered
how they died. Who were they.
Who remembers.

Turning Sixty

It isn't that I fear
growing older—such things as fear,
reluctance or desire
play no part at all
except as light and shadow sweep a hillside

on a Sunday afternoon,
astonishing the eye but passing on
at sunset with the land
still unchanged: the same rocks,
the same trees, tall grass gently drifting—
merely that I do not understand
how my age has come to me
or what it means.

It's almost like some small
forest creature one might find
outside the door some frosty autumn morning,
tired, lame, uncomprehending,
almost calm.
You want to stroke its fur,
pick it up, mend the leg and send it
scampering away—but something
in its eyes says, "No,
this is how I live, and how I die."
And so, a little sad, you let it be.
Later when you look,
the thing is gone.

And just like that these
sixty years have come and gone,
and I do not understand at all
why I see a gray-haired man
inside the mirror when a small
boy still lives inside this body
wondering
what causes laughter, why
nations go to war, who paints the startling
colors of the rainbow on a gray vaulted sky,
and when I will be old enough
to know.

2008

What Makes a Man

Even as my dad lay dying, cancer
back a second time and moving fast,
he blurted out, "I should have fought!"
Apropos of nothing. Out of nowhere
but the secret reservoir of memory
and shame he'd carried all his life, the weight
of it I never fully understood
until that moment. World War II, he meant.

The two of us alone: a man who'd missed
the great adventure of his generation,
Ike's Great Crusade, the crucible for all
those other men around him all his life,
the test they'd passed, the club he couldn't join;
his son, the ex-Marine, the one who'd come
back home from Vietnam insisting it was
all just bullshit, just a lethal scam
that only proves how gullible
each generation's cannon fodder is.

Only in that moment in that room
did I begin to grasp how impotent
my father must have felt through all those years,
how much he must have taken my enlistment
as a personal rebuke, and how my
subsequent insistence that I'd
validated nothing in myself
must have been to him a kind of treason.

Dying now, in 1988, he still
could not let go of Cousin Bob
who'd been dismantled by a German mine
but died a man in 1945,
not like this: wasted, helpless, haunted
by the shades of what he thought he was
and what he wished he'd been, a nurse's aide
to change his bedpan, too much time to think,
and nothing either one of us could do
to change a thing.

Extra! Extra!

Done before I knew it had begun.
The Yom Kippur War, that is.
I was working on a tanker out of Long Beach;
we'd been at sea for a couple of weeks,
and by the time I heard the news,
it was all over. How 'bout that,
I thought, a war come and gone and me
none the wiser—nor any the worse for wear.

That's when I began to think
the news is overrated. Most of it
is bad, in any case, and most of it
you can't do anything about
but brood. And all that paper. All those
trees. Chemicals they use to make the ink.

Epiphany

for Anne,
28 years later

What I remember is you at twenty-six
in the shower naked beside me,
soap cascading the length of that
heart-stopping eye-popping sight,
me like a kid in a candy shop:
most beautiful woman in all the world
and mine. All mine. All I see to this day.

The Secret Lives of Boys

Nothing the boy wanted
ever came true. Not the chance
to be a World War Two fighter ace
in 1958. Not the chance to save
beautiful Ursula Netcher
from pirates. Not the ability
to leap tall buildings
in a single bound.

Okay, he got that plastic
tripod-mounted battery-powered
machinegun for Christmas one year,
but it broke two days later.

And he got to pick the football helmet
with the plexiglass face mask
for selling the most
YMCA oatmeal cookies,
but it didn't make him
any better at football.

He got the job
handing out skates and changing records
on Sunday afternoons at the roller rink.

But he never got the things
that really mattered.
The courage to defend himself
from the playground bullies.
Parents who didn't show
one face to the world,
another inside the home.
The chance not to be
the preacher's kid
in a town where you couldn't hide.

He got the double chin.
He got C's in gym class.
He got his brothers' hand-me-down clothes.

He wanted to be a Wildcat pilot,
or maybe a ball turret gunner.

He wanted to rescue beautiful Pam Magee
from pirates. Or maybe Comanches.

He wanted to be
anything
but what he was.

2009

Burning Leaves

Something you just don't smell anymore:
burning leaves. Rake them into the street
and set them on fire. That was the way
we used to get rid of them. That was the way
you knew it was autumn. Football season.

Friday night, and the whole small town,
the young and the old and the in-between,
cousins and aunts and greats and grands,
the high school band and the cheerleading squad
packed into Poppy Yoder Stadium,

even the hoods and the rebels without a cause
under the stands in the shadows
smoking Winston and Kool,

out on the field, under the lights,
the hometown boys, the Pennridge Rams,
in victory or defeat, warrior heroes.

Then the long walk home beneath the stars,
the smell of burning leaves in the knife-
edged air of October, even the Milky Way
still visible, then, when I was a kid.

There must be something I can't remember.
It wasn't that way. It wasn't a Norman
Rockwell painting: boy with a banged-up knee
and a kindly cop seeing him safely home.

But things like that really happened.

Now-days, burn your leaves in the street,
cops show up and threaten to take you away.

Life in the Neighborhood

The cop on the corner stood there and watched
while a pink rhinoceros trampled the tulips

in Mrs. Palmer's yard. "Yo!" I hollered,
"Why don't you put a stop to that?"
"Whaddaya want me to do?" the cop replied,
"Cuff 'im and run 'im in?" *Oh, swell*, I thought,
if you want to get something done around here,
you've got to do it yourself. So I went to the kitchen
and grabbed a bucket of cottage cheese, walked
across the street, and held it out to the rhino
—I'd read in a book that rhinos are suckers
for cottage cheese—and it worked:
he forgot all about the tulips and dug right in,
so I grabbed his horn and flipped him over my shoulder,
rolled him onto his back, and tickled the underside
of his chin till he finally fell asleep. "My hero,"
Mrs. Palmer sighed. The cop just shook his head.

2010

Redipuglia

What once had been a ramshackle
cemetery dotted with the detritus
of battle—barbed wire, battered helmets,
trenching tools, broken rifle butts—
Mussolini in his fascist grandiosity
recreated as a pristine staircase
of the dead: twenty-two giant steps,
each one-hundred-forty meters wide,
twenty feet deep, and nine feet high,
rising to the crest of Mount Sei Busi,
three giant crosses crowning all.

Twenty-one steps are faced with small
brass plates, 1900 plates per step,
each plate the name of someone dead:
    Fabio Bernardi, Terza compagnia,
        Ventunesimo battaglione del Bersaglieri,
        3rd Company, 21st Battalion of Bersaglieri;

Mario Bottino, Sessantottesimo batteria,
    Artiglieria del mulo,
    68th Battery, Mule Artillery;
Paolo Barbieri, Primo Reparti d'assalto;
Ottavio Cavallo, Sardo granatieri, Gruppa Pistoia.

Behind each plate, the dead man's bones:
    Marco Esposito, Ottantatresimo compagnia
        di assistenti tecnici,
        83rd Company of Engineers;
    Allesandro Forni, Nono reggimento
        di fanteria chiara di Bersaglieri,
        9th Bersaglieri Light Infantry Regiment;
    Carlo Selvaggio, Quinto reggimento del Alpini;
    Pietro Allegreti, Arma dei Carabinieri.

Many plates are incomplete, containing
only what could be recovered of the man:
    Luigi -----, Fusiliers;
    ----- Trovato, 28th Infantry, Pavia Brigade.
The bones and names of 40,000 dead.

The twenty-second step contains
the bones of 60,000 more
whose names were taken with their lives.

The hill contains, in all, 100,187 dead.

Across the top of every step in huge
block granite print a dozen times
and more: a single word. PRESENTE
Silent roll call of the dead:
PRESENTE Present. We are here.

Emilio Morelli, 6th Company,
    142nd Infantry, Catanzaro Brigade;
Roberto Pappalardo, 132nd Infantry Regiment,
    Lazio Brigade, 29th Division;
Vittore Maggio, 3rd Battalion,
    58th Infantry, Abruzzi Brigade:
PRESENTE Present. We are here.

Young men:
    Stefano Tenaglia, 14th Regiment,
        4th Bersaglieri Brigade;

Giani Caltibiano, 75th Alpino Division;
Umberto Testa, 22nd Arditi:
PRESENTE Present. We are here.

Young men:
Cristiano Martelli, 19th Infantry, Brescia Brigade;
Battista Grassello, 48th Regiment, Ferrara Brigade;
Claudio Conti, 28th Infantry, Pavia Brigade:
PRESENTE Present. We are here.

Young men:
Raffaello, Firenze Brigade;
Leonardo, Novara Lancers;
Gino, 52nd Alpine Infantry Division:
PRESENTE Present. We are here.

If you stand at the base of the steps
looking up, the steps are so arranged
that all you see is the single word PRESENTE
rising out of the stone
over again, and over and over again,
marching up to the heavens,
mocking the *Duce*'s own design,
mocking the millions who come to worship here,
mocking the empty promise of salvation,
whispering, murmuring, muttering:

PRESENTE Present. We are here.

Children of Adam & Eve

for Lisa Coffman

So now we're almost brother and sister,
partners, lovers, penpals of pain:
you with your Tennessee freeze-tag foot,
wrecked tendons, hobbling around on crutches;
me with my gimpy won't-be-doing-the-ten-
mile-Broad-Street-Run-this-year aching hip.

What a pair we make, traversing
together the odd terrain of the invalid,
learning at last what it means to be
Adam and Eve's descendants, kicked

out of Eden and forced to wander
a world that renews itself every spring
while you and I are ever more at odds
with our stubbornly mortal bodies.

As I write this, April daffodils;
irises, tulips, and everywhere
that iridescent yellowy green
of new deciduous leaves on trees
so vibrantly irrepressible I
don't know whether we ought to laugh or cry.

2011

How History Gets Written

Say I discover a cure for cancer;
say that it's cheap and never fails.
Say I restore the Arctic ice pack.
Say I preserve the Amazon.

Say I eliminate fossil fuels
and turn the babble of politicians
into an endless supply of energy,
non-polluting and free to all.

Maybe I guarantee every child
parents and schools and shelter and love.
Maybe I make mean people suck
on their thumbs. Maybe I save the whales.

What if I build a gun that doesn't shoot,
a bomb that doesn't explode, a bright pink tank?
What if I find clean water for those in need?
What if I put an end to poverty?

Say that I learn the secret of harmony,
teach the nations to live in peace.
Say I can tell you how many angels
dance on the head of a pin.

What if I line up the stars like pearls
and drape them across the Himalayas?
What would you think? What would you do?
What would you write in your history books?

2012

Patrick

He can't get out of his head the horrors he's seen
picking the pieces up and stuffing them back.
Like Lady Macbeth, his hands will never be clean.

But not like her: she murdered a king;
he was only an army medic, but now
he can't get out of his head the violence he's seen.

He only tried to put the pieces back
into broken bodies. It wasn't his fault,
but now he thinks his hands will never be clean.

His unit invaded Fallujah;
urban fighting's as ugly as fighting gets.
He can't get out of his head the havoc he's seen.

He can't sit still or even look at his hands.
He tried to save his friends, the dead and the maimed.
Now he's sure his hands will never be clean.

The army said he was fine and sent him home
with so much blood his hands will never be clean.
The VA gives him pills. Frozen in time,
he can't get out of his head the carnage he's seen.

Judas Joyful

What holds back the hand? What iron
bone-deep prohibition so ingrained it
stays the urge to strike down what

you'd gladly celebrate the death of
can't you overcome? One you once believed
you loved. Some Judas. Or a Genghis Khan.
The last lost ladder rung to heaven.
Banner-waving freedom-loving fraud.
This is how the clan survives. The tribe.
The race. The little fragile single
thread that keeps us from collapsing
into utter chaos, blood for blood,
a universe inside each grain of sand.

And what lets go when us and them,
when famine, fire, pestilence and war
lay waste to all we nurture or desire?
Our history books are full of it.
Destruction is a kind of joy,
let's face it, existential fun,
let anyone deny it if they dare.
You'd have to be delusional
or tree-stump dumb to think we've got
a snowball's chance in hell of breaking
free of what and how we are,
the universe inside a grain of sand.

Cheating the Reaper

for Kazunori Takenaga
February 5th, 1968
June 23rd, 2011

This is the building, Ken.
This is the place
where our lives nearly ended.
My fault. I got careless.
That NVA gunner was aiming at me,
but all I got was a hell of a headache,
a couple of cuts, tinnitus,
a cheap Purple Heart.
You got a gaping gash in your head
and nearly lost an arm.
Both of us a rice shoot away
from buying the farm.

But here we are in a vibrant city
forty-three years later:
two ex–Marines shaking our heads
in wonder at what we survived
and what we are seeing now:
a five-story four-star hotel,
scooter rental and coffee shop
instead of a house we'd commandeered
for a makeshift battalion CP,
a cinderblock wall
enclosing a littered yard.

Who would have thought
the day that RPG exploded
we'd live to see this day,
this house, this city, this Vietnam?
Who would have thought
we'd ever want to come back
or be happy because we'd lost?

This is the very building, Ken.
This is where we almost died
for nothing that mattered,
but didn't.

2013

What It Signifies

The lines you draw divide the land;
you think you have the upper hand.
The walls go up, the banners, too.
No sentry questions if it's true.
One asks for roses, bread and guns;
another for the double sun.
A broken vase, the sulfur smell
of angry mother, iron hell.
Two riders who, approaching fast
across the open valley, cast

the shadow of a fractured moon
on water where a single loon
cry quavers on the air, dismount
and call the sentries to account.
The gate stays closed, the lights go out;
somewhere in the dark a shout
of anguish, or alarm, or fear
disturbs the dreams of those who hear
while others sleep, oblivious
to what it means, though some of us
have seen this all before. What's more,
we know the way it always ends
in perfect sadness that offends
just empty cold and nothingness.
The rest is of no consequence.

First Day of School

at the Haverford School for Boys

One more time the madness begins:
four hundred bursting bundles
of testosterone in search of who
they are and who they want to be,
belligerent, bodacious, boisterous,
bad-ass, bollixed and befuddled,
curious and choir-boy sweet,
each one a Gordian knot.

Four hundred teenaged boys you'd
swear were put on Earth by some
demented God to punish you for
some horrendous sin you can't quite
put your finger on. Breathing?
Waking up this morning? Thinking
you have anything to offer they
might use to find their way?

And yet you still keep coming back
for more, year on year on year.
And every year you just keep getting
older while the boys you teach are
still the age they were last year,

still eager, still exuberant, still
full of all the worlds the future holds.

Miraculous phenomenon:
the boys you teach never grow old.
Maybe that's the reason you
keep coming back: you've found
the secret of eternal youth.

2014

The Baby in the Box

What if you find a baby in a box?
What if you find it right on your doorstep?
What if the baby is crying?
What if the baby is hungry?
The baby is helpless.
Lying in its own filth.
Crying.
A baby.
A baby in a box.

What if its mother has left it there?
What if its mother has died of ebola?
What if the baby has ebola?
Or not.
You don't know.
The baby is crying.
The baby needs someone to care.
The baby is a baby.
The baby needs you to care.

What are you going to do?
The baby is hungry.
The baby is crying.
The baby is lying in its own filth.
Helpless.
It is only a baby.

A baby in a box.
It might kill you.
What are you going to do?

Long Time Gone

The boy on the bench on the boardwalk
just got back from the war. He watches
the waves washing the shore, the shore birds
pecking at tiny crabs in the sand
or diving for fish in the shallow surf.
There was sand where he'd been, but a long
walk to the beach, and the pecking birds
were snipers, the diving birds IEDs.
Now that he's home, and home isn't home,
what will he do with himself?
Maybe he'll go to college. Or trade school.
Maybe he'll re-enlist. He lifts
his gaze to the distant horizon
where sea meets sky at the edge of the world.
He wonders how far he could swim.

2015

Praying at the Altar

I like pagodas.
There's something—I don't know—
secretive about them,
soul-soothing, mind-easing.
Inside, if only for a moment,
life's clutter disappears.

Once, long ago, we destroyed one:
collapsed the walls
'til the roof caved in.
Just a small one, all by itself

in the middle of nowhere,
and we were young. And bored.
Armed to the teeth.
And too much time on our hands.

Now whenever I see a pagoda,
I always go in.
I'm not a religious man,
but I light three joss sticks,
bow three times to the Buddha,
pray for my wife and daughter.
I place the burning sticks
in the vase before the altar.

In Vung Tau, I was praying
at the Temple of the Sleeping Buddha
when an old monk appeared.
He struck a large bronze bell
with a wooden mallet.
He was waking up the spirits
to receive my prayers.

Spontaneous Combustion

So, a hot summer night
in our quiet little town;
bunch of us just hanging around
the picnic pavilion in the park.
Somebody's brought a radio.
"Bristol Stomp" comes on.
Somebody cranks the volume up.
Fifteen or twenty teenaged kids
start dancing on tables, stomping
the wooden picnic deck,
singing for all we're worth:
"Kids in Bristol are sharp as a pistol
when they do the Bristol Stomp!"

Chief Nase comes roaring up
in the town's only cop car.
"Turn that off and go home," he yells.
Somebody shouts, "Fuck you, Fatso."
The chief struggles out of the car,

but we've scattered like pigeons
and he's left standing all alone
with his pistol drawn
like he's actually going to shoot somebody.

After he leaves, we all sneak back,
light up cigarettes.
Somebody pops a beer.

It's About You

for Leela

Flesh of my flesh,
my blood in your veins,
you are my daughter,
my own and only child,
but after all these years
I still don't know what to say.

I could tell you I spent my twenties
convinced that alone was permanent,
certain I somehow deserved it,
my life a joke on me,
the whole cosmos laughing.

I could tell you it does get better,
but why should you believe me?
Words are just words;
the pain is palpable.

If I knew how to make you happy,
I'd be the happiest person alive.
But it's not about me.

In Sanskrit Leela means "playful."
In Arabic, "night beauty."

In the language of love,
it means you.

The Amish Boys on Sunday

Amish country. January
afternoon. Crackling crisp and clear.

Families in their winter buggies:
boxes, black, on wheels, each buggy
with a single easygoing horse
unperturbed by cars, trucks, traffic
lights, the smell of gasoline exhaust.
A two-lane highway, buggies
on their way to worship, or,
service over, coming home,
in no particular hurry, the very
Amish attitude toward progress.

Around a bend and up ahead,
three Amish boys are walking
toward me on the shoulder.
Two maybe twelve, the other ten,
all dressed in Sunday best:
black pants and coats, white shirts
and broad-brimmed flat black hats.
I'm driving slow, and as I pass,
all three doff their hats in unison
and bow like gallant cavaliers,
grinning like they've got a secret
wouldn't I like to know.

2016

Here's to Us

So here we are, the two of us,
gray-haired and feeling aches and pains
in body parts we never even knew
we had when we were young.
And we were young, once. Sometimes
it seems like only yesterday;
other times, a long time ago.
Let's just say we're not the svelte
athletic pair who used to run
10K or dance to Balkan music

all night long. Dancing's work, and as
for me, a thirty-minute walk
I call a workout.
                    Some people
call it getting old; I call it
growing old together, wouldn't
wish it any other way.
In bed at night, sound asleep,
you turn to match my turning, reach
an arm across my body, pull
yourself up close, belly to back,
hip to hip, a perfect fit;
a perfect pair for all the slings
and arrows of outrageous fortune
life has thrown our way, we're more
in love than when we started,
more content than people half
our age could ever understand.

I Dream of Alternate Histories

Just imagine if Woodrow Wilson
had met with Ho Chi Minh at Versailles
in nineteen nineteen, decided Ho
was right, and told the French, "I told the world,
'Self-determination.' Not just for whites;
for everyone; I'm going to keep my word."

Or what if Roosevelt had lived. FDR,
who said the French had ruled in Vietnam
for eighty years and only left its people
worse off now than when they first arrived.
What would FDR have done when Ho
declared his country independent?

But Harry Truman got the nod instead,
and authorized the use of US ships
to ship French soldiers back to Vietnam
to wage an eight-year war against a people
who had had enough of *vive la France*.
What if Harry S had told the French to swim?

Or what if, after Dien Bien Phu had fallen
and the French had had enough of Vietnam,
Eisenhower had ordered Foster Dulles
to agree the Maryknolls could keep Diem,
the Virgin Mary wasn't coming south,
and Ho Chi Minh could have his country.

Imagine John F. Kennedy in August
nineteen sixty-three, hearing of the raids
on Buddhist temples by the Saigon
thugs of Ngo Dinh Nhu, had said, "That's it.
These clowns are hopeless. Let's go home
and cut our losses while we can."

Or good old LBJ. What if he,
confronted with a much-provoked attack
on US warships in the Tonkin Gulf,
had had a revelation: "No more lies!
Let's build a Great Society at home
and export that instead of wars."

And then there's Richard Milhous Nixon.
Dick who promised Peace with Honor,
gave us Watergate instead. What if
Eisenhower had dumped him? What if he'd
been stoned to death in Venezuela
back in nineteen fifty-eight?

Old Men Bodysurfing

for Joe & Dale & Me

You should have seen the three of them:
sixty-five, seventy, maybe older,
pot-bellied, gray-haired, wrinkled
like God had given them skin two sizes
too big, riding wave after wave after wave
all the way in to the surf line,
giving each other the thumbs up,
then doddering back into the ocean
to catch the next wave. Shameless
exhibitionists. Acting like kids.
One of them had a ponytail, for chrissake.

The Poetry of Science

"Science is the poetry of reality."
—Richard Dawkins

Was it Ptolemy who posited
the music of the spheres?
Aristotle guessed there must be atoms.
Galen gave us medicine
while Archimedes gave the world "Eureka!"
Galileo used a glass to prove
Copernicus and Kepler had it right.
Leonardo knew that men would fly.
Descartes, the French philosopher,
could think because he was,
and what is science, after all,
but natural philosophy?
An apple fell on Newton's head,
symbolism Isaac took to heart.
Smith's map of Britain changed the world.
Darwin grasped that men and monkeys
aren't so different as we'd like to think
while Lister gave us more than Listerine.
Indeed, the world would be bereft
of poetry if mass times speed times
speed again were not the perfect poem.
And if you're not convinced, consider this:
Madame Curie's burning passion killed her.
How much more poetic can you get?

Lunch at the A&N Diner

for Linda Titus
November 5th, 2016

Miss Bowers? Holy cow! Fourth grade
was sixty years ago. Surprised we still
remember back that far. Mrs. Vera.
Mrs. Kulp. Then junior high
and high school: Pennridge Rams.
So much we shared while we were
growing up, good times and bad.
But every generation comes of age.

And then grows old, looks back,
and wonders how it all went by
so quickly. And so long ago.
Suzie died before she started college.
Kenny died in Vietnam. That brilliant
girl who played the flute became
an alcoholic. Gareth died of AIDS.
But that's the way it goes.
I'd rather think about one
summer night we spent together
after I came back from war and you
from school, old friends already,
even then, though youngsters still,
come morning went our separate ways.
Yet here we are again. Just you and me.
What lunchtime crowd? They don't exist.
That night was refuge from the storm
that raged inside of me for years.
The war was undescribable.
Being home was worse.
You were playing a harp.
You had wings that night.
And a halo.
You still do.

Making America Great Again

> a found poem of Trump products
> & where they are made

I. Bangladesh: shirts

II. Canada: facial soap

III. China:
bath towels, body wash, ceramics & conditioners
eyeglasses, kitchenware, laundry bags & light fixtures
moisturizers, mirrors & neckties
pens, pet collars & pet leashes
shampoo, shirts, shower caps & suits

IV. Germany: brass fittings

V. Honduras: shirts

VI. India: sport coats

VII. Indonesia: neckties

VIII. Mexico: suits

IX. Netherlands: vodka

X. Turkey: furniture

XI. Slovenia: barware

XII. Vietnam: neckties & shirts

XIII. United States of America:
"Make America Great Again" campaign hats

2017

Dancing in the Streets

for Martha & the Vandellas

The summer I was fifteen, I discovered
girls, and beer, and cigarettes,
how to dance, and how to lie
and get away with it. That summer,
everyone around the world
was dancing in the streets.
Except in Perkasie, a one-horse town
without so much as a traffic light
where fun was watching Lawrence Welk
or listening to the corn grow.
Christ, my mother didn't get it,
wouldn't even let me go
seven miles to Quakertown to dance.
St. Isadore's, for cryin' in a bucket.
Teen dance at a Catholic Church
chaperoned by priests and nuns.
"There's lots to do in Perkasie," she said.
What did she know? Lawrence Welk.

So I just said I'd be at Larry Rush's house,
hitchhiked up to Quakertown instead,
danced with Andrea Jenkins, had
the best time ever in my life,
concluded what my parents didn't know
wouldn't hurt them. Freedom!
What a heady feeling. All the world
at my disposal; all I had to do was lie.
This was 1964. What did I know?
Selma, Watts, Detroit, Khe Sanh, My Lai,
the cost and consequence of lies
had not yet come collecting what was due.

Silver Linings

My daughter says she isn't ready yet
for me to die. That's nice to know,
considering that more than once I'm sure
she would have liked to do the deed herself.

Things get complicated. Raising children
doesn't come with *Raising Kids for Dummies*.
One just has to do the best one can,
which all too often isn't good enough

by half, but by the time you realize
you've screwed things up, it's much too late
for anything but wishing you were
anyone but who you are: someone smart,

someone self-aware enough to know
the damage you can do to those you love
the most. And then you get to live with who
you are and what you've done and haven't done.

So now I've got this cancer diagnosis.
I'm pretty sure it isn't going to kill me,
but it's nice to know my daughter
isn't ready yet for me to die.

2018

The Right to Bear Arms

I. Anno Domini 1789

Typical weapon of the time:
Land Pattern Musket (aka "Brown Bess")
Length: 4 feet, 8 inches
Weight: 10 & ½ pounds
Action: muzzle-loaded flintlock
Rate of fire: 3 rounds per minute in very skilled hands
Muzzle velocity: 785 feet per second
Effective range: 50 yards

II. 2018 Christian Era

Typical weapon of the time:
AR-15 (aka "America's Rifle")*
Length: 3 feet, 3 inches
Weight: 7 & ½ pounds
Action: semi-automatic with 10, 20, or 30-round magazine
Rate of fire: 60 rounds a minute (in the hands of a rank amateur)
120 rounds a minute (in the hands of an adrenalin-charged killer)
Muzzle velocity: 3,300 feet per second
Effective range: 600 meters

*nickname coined by the National Rifle Association

Playing It Safe

I never know what's going to set you off.
Well, not "set off" exactly. Much more quiet.
Silent. Turning inward scary. Wraith
or shadow or a nothing-at-all-but-just-there,
yet real as frown or sneer or snort or slow
how-can-you-be-so-stupid shake of the head.

I'd have a hard time trying to enumerate
the ways you've graced my life these thirty years,
a life more fun, more meaningful, more worth
the trouble than it would have been without you.

But there's something bewildering about the way
I inadvertently offend you now and then

by being who I am. Am I obtuse?
I often feel as if I've trespassed
on some private property that isn't marked
and yet the owner acts as if it's obvious,
I should have known, what's wrong with me.

This last time's left me wondering
if I should stick to sports and weather.
How 'bout dem Eagles? Looks like rain today.

Thank You for Your Service

Yes, of course; it's what you say these days.
Like genuflecting in a Catholic church.
Like saying "bless you" to a sneeze.
A superstitious reflex, but, of course,
sincere. Or is it just to ease the guilt
of sending someone else to do
the dirty work? Whatever. I just say,
"You're welcome," let it go at that,
when what I'd really like to say is,
"Thank you for my fucking service
in that fucking war I've dragged
from day to day for fifty fucking years
like a fucking corpse that won't stay dead?
That fucking nightmare that my
fucking country told me was my fucking
patriotic duty to fight? For what,
exactly, do you think you're thanking me?
Service to my country? You empty-headed
idiot. You think I want your thanks
for what I did? You shallow, superficial
twit. You've no idea what I did, or why,
or what it cost a people who had
never done us any harm nor ever
would or could. You can take your
thank you for my service, shove it
where the sun doesn't shine."
But you wouldn't understand.
You'd only get insulted if I told you
what I'd really like to say. So I just say,
"You're welcome." Smile. Walk away.

Also by W. D. Ehrhart

Poetry

Books

From the Bark of the Daphne Tree, Adastra Press, 2013.
The Bodies Beneath the Table, Adastra Press, 2010.
Beautiful Wreckage: New & Selected Poems, Adastra Press, 1999.
The Distance We Travel, Adastra Press, 1993.
Just for Laughs, Viet Nam Generation & Burning Cities Press, 1990.
The Outer Banks & Other Poems, Adastra Press, 1984.
To Those Who Have Gone Home Tired, Thunder's Mouth Press, 1984.
The Samisdat Poems, Samisdat, 1980.
A Generation of Peace, New Voices Publishing Company, 1975.

Chapbooks

Praying at the Altar, Adastra Press, 2017.
Sleeping with the Dead, Adastra Press, 2006.
A Sort of Peace: Echoes and Images of the Vietnam War, with photographer Don
    Fox, Fox Studio Arts, 2005.
Greatest Hits: 1970–2000, Puddinghouse Press, 2001.
Mostly Nothing Happens, Adastra Press, 1996.
Winter Bells, Adastra Press, 1988.
Matters of the Heart, Adastra Press, 1981.
Empire, Samisdat, 1978.
Rootless, Samisdat, 1977.
A Generation of Peace (Revised), Samisdat, 1977.

Editor

Unaccustomed Mercy: Soldier-Poets of the Vietnam War, Texas Tech Press, 1989.
Carrying the Darkness: Poetry of the Vietnam War, Texas Tech Press, 1989.

Co-Editor

Retrieving Bones: Stories & Poems of the Korean War, with Philip K. Jason, Rutgers University Press, 1999

Demilitarized Zones: Veterans After Vietnam, with Jan Barry, East River Anthology, 1976.

Other Books

Nonfiction

Ordinary Lives: Platoon 1005 and the Vietnam War, Temple University Press, 1999.

Busted: A Vietnam Veteran in Nixon's America, University of Massachusetts Press, 1995.

Passing Time: Memoir of a Vietnam Veteran Against the War, McFarland, 1989.

Going Back: An Ex-Marine Returns to Vietnam, McFarland, 1987.

Vietnam–Perkasie: A Combat Marine Memoir, McFarland, 1983.

Essays

Dead on a High Hill: Essays on War, Literature and Living, McFarland, 2012.

The Madness of It All: Essays on War, Literature and American Life, McFarland, 2002.

In the Shadow of Vietnam: Essays, 1977–1991, McFarland, 1991.

Miscellaneous

W. D. Ehrhart in Conversation: Vietnam, America and the Written Word, Jean-Jacques Malo, ed., McFarland, 2017.

About

The Last Time I Dreamed About the War: Essays on the Life and Writing of W. D. Ehrhart, Jean-Jacques Malo, ed., McFarland, 2014.

Military History of W. D. Ehrhart

W. D. Ehrhart enlisted in the United States Marine Corps on 11 April 1966, while still in high school, beginning active duty on 17 June. He graduated from basic recruit training at the Marine Corps Recruit Depot, Parris Island, South Carolina, on 12 August, receiving a meritorious promotion to private first class, and completed basic infantry training at Camp Lejeune, North Carolina, on 12 September 1966. (While at Parris Island, he qualified as a rifle sharpshooter on 18 July 1966, subsequently qualifying as a rifle expert on 11 April 1968 and as a pistol sharpshooter on 24 April 1969.)

Assigned to the field of combat intelligence, Ehrhart spent 10 October to 15 December 1966 with Marine Air Group 26, a helicopter unit based at New River Marine Corps Air Facility, North Carolina, meanwhile completing a clerk typist course at Camp Lejeune in November 1966 and graduating first in his class from the Enlisted Basic Amphibious Intelligence School at Little Creek Amphibious Base, Norfolk, Virginia, in December 1966. He also completed a Marine Corps Institute combat intelligence correspondence course in December while at New River.

Before leaving for Vietnam on 9 February 1967, Ehrhart received additional combat training with the 3rd Replacement Company, Staging Battalion, Camp Pendleton, California, in January and February. Upon arrival in Vietnam, he was assigned to the 1st Battalion, 1st Marine Regiment, first as an intelligence assistant, later as assistant intelligence chief. In March 1967, he was temporarily assigned to the Sukiran Army Education Center, Okinawa, where he graduated first in his class from a course in basic Vietnamese terminology before returning to permanent assignment.

While in Vietnam, Ehrhart participated in the following combat operations: Stone, Lafayette, Early, Canyon, Calhoun, Pike, Medina, Lancaster, Kentucky I, Kentucky II, Kentucky III, Con Thien, Newton, Osceola II, and Hue City. He was promoted to lance corporal on 1 April 1967 and meritoriously promoted to corporal on 1 July 1967.

Ehrhart was awarded the Purple Heart Medal for wounds received in action in Hue City during the Tet Offensive, a commendation from Major General Donn J. Robertson commanding the 1st Marine Division, two

Presidential Unit Citations, the Navy Combat Action Ribbon, the Vietnam Service Medal with three stars, the Vietnamese Campaign Medal, a Cross of Gallantry Meritorious Unit Citation, and a Civil Action Meritorious Unit Citation.

Ehrhart was next assigned to the 2nd Marine Air Wing Headquarters Group at Cherry Point Marine Corps Air Station, North Carolina, from 30 March to 10 June 1968, where he was promoted to sergeant on 1 April. After a brief assignment with the Headquarters Squadron of Marine Air Group 15 based at Iwakuni Marine Corps Air Station, Japan, he was then reassigned to Marine Aerial Refueler Transport Squadron 152, Futema Marine Corps Air Facility, Okinawa, from 20 July to 30 October 1968, where he received a commanding officer's Meritorious Mast.

Ehrhart completed his active duty with Marine Fighter Attack Squadron 122, based alternately at Iwakuni and Cubi Point Naval Air Station, Philippines, from 31 October 1968 to 30 May 1969. While in the Philippines, he completed a field course on jungle environmental survival in February 1969.

On 10 June 1969, Ehrhart was separated from active duty, receiving the Good Conduct Medal. While on inactive reserve, he was promoted to staff sergeant on 1 July 1971. He received an honorable discharge on 10 April 1972.

About the Poet

W. D. Ehrhart was born in western Pennsylvania in 1948 but grew up in the rural southeastern part of that state. After graduating from Pennridge High School, in Perkasie, 1966, where he received the Pearl S. Buck Literary Achievement Award, he served three years on active duty with the Marines. He subsequently earned a BA from Swarthmore College in 1973, where he won an Academy of American Poets Collegiate Prize; an MA from the University of Illinois at Chicago Circle in 1978; and a PhD from the University of Wales, Swansea, UK, in 2000.

Over the years, Ehrhart has earned his living as a construction worker, merchant seaman, forklift operator, legal aide, newspaper reporter, magazine writer, high school teacher, and adjunct professor. In 1990, he was Visiting Professor of War and Social Consequences at the University of Massachusetts in Boston. Since 2001, he has been a Master Teacher of History and English at the Haverford School for Boys in suburban Philadelphia. He will retire in June 2019.

Ehrhart has been awarded a Mary Roberts Rinehart Foundation grant, two Pennsylvania Council on the Arts fellowships (one each for prose and poetry), the President's Medal from Veterans for Peace, a Pew Fellowship in the Arts, and Distinction in the Arts from Vietnam Veterans of America. As a teacher, he was presented the Rafael Laserna Outstanding Teacher Award by the Haverford Class of 2011.

He has been married since 1981 to the former Anne Senter Gulick, and their daughter Leela was born in 1986.

Index of Titles

Adoquinas 123
Afraid of the Dark 79
After the Fire 53
After the Latest Victory 157
After the Winter of 1994 185
Again, Rehoboth 71
All About Death 226
All About Love 227
The Ambush 17
America Enters the 1990s 142
America in the Late 20th Century 160
The Amish Boys on Sunday 254
Animal Instinct
Another Life 18
Another Way of Seeing 76
Appearances 113
Apples 119
Artsy Fartsy Whiskey & Girls 204

The Baby in the Box 251
Beautiful Wreckage 180
Because It's Important 198
The Beech Tree 124
Bicentennial 36
The Blizzard of Sixty-six 98
The Bob Hope Christmas Special 19
The Bodies Beneath the Table 237
The Bombing of Afghanistan 216
Breakfast with You and Emily Dickinson 220
Briana 90
Burning Leaves 242

Canoeing the Potomac 103
Cascais 47
Cast Out 54
Channel Fever 85
Charleston 26
Chasing Locomotives 134
Cheating the Reaper 248
Children of Adam & Eve 245
The Children of Hanoi 152
Christ 5
Christmas Miracles 188
Cliches Become Cliches Because They're
   True 202

Climbing to Heaven 110
Coaching Winter Track in Time of War
   229
Colorado 46
Coma 51
Coming Home 19
Companions 73
A Confirmation 63
Continuity 93
Cowgirls, Teachers & Dreams 102
The Cradle of Civilization 155
Cycling the Rosental 191

The Damage We Do 213
The Dancers 77
Dancing 6
Dancing in the Streets 260
The Death of Kings 45
Deer 96
Desire 54
Detroit River Blues 203
The Distance We Travel 163
Down and Out in Darfur 235
The Dream 79
Driving into the Future 81
Driving Through Wisconsin 66
Dropping Leela Off at School 184
Drought 186
The Ducks on Wissahickon Creek 121

Eighteen Months in Chicago 67
Empire 59
Epiphany 240
The Eruption of Mount St. Helens 88
Everett Dirksen, His Wife, You & Me 100
Excerpts from the Mind of the Writer 1
The Exercise of Power 161
An Exorcism 62
Extra! Extra! 240

The Facts of Life 146
The Farmer 83
Finding My Old Battalion Command Post
   156
First Day of School 250

The First French Kiss 189
The Flying Gypsy 29
Fog 75
The Fool 34
For a Coming Extinction 139
For Anne, Approaching Thirty-five 139
For Mrs. Na 120
For My Daughter, Alone in the World

Geese 35
The Generals' War 4
A Generation of Peace 22
Gettysburg 5
Ghosts 43
Gifts 91
Ginger 193
Going Down Off Columbia Bar 43
Going Home with the Monkeys 42
Golfing with My Father 228
Governor Rhodes Keeps His Word 162
Granddad 33
Gravestones at Oxwich Bay 208
Great Horned Owl 67
The Grim Art of Teaching 77
Growing Older Alone 56
Guatemala 170
Guerrilla War 16
Guns 153

The Hawk and Two Suns 17
The Heart of the Poem 147
Heather 124
Helpless 51
Here's to Us 255
High Country 101
Home Before Morning 219
Home on the Range 233
How History Gets Written 246
How I Live 145
How It All Comes Back 173
Hunting 5

I Dream of Alternate Histories 256
I Just Want You to Know 198
Imagine 22
In the Valley of the Shadow 144
The Invasion of Grenada 115
Is It Always This Hard? 195
It's About You 254

Jimmy 48
Jogging with the Philosopher 200
Judas Joyful 247
Just for Laughs 137

Keeping My Distance 136
Kosovo 222

The Last Day 31
Last of the Hard-hearted Ladies 74

The Last Prayer of Michelangelo 57
The Last Time I Dreamed About the War 172
Leaving the Guns Behind 50
Lenin 135
Letter 51
Letter from an Old Lover 112
Letter to the Survivors 99
Letters 47
Letting Go 210
Life in the Neighborhood 242
"… the light that cannot fade…" 104
Listening Post 3
The Living 24
Long Shot O'Leary Ain't Dead Yet 170
Long Time Gone 252
Lost at Sea 78
Lost Years 133
The Lotus Cutters of Hồ Tây 153
Love in an Evil Time 150
Lunch at the A&N Diner 258

Mail Call 14
Making America Great Again 259
Making Love in the Garden 168
Making the Children Behave 39
Manning the Walls 223
Matters of the Heart 89
A Meditation on Family Geography and a Prayer for My Daughter 201
Meditations on Pedagogy 225
Midnight at the Vietnam Veterans Memorial 171
Moments When the World Consents 111
Money in the Bank 37
More Than You Ever Imagined 160
Mostly Nothing Happens 176
Music Lessons 206
Myers, Messick & Me 30

Near-sighted 84
The Nest Step 15
New Jersey Pine Barrens 94
The Next World War 138
Nicaragua Libre 126
Night Patrol 15
Night Sailing 194
Not for You 181
Not Your Problem 138
Nothing Profound

The Obsession 31
Oh, Canada 231
Old Men Bodysurfing 257
Old Myths 21
The Old Soldiers 150
On Any Given Day 169
On the Eve of Destruction 212
On the Right to Vote 115
One Night on Guard Duty 4

The One That Died 14
The Open Door 162
The Origins of Passion 141
The Orphan 206
The Outer Banks 105

Pabst Blue Ribbon Beer 205
Pagan 95
Parade 117
Patrick 247
Peary & Henson Reach the North Pole
   68
Perimeter Guard 12
The Perversion of Faith 187
Playing It Safe 262
The Poet As Athlete 143
The Poetry of Science 258
Portrait of Friends 52
POW-MIA 118
Prayer for My Enemies 182
Praying at the Altar 252
Primitive Art 232
Purple Heart 174

The Rat 14
Reading Out Loud 188
The Reason Why 114
Red-tailed Hawks 175
Redipuglia 243
Reflections on the Papacy 230
Rehoboth 23
Rehoboth, One Last Time 194
A Relative Thing 20
Responsibility 113
Rhythm 29
The Right to Bear Arms 262
The Rocker 192
Rootless 46

Sanctuary 57
Sarajevo 183
A Scientific Treatise for My Wife 148
Second Thoughts 132
The Secret Lives of Boys 240
Secrets 134
Seminar on the Nature of Reality 218
September 25
September 11th 215
The Sergeant 199
Sergeant Jones 13
Shadows 38
The Silent 39
Silver Linings 261
The Simple Lives of Cats 157
Singing Hymns in Church 154
Sins of the Fathers 208
Sleeping with General Chi 166
Sleeping with the Dead 211
A Small Romance 151
Small Song for Daddy 130

Small Talk 173
The Sniper's Mark 4
So Much Time 1
Some Other World 125
Song for Leela, Bobby & Me 149
Sound Advice 92
Souvenirs 13
The Spiders' White Dream of Peace 61
Spontaneous Combustion 253
Star Light, Star Bright 159
Starships 6
Starting Over 131
The Storm 130
Strangers 180
Suffer the Little Children 182
The Suicide 110
Sunset 82
Surviving the Bomb One More Day 98

The Teacher 69
Temple Poem 235
Thank You for Your Service 263
Time on Target 16
To Maynard on the Long Road Home 44
To Swarthmore 7
To the Asian Victors 33
To Those Who Have Gone Home Tired
   41
The Traveler 32
The Trial 49
The Trouble with Poets 128
Turning Sixty 237
Turning Thirty 70
Twice Betrayed 121
Twodot, Montana 55

Variations on Squam Lake 186
Viet Nam—February 1967 2
Vietnam Veterans, After All 40
A Vietnamese Bidding Farewell to the Re-
   mains of an American 158
Vietnamese-Cambodian Border War 61
The Vision 87
Visiting My Parents' Graves 189

Waking Alone in Darkness 68
A Warning to My Students 96
Water 122
The Way Light Bends 142
Welcome 58
What Better Way to Begin 209
What Goes Around Comes Around 197
What I Know About Myself 168
What It Signifies 249
What Keeps Me Going 129
What Makes a Man 239
What the Fuss Is All About 234
What War Does 165
What We're Buying 147
What You Gave Me 140

Who Did What to Whom 152
Why I Don't Mind Rocking Leela to Sleep
  127
Winter Bells 116
The Work of Love 236

The World As It Is 86
The Wreckage Along the Road 212

Yours 26

Index of First Lines

A cold moon hangs 69
A dry spring after an April 122
A friend from college called today 212
A kind of blindness, that's what's needed now 142
A man with his hand on a trigger 138
Across the bay 47
After all these years, how strange 112
After awhile, he gave 206
After darkness 194
After the fire 53
After the streets fall silent 41
Again we pass that field 153
Age finally caught him from behind 48
Air heavy with rain and humidity 2
All around me 46
All these letters 47
All winter long 32
Alone in the basement, sorting clothes 139
Amish country. January 254
And then one night I left— 67
And then there's Sergeant Jones 13
Another day gone 42
Another night coats the nose and ears 15
As it is now 26
As rivers go, this one isn't much 103
"Ash fallout is the hot news here" 88
At night in the Seven-Eleven Club 199
Atlantic waves roil over reefs beyond the cut 111
Avoid this place 138

Bangladesh: shirts 259
Barbarian tribesmen 59
Because I love my wife, I've traveled 93
Because I love you, I wish for you 182
Because this street was washed with fire 152
Beginning in a dream 40
Believe in a raw wind scraping over the land 115
Biking at night with no lights 44
Brad pitched the tent beside the creek 101
"Bring me back a souvenir," the captain called 13

"Can you guess what it is?" you ask 119
Christy is eighteen 84
Citations, medals, warrants of promotion 21
Cold spring rain drums hollow rhythms 157
Crouched in a corner 12

Death comes knocking and the silence descends 90
Descending into Valley Green is easy 200
Do they think of me now 39
Donaldo, Stephen and I 68
Done before I knew it had begun 240
Don't look at me 77
Driving north on 95, I pass 43

Each day I go into the fields 83
Each room except the room you're in 134
Eighty-six years I have labored on the scaffold 57
Even as my dad lay dying, cancer 239
Even when we were nine 140
Everyone loves to hear about love 227

Fifty-eight thousand American dead 171
Flashing jagged teeth 14
Flesh of my flesh 254
For three days, iron cold gripped 98

Giant 45
Good morning 56
Grandfather Ehrhart 49

Having been where contrasts meet 6
He can't get out of his head the horrors he's seen 247
He seemed in a curious hurry 4
Here I was in Budapest, alone 236
He's giving up his paper route 160
Hysterical seagulls dart and soar 105

I always have to wash my hands 168
I always told myself 120
I am eight years old and naked 141
I am tired of philosophy 86
I bumped my head on the setting sun 145

I call myself a primitive 232
I call the sea. The wind calls back 157
I didn't want a monument 115
I don't know why I fell asleep 213
I dreamed about you again last night 211
I give you the worst gift first 91
I had never before seen anything die 186
I hated it. That inescapable 188
I have been walking all afternoon 46
I have never seen you naked before 168
I have stood by this bay before 71
I heard tonight a boy you knew 24
I knew that Sunday morning 55
I know what you hear most often is me 198
I like pagodas 252
I might have known trouble was coming 194
I never know what's going to set you off 262
I never thought I'd see the day 123
I read once that Everett Dirksen 100
I remember only a table 33
I saw the Crucified Christ three days ago 5
I still remember bicycle rides 133
I want a Cadillac 54
I was always afraid of you— 74
I was doing fine with God 195
I was jogging. It was cold 203
If life were fair, you'd be a millionaire 219
If you had told me thirty years ago 189
Illusion 17
I'm at this party 79
I'm sorry it's not a vacation for two 198
Impossibly sprawled 147
In the dark breath of February 116
In the heart of the night 95
In the jungle of years 118
In the language of people 78
In the photograph, my mother's slim 180
In the town of Freiburg, Germany 173
In Russia, everyone drinks vodka 114
Irregular motion 34
It can happen anywhere 87
It isn't like my daughter 130
It isn't that I fear 70
It isn't that I fear 237
It seemed so childish 31
It seems foolish now, but at the time 43
It was a hard winter 36
It's like when you see something ugly 165
It's never as simple as this, of course 121
It's only the wind, mothers 68
It's practically impossible 16
It's strange, the obstacles 14
I've forgotten the pain 189
I've had nightmares before—this 61
I've never seen a person dance with death 218

January, heavy snow 76
Jeff and I were eight or nine the day 205
Just imagine if Woodrow Wilson 256

Late afternoon: in the stillness 82
Leaving the party she takes my hand 188
Light sails west 50
Light surf breaks beneath clouds 54
Like a large cat rising out of a sleep 170

Midnight, and a rain falls black 130
Miss Bowers? Holy Cow! Fourth grade 258
My beat-up old VW tumbles 66
My daughter says she isn't ready yet 261
My daughter's reached an age 184
My father took up golf in middle age 228
My mother loved to sing 154
My name is Aysha Rahim 215
My neighbor leans across the fence 124
My orange kitty is a wicked little girl 193

Night comes down to a loon calling 186
Night drifts coldly into dawn 31
Nothing the boy wanted 240

Oh, give me a home where the buffalo roam
    233
Oh, how we wanted to be good 182
Okay, our father was a shit 197
Old Tom, your rasping low voice 89
Older than ancient, you shadow me 73
100 minus three is 97 is 94 is 91 is 88 is 85 is
    82 1
One look at him induces adjectives 143
One more time the madness begins 250
One wonders what the fuss is all about 234

Paper orders passed down and executed 4
Pressed down by the weight 129

Remember the time Jerry Doughty 92
Ruth and I were sitting in the kitchen 172

San Francisco airport— 19
Say I discover a cure for cancer 246
Say it's the way things are 161
Seven generations of Ehrharts 201
She sits each night near Market Street 29
She was rude, obnoxious, slovenly 79
Sighting down the long black barrel 5
Sitting at night on the porch 127
Sixty miles away, in New York City 94
Sixty-one years 37
Smoke from a single rifle shot 183
Snow all night, and then the temperature 75
Snow came early here, and hard 98
So, a hot summer night 253
So after I had read my poems 128
So here we are, the two of us 255
So many ways to waste one's time 225
So much time, so little to do 1
So now it has come to this 26
So now we're almost brother and sister 245
Solemn Douglas firs stride slowly 63

Some American soldier 121
Something made us bolt upright 144
Something you just don't smell anymore 242
Split the ribcage open 147
Standing where the water tumbles 206
Stories on the six o'clock news 61
Suddenly the woman fell down 62
Suddenly, to your surprise 151
Summer, winter, autumn, spring, Mrs. Ward 192
Suzie, you picked a hell of a time 104

Ten years after the last rooftop 117
That day we fished Coyote Creek 102
That evening you and I and Daniel 110
That winter the woman hurled herself 110
The afternoon we walked among 124
The ambush lasted only seconds 136
The ancients thought the world is flat 148
The audience knows 77
The B-1 bomber 96
The bay is calm tonight 23
The bodies beneath the table 237
The boy on the bench on the boardwalk 252
The boys are running "suicides" 229
The boys with pistols and shotguns 222
The bullet entered between the eyes 173
The conversation turned to Vietnam 22
The cop on the corner stood there and watched 242
The day the towers came down, goggle-eyed 223
The day you flew to Tam Ky, I was green 149
The deceiver 113
The door was opened just enough 162
The first salvo is gone before I can turn 4
The girl kneels in the parking lot 162
The grass is wet 3
The great miscalculation 33
The hell it's not class war 170
The hunter awakes 67
The last time I saw my mother alive 210
The lies lie 142
The lines you draw divide the land 249
The long day's march is over 18
The long night hangs above these woods 25
The longest war is over, so they say 22
The lotus cutters gather morning 153
The man with your name and your life 181
The next step you take 15
The night I got here 7
The night Marie called home to say you'd freaked 220
The old general wants me to sleep 166
The old soldiers imagine themselves warriors 150
The remarkable thing 135
The rhythm 29
The River Drau flows swiftly here 191
The riverside banquet, extravagance 187

The silver hawk swoops 300 miles per hour 17
The stars are faces 6
The strange American steps out of the night 163
The summer I was fifteen, I discovered 260
The sun comes up each morning in silence 235
The sun taps on the kitchen table 113
The weekend Watts went up in flames 212
The wraith of a shadow shivered the air 174
There in that place the Americans bombed 152
There was a woman I knew 150
There's nothing here to commend your 204
These chattering children fill the woods 175
These guys who get themselves elected Pope 230
They are the dark ones 39
They went to Cam Ranh Bay 19
This is the ancient cathedral 57
This is the building, Ken 248
This paper cup I'm drinking from was made 231
Though you stand on the edge of darkness 207
Thought you killed me 51
Three men deliberately posed 30
To any who find this 99
Today my child came home from school in tears 208
Tonight I pull a plastic locomotive 134
Two white-tailed deer stood still 96
Typical weapon of the time 262

Under stars in late October cold 159

Vietnam. Not a day goes by 139

Walking home on Upsal Street 176
Was it Ptolemy who posited 258
Was there ever a moment 125
Was your plane on fire, or did you die 158
We are the ones you sent to fight a war 20
We never did talk much 81
We used to get intelligence reports 16
We walk together in a free land 2
What a day that was 52
What do you do when the blows keep coming 235
What holds back the hand? What iron 247
What I remember is you at twenty-six 240
What if I didn't shoot the old lady 180
What if you find a baby in a box 251
What once had been a ramshackle 243
What we came here to find 156
When I cast off in my small boat 85
When I was ten, I thought that I 137
"When the archangel's trump shall sound 208

When the creep who was different 169
When the first storm struck, we didn't com-
plain 185
When they dragged me out of sleep 126
When you have ridden once too often 58
When you went away 35
Where the Tigris and Euphrates meet 155
Why didn't you tell me 51
Winter, and a gray storm sea 146

Yankee day 5
Yes, of course: it's what you say these days
263
You bet we'll soon forget the one that died 14

You came back 38
You can just keep your rockets' red glare
209
You don't want me to tell you about death
226
You have to understand the way things are
202
You must be sitting down to eat 216
You should have seen the three of them 257
You wake to a pain in your right side 160
You watch with admiration as I roll 132
You were eight years old when you hunched
131
Your sister and mother and wife 51